ADVANCES IN LIBRARY ADMINISTRATION AND ORGANIZATION

ADVANCES IN LIBRARY ADMINISTRATION AND ORGANIZATION

Series Editors: Edward D. Garten and
Delmus E. Williams

Recent Volumes:

ADVANCES IN LIBRARY ADMINISTRATION
AND ORGANIZATION   VOLUME 21

ADVANCES IN LIBRARY ADMINISTRATION AND ORGANIZATION

EDITED BY

EDWARD D. GARTEN

Dean Emeritus, Libraries & Information Services,
University of Dayton, Dayton, Ohio, USA

DELMUS E. WILLIAMS

University of Akron Libraries, OH, USA

JAMES M. NYCE

School of Library and Information Management,
Emporia State University, USA

2004

ELSEVIER
JAI

Amsterdam – Boston – Heidelberg – London – New York – Oxford
Paris – San Diego – San Francisco – Singapore – Sydney – Tokyo

ELSEVIER B.V.	ELSEVIER Inc.	**ELSEVIER Ltd**	ELSEVIER Ltd
Sara Burgerhartstraat 25	525 B Street, Suite 1900	**The Boulevard, Langford**	84 Theobalds Road
P.O. Box 211	San Diego	**Lane, Kidlington**	London
1000 AE Amsterdam	CA 92101-4495	**Oxford OX5 1GB**	WC1X 8RR
The Netherlands	USA	**UK**	UK

First edition 2004

British Library Cataloguing in Publication Data
A catalogue record is available from the British Library.

ISBN: 0-7623-1121-5
ISSN: 0732-0671 (Series)

♾ The paper used in this publication meets the requirements of ANSI/NISO Z39.48-1992 (Permanence of Paper). Printed in The Netherlands.

Working together to grow
libraries in developing countries

www.elsevier.com | www.bookaid.org | www.sabre.org

ELSEVIER   BOOK AID
International   Sabre Foundation

CONTENTS

v

PART II

SYMPOSIUM PAPERS THE CHANGING
FACE OF SERVICE: PAPERS FROM
THE FIFTH ANNUAL JOHANNAH SHERRER
MEMORIAL LECTURE, LEWIS & CLARK COLLEGE,
OCTOBER 2003

PART III

INTRODUCTION

Putting together a volume of *Advances* is an interesting effort that combines a little planning and a lot of serendipity. In the years that we have been editing this annual, Ed Garten and I have spent considerable time searching through tools like *Dissertation Abstracts* for research studies of interest, tracking people who are doing interesting work, and commissioning articles in contemporary areas of interest. But, as often as not, some of the best of our articles have come about as a result of a chance meeting at a conference, a consulting gig, a conversation with a colleague, or some other happenstance. The papers included here are no different, reflecting both heavy scholarship and more practical information about how we as a profession administer our libraries, the programs we offer, and the work we do. As in past volumes, the context is international in scope, and the strength of the volume may be that it reinforces the idea that, while libraries (and other organizations) in Sweden, Thailand, Canada, South Africa and the United States are very different, the challenges faced and techniques used by managers are not. As a result, we the editors present these articles to you in hopes that they provide some grist for the mill as you try to bring order to your part of the world.

In the first article, Janet Carson presents an analysis of the population of librarians in Canada. It is her view that a full understanding of problems facing contemporary information professionals requires an analysis of the laboring aspects as well as the professional nature of their work. As a result, she has developed a comprehensive study of work in libraries with special emphasis on power and expertise that illuminates what librarians do and how they perceive themselves and are perceived. The results are something we can all identify with and should inform anyone looking at the future of any group of knowledge workers who are in an environment affected by expanding information technologies, constricted economic resources, and globalization.

The next four papers collectively represent an exploration of leadership and organizational models around which library administrators might organize their efforts. While the focus of all of the pieces is on libraries, they combine information gleaned from library environments with studies stemming from other types of organizations. Richard Bowman and Ed Garten begin with a piece that considers the concept of servant leadership as reflected in the management structure at the University of Dayton and its library and in Department of Education at Winona

State University in Minnesota. The dialog that results provides an insight into how this management style works as people in leadership roles work to facilitate the efforts of their colleagues.

The next paper is presented by Ellen and Nico Martins and Fransie Terblanche and addresses the factors within organizational cultures that have an impact on creativity and innovation. The resulting model, based on a research study done in South Africa, provides guidance to those who want to develop a culture that can adapt to the changing needs of the library as an organization and to the changing demands placed on it by its constituencies.

The next piece in this set comes from what might at first appear to be an odd source. Per-Arne Persson is an officer in the Swedish army charged with introducing systems technology into "command work" in the military. The ethnographic study that he presents relates to the specific problems that arise when one tries to introduce innovation of this sort into a bureaucracy that is typically led by people who try to combine charismatic and rational leadership. In Persson's view, efforts to use technology to further rationalize operations must take into the account the uncertainty of battlefield conditions, and, as a result, there will always be sufficient uncertainty to require charismatic leadership. Most librarians would conclude early on that libraries are not military units, and they would be right. However, as one seeks dependability in the face of change, it is useful to return to military organizations that served as models for modern bureaucratic management as a point of departure in any discussion that talks about technological innovation.

The final paper in this series is an article by Cindy Klinck that describes the application of organizational transformation within a public library that is regularly cited as being among the best of its size in the United States. Klinck describes the evolution of her organization as it moved from a traditional bureaucratic structure to a team based management approach. It is a descriptive case study that describes a thoughtful approach to organizational change that has served Ohio's Washington-Centerville Public Library well.

The next group of papers was compiled by Jim Kopp, the Director of the Lewis & Clark College Library, and reflects papers presented at the 5th Annual Johannah Sherrer Memorial Lectures held in October 2003. Sherrer was a well regarded reference librarian and college library administrator who had much influence on the service philosophy of her generation, and the lectures reflect a commentary on her views and their place in contemporary public service programs.

This is followed by two case studies developed by Jean Donham from Cornell College in Iowa and Kathleen Tiller from the University of Dayton. These are accompanied by an article by Nancy Thomas, a member of the faculty of the School of Library and Information management at Emporia State University, who provides a grounding in the literature for the pieces and a critique of the programs that have developed in these two libraries. The three pieces taken together provide an interesting set of views on a much discussed topic. While it is unlikely that this will be the last word in this discussion, these papers have much to contribute to the continuing dialog.

The final two papers in this volume relate to assessment. The first is an article written by Lisa Blankenship and Adonna Fleming on the assessment program that has developed over the 1990s at the University of Northern Colorado. UNC has systematically worked through a library faculty committee to tailor assessment tools to meet the specific needs of their institution. The result has been a well considered program that is worth emulating, and the twists and turns that UNC took in getting to that result is well worth your consideration. Then Malivan Praditteera reports on a survey conducted in Thai university libraries that was designed to assess the application of ISO9000 standards for quality in those institutions to meet assessment criteria set by the government of Thailand. This is particularly interesting as it addresses efforts in a less developed nation to introduce quality standards in a uniform way.

I would like to make one final comment as we introduce this volume. Beginning with Volume 21, James M. Nyce from the School of Library and Information Management faculty at Emporia State University will join Ed Garten and me as editors of *ALAO*. Jim is a cultural anthropologist with a wide circle of contacts in this country and abroad, and brings a fresh perspective to the table. Ed and I been pleased with his contribution so far, and look forward to having another sets of eyes involved in developing these volumes in the years to come. Welcome, Jim.

In conclusion, let me say that we the editors hope you find reading the papers presented here as stimulating as we have in bringing them together. Thank you for your continuing support of this effort.

Delmus E. Williams
Co-editor

PART I

PROFESSIONAL PRACTICE AND THE LABOUR PROCESS: ACADEMIC LIBRARIANSHIP AT THE MILLENNIUM

Janet Carson

OBJECTIVES

This study takes the position that the vitality of academic libraries is grounded in the working experiences of its librarians. It suggests that a full understanding of problems facing contemporary information professionals in the post-industrial workplace requires an analysis of the labouring aspects as well as the professional nature of their work. The study of changes in the academic library work experience thus depicts the state of the library, and has implications for other intellectual workers in a social environment characterized by expanding information technologies, constricted economic resources, and the globalization of information production. Academic librarians have long recognized that their vocation lies not only in the classical role in information collection, organization, and dissemination, but also in collaboration with faculty in the teaching and research process, and in the contribution to university governance. They are becoming increasingly active in the protection of information access and assurance of information quality in view of information degradation on the Internet and various compromises necessitated by interaction with third party commercial information producers.

Advances in Library Administration and Organization
Advances in Library Administration and Organization, Volume 21, 3–59
Copyright © 2004 by Elsevier Ltd.
All rights of reproduction in any form reserved
ISSN: 0732-0671/doi:10.1016/S0732-0671(04)21001-X

The paper isolates expertise and power as key components of the professional labour process. Professionalism conventionally suggests the characteristics of knowledge base, expertise, professional development, social responsibility, autonomy, self-regulation, social closure, and the protection of jurisdiction or the market. The labour process focuses on job characteristics, the internal and external labour markets, power, authority, and worker rights, and notes the separation of conception and execution. The paper is not concerned with theoretical differences, but with common areas related to the possession of expertise and the assertion of power in librarianship. It is guided by the historically-specific experiences of Canadian working librarians which suggest that a combination of perspectives is needed to fully analyze the situation.

The paper begins by noting the competing perceptions of a promising future vs. increasing control or deskilling in academic libraries. To resolve these discrepant claims, it refines the problem from the perspective of librarians at the "point of production" through ethnographic techniques. With this grounded information, it clarifies the characteristics of the working environment, and obtains details that help problematize the expertise and power aspects of professional labour. On the strength of the accounts of working experiences, it advances that librarians have been emphasizing skill factors at the expense of those that bring control. It then presents data on statistical trends in the labour situation and in-depth working experiences from the librarians' narratives, identifies areas of disagreement between them, and determines the need to examine labour market factors outside the library for a comprehensive triangulation of information. Documentary data on the acquisition of expertise are obtained from credentialling institutions, and on the demand for expertise from position ads. There is agreement that the intensification of skill does not compensate for lack of power, and that the interaction of corporate forces external to the library with the labour process contributes to additional loss of power for librarians.

COMPETING VISIONS: INTELLECTUAL CLASS OR TECHNOLOGICAL DOMINATION?

There has been much research on the impacts of technological change and rationalization upon professional and semi-professional work, as well as manual, clerical and technical work (e.g. Brewer, 1996; DiPrete, 1988; Krause, 1996; Macdonald, 1995; McDonald, 1995; Murphy, 1990; Novek, 1998; Sinclair et al., 1996; Smith, 1997; Vallas, 1999). The competing views of Bell (1973) about the new knowledge class and Braverman (1974) about the deskilling of manual and technical work are easily seen in claims and critiques about the work of professional librarians. In Bell's vein, librarians are experiencing an up-skilling of their work, or are undergoing re-professionalization. Their jobs are enriched with new challenges related to the expanding information universe and its electronic means of production. Information technology, for example, challenges librarians to create better web pages, to mine the rich fund of information resources on the Internet, or to develop more capable and user-friendly information retrieval systems. This view is typical of that of library educators and of general public opinion. In Braverman's vein, librarians are experiencing degradation in their work, as it becomes routinized and allocated to less qualified staff. In some circumstances, there is a threat that librarians may be replaced by electronic resources, if Perrolle's (1986) foreboding of "intellectual assembly lines" is accurate. The eclipse of professional expertise by the diffusion of information resources on the web and end-user access of them is an illustration of this projection. In Bell's view, knowledge appears to be the predominant factor, and, in the case of Braverman, control. Emergent questions concern not only changes in the quality of working life of librarians, but also the diminution of their professional contribution to society.

The literature of librarianship reflects similar discordant views on the digital revolution in libraries, from the fear of "techno vandals" (Gorman, 1994), to the wise mix of print and digital (Crawford, 1999), to the need to consider the opportunity costs and to aggressively address the needs of electronically sophisticated users (Harris & Hannah, 1996). Comprehensive approaches to changes in contemporary librarianship include Buschman's (1993) critical political, economic, and social perspectives on information technology in libraries; Winter's (1996) conceptual, interdisciplinary account of the political economy of knowledge; and Harris, Hannah and Harris' (1998) location of postindustrial librarianship within social phenomena and labour theory. Studies in librarianship have not focused specifically on labour in academic libraries, nor have they used the insights of working librarians as qualitative data to suggest the larger sociological, economic, political, and cultural forces in which they work.

THE GROUNDED PROBLEM: INSIGHTS FROM "THE TRENCHES"

The research contributes to the study of academic librarianship by focusing on the *experience* of professional labourers, and specifying the problem from a grounded perspective. This approach was taken because of a lack of conclusiveness in the literature about the vitality of the profession. It could not replicate the research of other professions or semi-professions because the nature of skills and workplace relations within each profession are different. For this study, the librarians themselves provided context-specific information at the point of production for both the research problem and the analysis.

The research methodology involved semi-structured in-depth interviews with a sample of Canadian university librarians. My interviews were guided by my own experience as a working academic librarian and my education as a sociologist, enriched by systematic observations between 1997 and 1998 at my workplace. The site of observation was a medium-sized research university in central Canada. My data included conversations, meetings, interactions, computer use, and selected work-related documents, and noted visual manifestations such as stress indicators, collaborative efforts, and reactions to technology. The observations represented workers making sense of the contradictory forces of technological expansion alongside economic retraction. Being tentative, local, and somewhat subjective, the identified problem areas of staff relations, staff shortage, and expanded knowledge base were viewed as preliminary to a more rigorous and verifiable form of information gathering.

For substantive and more broadly based qualitative input on work-related information, I talked to the librarians themselves. This was done in a series of twenty semi-structured in-depth interviews conducted between 1998 and 2000. I began with the question: "What factors do you think facilitate change in academic libraries, and what factors inhibit it?" All of the interviewees were articulate, reflective, and accomplished in their field, thus constituting an expert pool. The response rate of 100% and the openness of their conversation manifested, not only an interest in the research topic and professional tendency to be helpful, but also a wish to be heard. The data from the interviews was rich, and enabled three successful levels of interpretation: the answer to the question, the labour process interpretation of issues in the narratives, and substantive labour process information. The first two, the institutional environment and the labouring situation, contributed to the refinement of my research problem, and are detailed below. The third, the detailed relational information about labour, is covered later.

Interview Data: The Institutional Environment

There was widespread agreement that the information technology revolution, economic factors internal to the institution, and social factors external to the institution were the greatest factors affecting change in academic libraries. After a while the distinction between what facilitated and what inhibited change made little difference, as both perspectives focused on the issues. Table 1 itemizes the major issues identified by respondents within their labouring environment, in order of response frequency.

Table 1.   Factors Affecting Change and Continuity in Canadian Academic Libraries ($n = 20$: 15 female, 5 male).

Factor	Total	Fem	Male
New information and communication technologies; The Internet			
Revolutionary; pervasive			
Internet "*supplice*" [ordeal; uncertainty; torture]; fear of technology	15	10	5
Learning curve for IT; limitations on time and teachers			
Need to "ramp up mid-career"			
Must be self-taught/motivated	12	10	2
Workload; Staff shortage; Inability to hire (especially technology-related jobs)	11	9	2
Larger social factors; Outside forces; Societal change			
Neo-conservative economy			
Constancy and rapidity of change			
"Different landscape"			
"Boomers" are entrenched	11	6	5
Economic/budgetary factors			
Problematic; except for technological equipment & personnel, according to some	10	8	2
Age or technological orientation of librarians; Recency of training			
"My colleagues who are no longer young lack energy, dynamism, and ability to find new solutions"	8	5	3
Library management style			
Entrenched and old-fashioned			
So many decisions and overlaps; "no right choice for managers"	8	6	2
Library clients			
Literacy level: information rich and information poor			
Expectations, such as for high speed and immediacy	7	5	2
Gender [probed with male interviewees]			
Gender *may be* related to comfort with technology; drive			
More male/female egalitarianism, fewer gender differences in francophone institutions; there are French/English differences here			
"*Ici c'est les femmes!*"; "women are as combative as men," vs. "a group of women is easier to work with than one of men"	4	1	3
Networking and cooperation			
Joint ventures & consortia share electronic subscription costs			
Documentation or telecommunications standards are often forces that inhibit positive change	5	5	
Library structural factors			
"The institution"			
The outmoded building	4	3	1
Other actors in the university (faculty; union contracts)	3	2	1

Economic or Structural Factors Within the Library

Economic stringency and other constraints on library operations are identified most frequently by librarians as inhibitors of progressive change, or reasons for altering library work in negative ways. For many respondents, the short answer was, "Money!" The lack of general economic and budgetary resources includes money for books, electronic information materials, and improvements to the building. Connected with fiscal concerns were personnel-related issues such as excessive workload, staff shortage, and an inability to hire. Competition for scarce resources ensues. The perceived support for information technologies varies among the universities. A representative of a well-endowed university provided this perspective:

> Money is a two-edged sword. More money has been spent in the central system on information technology and the IT Department, and siphoning people off other departments, and is growing. We are not downsizing . . .. It is easier to get outlets than lighting improvement! . . . Money is not being spent on staff.

Library management style is another structural aspect that may inhibit change or that needs to change, because it is entrenched and outmoded. A section head reflects:

> The structures of [my university] work against the meaningful participation of librarians in critical decision-making [related to the budget]. This university has an extremely hierarchical and old-fashioned idea of management . . .. It would be better if there were consultation, or committee representation . . .. There is almost non-existent communication!

A former chief of a small library asserts:

> The institutional will to change has been inhibited by existing structures. These structures have inhibited our ability to innovate throughout the organization, and prevented us from seeing outside the box. Translate these through the rules and regulations of bureaucracy, which has been my experience. Having been there, I'm quite happy not to do it anymore.

The management of contemporary academic libraries also involves so many decisions and overlapping considerations. A senior manager recognizes that:

> Even managers and university librarians cannot make decisions without looking at overlapping areas: technical needs, service considerations, economic realities, political issues . . . leaving no right choice for library managers.

Another dimension of these structural constraints involves interlibrary relationships such as joint ventures, consortia, and documentation standards, and the compromises that are required to enjoy their collective benefits. Thus, this comprehensive theme of economic and structural constraint reinforces and expands my observations on staff tension and staff shortages in the preliminary phase of the research. Underlying the issues related to staff shortage, institutional inadequacies, and fiscal limitations is the divisive effect of information technology, particularly upon staff. Technology is the second major controversial area found through the interviews.

Technological Revolution

New computer and telecommunications technologies and their diffusion to staff and patrons are regularly identified as the most evident change in this collection of issues. This category is not as differentiated as the first. The most dominant aspect of technological change is the speed and pervasiveness of that change, especially the growth of Internet-based information resources. A librarian who works with technology summarizes the situation:

> Every time you slow down or get out of the stream, technology keeps moving; it just doesn't stop.... It is hard enough to stay on top of one thing, let alone everything, and how they interrelate. One can't keep up for a long period of time.

A danger of this, warns another, is:

> We have become infatuated with technology and process rather than content . . . We do clerical work, both in the traditional sense, and now with technology. We're pretty expensive help.

A second aspect is the continuous learning curve for mastering these technologies, against limitations of time and the availability of mentors or teachers. A reference and instructional librarian articulates this for many others:

> I have been close to tears if help with technology was not available. We should not be embarrassed, or made to feel stupid.

In an environment restricted by a lack of institutional support, self-taught or self-motivated staff are considered to be the most successful, because they transcend the ignorance gap, "ramp up mid-career," and are dependent on no one. One solution is having the right attitude:

> I don't get worried about it any more. If you miss a couple of generations [i.e. two months], you can get back in.

Related to the revolutionary and unfamiliar aspects of new information technologies is the third aspect of technological change, its association with age. "Age" actually implies recency of training, which usually refers to librarians in their late twenties or early thirties. Respondents normally believe that recent information studies graduates arrive to the job with high computer literacy, or, at the very least, comfort with an electronic information environment and willingness to do things differently. This perception is captured in the contribution of a middle-aged male respondent, who admits:

My colleagues who are no longer young lack energy, dynamism, and ability to find new solutions.

A younger counterpart cynically admits:

It's technology that gets everyone in.... It's locked solid. You're not getting in there till the forthcoming wave of retirements.... [New librarians are] refreshed, recently trained, have enthusiasm for the profession, and are closer to the student population.

It is unclear whether the impacts of the age of librarians upon technology are based on their unenthusiastic attitudes or concrete skill deficiencies. In either case, there may be an interaction with the labour process.

The implications of technological change upon work thus tend to centre on changes in skill requirements, the need for additional training, and feelings of insecurity in an expansive and electronically mediated information universe. The interview responses in this category suggest that technology is more than wizardry, and is associated with both staff expertise and with relations of authority in the workplace. In addition to being integral to labour process, these expertise and control factors point to the third area mentioned by librarians, the social climate.

Social Factors Outside the Institution

According to interview responses, the third thematic area affecting change in academic libraries is actually a collection of factors associated with a "climate of change" or "the social structure." These include forces outside the library such as the economy, and the more specific influences of various social groups on the work of librarians. Unlike the first interview category, which includes internal fiscal strictures, a consideration of the social structure involves the general economic, social, and political climate of late capitalist society. Although respondents provided neither specific concepts nor contextual situations, an example might be the increasing availability of distance education, which impacts on funding, resources, and staffing. In contrast with the other two categories, there is no strong agreement about specifics for this one, which provides interesting areas of contestation for further analysis: a "different landscape" suggests progressive social forces; "constancy of change" is neutral; and "entrenched boomers" or "neo-conservative economy" suggest inhibiting forces.

Library clients have input to change. Students, in particular, have higher expectations for speed and immediacy. Many librarians feel that they must sustain the media-saturated environment to which the students are accustomed, or provide such an environment for those from economically or socially deprived backgrounds. There is concern for the polarization of student literacy in terms of "information-rich" or "information-poor," suggesting that there are larger social class issues connected with literacy in an educational context. It is clear from the few interview remarks about faculty, that, like librarians, they may be characterized as either "enthusiastic" or "entrenched" about the dynamics of contemporary libraries, and thus capable of either supporting or retarding library development in times of transition. In truth, faculty are not perceived to understand what a professional librarian really does, from either a negative or positive viewpoint:

> Few have seen us in our professional role, for example, instructing a classroom of students in bibliographic research skills. Those who have not seen us in our professional role would not suspect that this is our role. They think we're there to help students to find books.

Or,

> Those who do come to us are impressed, especially with electronic technology. For a library seminar for his class, one professor requested, 'I want you to do what you do . . . I want you to dazzle with all that computer stuff.'

Conspicuously absent is mention of the gender imbalance among librarians, so I probed that topic in later interviews, particularly with the men. One male responded, "Oh, you're going there!" This suggested he either did not expect to talk about gender, or thought it was irrelevant to the discussion. While it is conventionally assumed that library managers are more frequently male, male respondents suggest it is comfortable to work for female bosses. They also normally find it congenial to work alongside women. Young men suggest that gender is not an issue, and view women as strong or compatible associates:

> It doesn't bother me at all. I have no objections working with women. I have no objections working *for* women in positions of authority. I have worked in all-male environments before, and would choose women. A whole different dynamic. Best with a mix.

The articulated information from the workers in my sample shows that the gender factor provides little conclusive input on the question of change in the labouring environment. The females do not introduce it as an inhibitor or a facilitator of change. The males downplay it, indicate they are not uncomfortable with their minority status at the working level, or do not own that men are more likely to rise to management.[1] This contradicts the popular perception that men are a dominant minority (Smart, 1975). Thus, while the gendering of the labour process is normally integral to a political economic analysis, the defining subjects do not acknowledge the issue. It is, therefore, not problematized here, though gender balance is noted where the data are available.

Under the rubric of social factors, this third category of interview responses signals that librarians possess a general sensitivity to societal change, along with a strong awareness of the modification of library services, the interplay of library clients, and cultural dynamics. Telecommunications technologies and gender are other factors that interact with these changing forces, whether identified or implied by the respondents. These larger social forces underlie the other two major categories affecting change in libraries, structural constraints within the library and the technological revolution.

Summary of Interviews with the Librarians
Through the in-depth interviews, librarians provided grounded information about professional expertise and power associated with the retraction of resources, the interaction of technology, and changes in perceptions of knowledge and library service. The economic, technological, and social themes are complementary. First, there is an economic basis to most structural constraints which equally affect the individual worker, the institution, and interlibrary and other external relationships. Second, technologically-mediated information resources affect professional skill, which, in turn, connects with relations of authority. Third, apparent cultural changes that are popularly perceived as "lifestyle" disjunctions, such as increased speed and shifting time, involve social continuities when analyzed in terms of ownership and control.

In the next step in the analysis, these library problem data are transformed into labour process phenomena. The interview data are re-classified into professional labour categories of expertise and control. It will be seen later that the data in this problem identification phase link to larger forces related to ownership, control, buying power of money, and the labour market.

Interview Data: Labour Process Interpretation

Embedded in the discussions of the social situation are important statements about the problems of labour. In their discussions of millennial change, respondents place an overwhelming emphasis on skill sets, exemplified by keeping abreast of increasingly sophisticated technologies, responding to a greater diversification of patron needs, and juggling the many facets of an expanding knowledge base. The common denominator is a preoccupation with service in both the public and technical arenas. Yet the interviews do not reflect much sensitivity or concern about the degree to which librarians control their work, apart from control of time and quality. This section seeks to move beyond the structural and social factors that enable and inhibit change in academic libraries. It articulates the nature of professional expertise within the conception of the labour process in a professional environment, that is, within changing social relations of production. It also expands on the *value* of the expertise of librarians for patrons and other staff, and the *control* of their situation.

Expertise and control are key elements to the theoretical conceptualization of professional labour. Ehrenreich and Ehrenreich (1979) used skill as a defining characteristic of the professional-managerial class. In their framework for analysis of the relations of ruling in the post-industrial workplace, Clement and Myles (1994) used job skill and degree of control as the prime dimensions in their aggregate class factors. Wright (1997) also regarded expertise and power as two of the three dimensions of the knowledge class. The third, property, is not relevant to workers in this setting. In these views, labour is constitutive of social class in the neo-Marxian tradition, because the relations of production at the workplace are reproduced in society. The Marxian tradition is important to professional information work because of its relational approach to power, between expertise and control, and between librarians and other classes of workers.

Expertise may also accord status through credentialling (Collins, 1979) or social closure (Murphy, 1988). Collins viewed professional credentials as a firm dividing line between privilege and exclusion. Murphy addressed the issue of professional monopolization through exclusion. Abbott (1988) contested the permeability of closure by looking at the appropriation of professional duties by non-professional staff and at new hybrid professions. In these views, professional status is based on a set of characteristics, such as education and autonomy, in the neo-Weberian tradition, because professional powers are viewed through self-regulation and control of the marketplace. The Weberian tradition is important to professional information work not only for its conceptualization of occupational closure, but also for its articulation of the theoretical foundation of bureaucracy as a form of workplace control.

The grounded categories from the interviews provide rich circumstantial details about library professionalism and the labour process. In view of the wide dimensionality of job skills covered in the interviews with librarians and earlier observations about skill and power relations at the point of production, the library-based categories are reorganized into areas of skill and control, to provide a better understanding of social relations in the workplace.

Skill Characteristics
From the interview comments about the challenges of change in the contemporary academic library, I identified six characteristics that reflect professional expertise. They are complexity, knowledge base, service ethic, esteem, professional contribution, and rewards. The associated characteristic of certification did not emerge, because it did not apply to academic librarians.

Complexity was normally not articulated but implied by reference to the numerous skills that comprise their expertise. At the fundamental level, these include theory and practice in information studies, disciplinary knowledge, and the command of electronic resources. A management librarian summarizes the increase in job complexity in the post-industrial library:

> There is a movement toward generalists across functions. However unrealistic, a specialization in subjects and languages is needed. We also want management skills, communications and interpersonal skills, teamwork capabilities. Now everything overlaps. Black and white is very minimal, and there is a whole lot of grey.

It is clear that increased complexity brings greater intensity, and adds to the stresses as well as the challenges of today's job. Its generalist, cross-disciplinary nature also makes library work less highly regarded in academic and professional spheres where breadth tends not to be as highly regarded as depth or specialization.

The knowledge base of information specialists was frequently mentioned in the conversations. This suggested that the respondents felt particularly susceptible to the expansion of their knowledge base, since their business was to be expert in knowledge. There was divergence in what constituted professional knowledge, from attention to basic information service to proactive systems development within the community. The numerous remarks about the mechanisms of new information and communication technologies suggested that the conceptual understanding of information might be diminished by a preoccupation with the instrumental. According to a perceptive librarian working in a technological job:

> I think this whole mouse-push, this illiterate pointing at the stuff you want in the Windows interface, I don't think that is very conducive to having an articulate mind. I think it gives you an instrumental mind, and you know what you want and you know how to get it . . .. You can't articulate ideas as well, it seems to me. I don't really know. I don't really talk to many 14-year olds.

A strong commitment to service underlies librarians' expressed concerns about the rapidity of change, time management, and upgrading skill sets. In an evolving workplace, professional service may involve major system design initiatives or the "running to catch up" activities of public service work. While the former are proactive, the latter are responsive, and tend to characterize librarianship as a supportive profession. As a male librarian reflected:

> The profession has more feminine qualities: doing things for other people, selfless, gatherer rather than hunter.

The interviews suggest that the service aspect is a defining trait of professional expertise. This is characteristic of the classic social responsibility perspective on professionalism, which is being sustained among librarians in their bibliographic instruction, outreach to special groups, maintenance of quality control, and protection of intellectual property and privacy.

Professional esteem was frequently mentioned by the librarians, particularly in the context of collaboration with faculty. Librarians were in agreement that, while the cognitive base of information studies was complex, they did not have doctorates in this or any other discipline. In the words of one proactive interviewee, they were "similar but not the same." On collegiality with faculty, another ambitious librarian commented:

> Faculty regard us as strange creatures, handmaidens. Hard to have collegial relationships based on subject knowledge. We're not in the same ballpark. Working on more committees gives them a new way to see you.

With increasing threats to professional survival by staff attrition, and with the increasing use of paraprofessionals or end-user electronically-mediated information resources, information studies professionals now talk about re-inventing themselves in varying degrees through alternative venues. This has been achieved through a shift toward information systems specialization, Internet or web page development, or consulting. Others leave the university altogether to market their expertise in the commercial arena. Thus the comments suggest that, for academic librarians who are not managers or systems specialists, full esteem is gained outside the library itself. If their intellectual labour remains within the institution, the consequences may include alienation or job degradation.

The professional activities of academic librarians are, again, "similar but not the same" as those of faculty, their closest comparison group. While they have numerous national, regional, and specialized associations and journals, and are often active in public forums related to information access issues, they feel that these are not regarded as essential to the job. Whether time-wise or conceptually, the daily job takes priority, and even promotion through the ranks considers professional writing, organizing, and social action as only one aspect for consideration. Further, while contractual arrangements among Canadian libraries vary, few librarians have inviolate release time to do serious research and writing. Additionally, their intensive working days prevent them from working professional activities into their spare time. Opportunity for professional growth and academic status on a plain with faculty are theoretically possible, but the institutional situation leaves few openings for librarians to achieve that status, and regards them as workers "in the trenches."

The last dimension related to librarians' skill sets is rewards in the form of salary and benefits. Unlike the above expertise categories, they were not highlighted as problem areas by the interviewees, even after probes about the value of their work. The silence about salary issues may be due to a variety of factors, such as satisfaction, lack of awareness, a reticence to discuss the issue, or a fear of criticism.

Since salary and benefits are measurable, they are verified with administrative statistics, collective agreements, and labour market information.

The dimensions of professional library expertise, as delimited in the narratives of librarians are knowledge base, complexity, service ethic, esteem, professionalizing activities, and rewards structures. Details on what constitutes this knowledge component range from the ideal-typical view to the changing post-industrial reality, and come from the lived experiences of the librarians. The connecting theme is confrontation with social change, that is, the retention of core aspects of skill or adaptation to change. Thus skill conceptualization and change is an important component in the interrogation of the historical continuity of labour process. The following section shows that possession and exercise of expertise are related to concepts of power.

Control Characteristics
Control, or power, is more directly integrated into the workings of the labour process than skill, and has been more elusive in the interview comments. While skill can be perceived categorically, through measures such as education, power is relational and is perceived in relationships between workers. It is better assessed through indicators that convey these relationships and the power they generate. In the reworking of the interview categories, distinct issues of control and power emerge. Following is a breakdown of areas that demonstrate the professional worker's degrees of control in the library labour process, as informed by the comments in the interviews. They include control over the spheres of work, acquisitions, innovations, staff, quality, time, and conditions, plus enabling factors of demographic composition in the workplace. The information becomes more interesting when put in perspective of what has remained consistent over time, and what is in the process of change.

Control over the work was a dominant issue for librarians, as indicated by numerous comments about challenges in responding to student and faculty needs, to the provision of electronic information, and to cooperative projects involving other libraries. Working in a mode of response, the majority were not inclined to put themselves forward on social or instructional issues related to their expertise, as also noted above in the context of skill. According to one interviewee:

> It could be [1] gender, [2] waits rather than tells, or [3] absence of ego and unwillingness to pass judgment . . . . Librarians have a useful role, but are not always appreciated.

This occurs in relationships with faculty, where librarians may not have the credibility or confidence to assert their knowledge or promote themselves as collaborators. It also occurs in relationships with publishers, system vendors, and middle-men, who constrain librarians' freedom of choice of materials with inflexible packages of information, service, and pricing. Often, major purchasing decisions have budgetary and policy implications for administrators, so librarians as consumers also engage with their administrators to make a case for spending money.

Control over acquisitions has become a complex power issue in the age of costly electronic purchases, cooperative ventures, and deselection, and relies more than ever on the ability to exercise selection expertise. The free exercise of this knowledge cannot always be taken for granted, as trenchantly summarized by a subject specialist librarian:

> In earlier days, there was a lack of well-rounded collections due to too much reliance on faculty collection building. Nowadays, there is a homogenized collection due to outside corporate pressures. In either case, it is not strongly controlled from within.

In addition to the economic strictures affecting the freedom to spend money on acquisitions, in today's academic libraries the constraints include limited availability from publishers, vendor monopolies, institutional agreements with corporations, and negotiated consortium decisions.

The control of innovation is an important extension of control of the work, and the pressures upon librarians in this area are great. Some of the impetus to innovate comes from clients, and even from other libraries. According to a systems librarian:

> There is strong client demand, especially for greater speed . . . Sometimes a system is introduced so a library can be competitive with other institutions.

Academic librarians cannot elect to ignore developments in information technology, because, unlike university faculty, their work consists of mastering the dynamics of bibliographic control and dissemination as well as the generation of information. Librarians' mastery of innovation is increasingly interconnected with development initiatives in the corporate sector, and they may be treated as secondary players:

> Lack of consultation with the producers . . . I guess there wasn't the valuation of what we [the consumers] could have contributed to the project. . . . They are being driven by their own agendas, and they don't view us as players or partners in the creation, too.

Frequent remarks suggest that the professional workers cannot control the speed of innovation, nor make available the time to become competent or catch up.

In the area of control over staff, librarians expressed more concern about management attitudes toward them than about their decreasing control over subordinate staff due to the flattening of the middle ranges of the establishment. A frequent complaint among experienced librarians was the patriarchal attitude of senior management toward them. Notes one who was assertive in many spheres of the university:

Our management style is paternal, hierarchical, not collegial, which is surprising in an academic
setting. But the academy is also hierarchical.

This perception inevitably influences the attitudes of faculty about the expertise
and status of library professionals.

Interconnected with corporate sector involvement in information production is
quality control. While some database and systems vendors increasingly employ
professional librarians on their marketing staff, one systems librarian is distrustful:

Middlemen – internet, databases, whatever – but middlemen! Intermediaries will have to be
damn good and very reasonable. Middlemen play a good role if no one else can provide it better
or cheaper.

Areas where librarians strive for quality control, with greater optimism, are
in the regularization of documentation standards and system interconnectivity.
The public production of information sources on the Internet, and the resultant
anarchy, is another area where librarians have little control. Here they strive to
ensure that relevant scholarly information is retrieved by users, with numerous
remarks about instruction and accountability.

Control over time is connected with intensified workload and reduced staff.
Many respondents recognized that the technological fix was a myth:

Internet instruction takes staff time . . . It's an irony that, with so few staff resources, the administration should direct the solution at technology.

This time involves contact time with patrons, and with learning the latest
technologies. If the changing perception of worker's time is perceived as an
indicator of the labour status of workers, then loss of control of time equates with
loss of control of conditions of work.

The working conditions of academic librarians are governed by the collective
agreements or handbooks of unions or staff associations. No mention was made
of issues so covered, such as salary, merit awards, benefits, leave, and sabbaticals
or equivalent. Issues that were highlighted, such as increasing workload and
decreasing sense of control, are hard to protect under present contractual
arrangements. Nor can union contracts prevent the interaction of corporate or
outside influences with relationships at the point of production in the library.

The final category related to the power dimension includes demographic factors,
specifically age and gender, that affect the labour force and interact with relations
of production. It was noted that a critical mass of classically trained librarians
with a breadth of knowledge and historical understanding of institutional practices
will retire at once. This will leave, it was expressed, an intellectual vacuum in
the library, which will have implications for quality control in service. What was
not articulated was an obvious fear of management re-engineering to innovate,

streamline operations, and diffuse technology more efficiently, without the critical responses to the "technological imperative" typical of many who represent the current demographic.

Concern about age is contentious, as it involves preconceptions about the competencies and motivational state of both seasoned librarians and recent graduates. One recent graduate exemplifies this position:

> This library is clogged with boomers. They could please start retiring and whatever and get out of the way. Boomers have been squeezing us for a long time and it's going to continue.

A significant demographic category is gender. It has already been noted that gender was not formally identified by the interviewees as a factor that inhibited or enabled change in academic libraries. There was marked silence on any stated relationship between gender and power. Since the objective of this research is based on problem refinement by the workers, gender will not be pursued in depth. The silence around gender, however, is suggestive, and could provide substance for a more comprehensive study.

In summary, the control factors identified in the interviews about the professional labour process included those related to the job, the library environment, and individual characteristics, such as seniority. Operational factors associated with the immediate job (work, acquisitions, and staff) were most frequently introduced. Professional factors associated with the overall library situation (quality, innovations, time, and conditions of work) were less frequently mentioned. Personal factors such as age, gender, date of entry into the profession, and length of tenure were introduced least often. All three aspects are essential to analyze the control dimension of the professional labour process. This can be done with supplementary institutional and documentary data, as well as the in-depth analysis of the relational components of the interviews.

Conclusions About the Grounded Problem

The grounded interview evidence includes numerous comments about work and its characteristics, and infrequent reference to a critical labour process view. Overall, it implies that, in spite of a complex complement of expertise, academic librarians have little autonomy in their work in relation to the criteria of professionalism. In addition to the "librarian image" and hierarchical environment, the evidence suggests that the nature of control (or loss of it) are shifting due to a "changing landscape" that includes technological, spatial, economic, and global forces, all structural forces. In response to these constraining forces, interviewees interested in greater control of their work or professional growth have taken the routes, respectively, of limited collective action through unions or activity in university committees, academic publishing, or consulting.

The larger concern about skill and control issues is best interpreted at an economic level. Corporate influence and control on librarians' work, for example through their domination of publishing, resource availability, and indirectly on university spending, have reduced the importance of professional input. Interviews have shown that managers need to spend money on materials rather than expensive salaries. Therefore, the qualitative data on academic library work, disclosed by librarians and analyzed in labour process terms, point to the need to investigate economic and political forces that influence their operation. This is done through examination of data about academic librarians and libraries.

TRENDS IN THE LABOUR OF ACADEMIC LIBRARIANS

The literature of information studies offers contested views of the status and future of academic librarianship, focusing on the optimistic perspective. Librarians working in a cross-national setting in Canada clarified the discrepancy by validating the claims of rapid development, but emphasizing insecurity and perceived loss of control in their labouring environment. To situate this information, I examine the objective labour situation within the library and the university as a whole. This is operationalized and extracted from administrative and survey statistics, plus selected documentary evidence from collective agreements. The administrative data provide information about funding for libraries and breakdowns therein, about staff, and about materials. Survey statistics provide selective demographic information. Collective agreements provide information on professional rights and job security. Information on expenditures for technology vs. those for staff, intuitively a good thing to examine given the interview remarks, was more elusive because of measurement inaccuracies, but could be approximated.

This trending information suggests a relatively stable position for professional academic library workers, considering the changing apportionment of library funds, the decrease in the number of jobs available, and the limitations in salary increases. Some specific figures about the library within the university, staff within the library, and professionals within the staff complement clarify this point. The focal point is the labour of librarians, particularly its value and the power it affords.

The Library Fiscal Environment

According to an analysis by the Canadian Association of Research Libraries (Emory, 1999), the apportionment of university funding for libraries has remained fairly constant at 6.75–7% of the university budget. Given the size of library budgets, a miniscule fluctuation up or down may make the difference of hundreds of thousands of dollars, equivalent to a few professional salaries or an entire serials budget! This is exacerbated by inflation, increasing materials prices, and, in Canada, the weak international position of the dollar. Within this general apportionment, salaries have represented over half of the budget. Between 1995 and 2000, a period of growth in technological development, this salary proportion has decreased about 7% in the national average, with regional variations, from 60 to 53% of the library budget.

Professional Labour Costs

In the area of professional labour costs, salary is a proxy for the value of the skill aspects of the job, and stability of the librarian component an indictor of their value to the establishment. For this and the remainder of the discussion, the annual statistics from the Canadian Association of Research Libraries, as analyzed by Carson (2002) are used, unless otherwise noted. The proportion of professional to total salaries increased during the 1990s from one third to about 40%, particularly in the last few years of the decade. This indicates that professionals represent for the library budget a considerable segment of the library salary budget. It is not decreasing at the same rate as other expenditures, such as serials budgets, which dropped on average over 50% between 1990 and 2000. While these data do not reflect the actual staff component, inferences can be made about the stability ensured by contractual arrangements and a mature staff of long tenure. With regular and early retirements and the hiring of junior staff, these proportions are expected to decrease. Similarly, salary figures provide general information only on trending. The average national increase in the average librarian's salary during the 1990s from $53,000 to $62,500, or 18%, barely kept up with inflation, and said little about variations in staff composition and salary levels within the libraries.

The Value of Professional Work

Continuing the analysis, the importance of professional work may be inferred to a limited degree by counts of professional librarians, percentage of staff, and students per librarian. The number of librarians has decreased by 5–15% across Canada, or two to nine librarians per institution, and the average professional staff complement was 42 in 1999–2000. This is somewhat consistent with the overall budgetary reductions for libraries and staff detailed above. These numbers, however, are not as important as librarian resilience in proportion to the rest of the staff. Proportionally, librarians have continued to constitute from about 20–22%

of the full-time equivalent staff in the national average. While the actual numbers have decreased, the proportions have remained fairly constant.

A concern implied in the interviews and from trends in the literature on workplace change is that professional work might be deskilled, and gradually passed on to less costly or more technologically oriented staff. Full-time equivalent support staff have comprised, on average, from 50 to 75% of the entire staff between 1990 and 2000. In most of the libraries, however, support staff ratios have either diminished or remained the same, in contrast with the continuing stability of the professional staff component.[2] It is clear that, while librarians enjoy more job security relative to support staff, they feel the impacts of not having assistance with their workload. The diminishing support staff ratios also show the greater volatility of their positions, in relation to librarians, both in terms of job security and continuity in the job.

The number of students per librarian would appear to give a general indication about the university's valuation of librarians vs. students, but has measurement flaws. The national average is 450, with an increase of 50 over the 1990s and much local variation due to differences in ratios between professional and non-professional staff. The loss of a single librarian, even in technical services, can account for a change in these ratios, and, therefore, it is not a meaningful measure. The narratives are a better indication of the actual service experience.

Labour Trends Summarized

Until the end of the 1990s, the socio-economic environment of university libraries in Canada has been one of gradual economic decline, but relative stability for the professional labour therein. University expenditures have minimally increased over this period, and even decreased between 1995–1996 and 1996–1997. The library portions have increased only a fraction of a percent, not enough to make up for rising materials costs such as serials subscriptions or increasing operating costs such as salaries. Total salaries as a portion of library expenditures have undergone consistent annual cuts, amounting to a reduction of 10 percentage points of overall expenses over the 1990s. This can be partially explained by a reduction in staff due to attrition, as total library staff numbers have reduced by 11% between 1991–1992 and 1996–1997 (Emory, 1999).

The value of professional labour is reflected not only though actual remuneration, but also through stability relative to the rest of the library staff. Here the figures are encouraging. Median professional salaries have increased minimally per year, often below inflation, though recent increases have been greater. According to staff counts, the rate of attrition of professionals between

1991–1992 and 1996–1997 is lower than that of the non-professional staff (Emory, 1999). Professionals have actually sustained a proportion of 20% of the staff complement, in spite of an annual reduction in numbers. This is counter-intuitive, because the effects of technology diffusion and job displacement would suggest that the complement of professionals goes down while that of non-professional and casual staff goes up. Indicators of control enjoyed by the library as a whole, in the context of the entire university, were mainly financial, for example expenditure on staff as a proportion of library expenditures. While general, they help to depict the power of librarians. This overview tells us that, toward the end of the 1990s, professional librarians appeared to have more security than other library staff. If factors such as remaining a stable proportion of the library staff were adequate reflections of the importance of their labour, librarians have actually fared *better* than non-professional staff in post-industrial academic libraries! Clearly, more factors need to be considered.

Staff Versus Technology?

The expenditure on librarians relative to that on technology was suggested as problematic in the librarians' narratives. This section considers both the library-wide apportionment of funds and the relative strength of professional library work discussed above. It must be stressed that there is no causal relationship between expenses on salary or technology. They are not comparable. They are derived not only from different budgetary areas, the materials budget and the operations budget, but also from different premises. Further, it is difficult to quantify expenses for electronic library services, or the extent to which money spent on electronics *may replace* that spent on staff or books. Moneys spent on a new database or electronic journals may be part of the serials or the electronic materials budget, which are often separate categories of the collections budget. Additionally, they may be part of the campus electronic infrastructure budget, which involves hardware and software allocations. Database allocations may be part of the interlibrary resource-sharing budget, which includes consortial arrangements and document delivery. Reporting categories for hardware and software, and for electronic information, are not mutually exclusive. Further, expenditures growth may not be consistent over the years, but may come in "waves," where a library incurs high expenses for a year or two for a complete system infras-tructure. Chief librarians capitalize on the most appropriate mechanisms to cover these expenses.

Comparisons over time, therefore, are not informative, particularly as a back-ground for labour expenses. Taking 1999–2000 as a meaningful year, because the interviews were held during this period, the median university library expenditures for computer hardware and software ranged regionally from under $200,000 to about $550,000. For electronic materials, the Canadian average was about $850,000, or 14% of all materials budgets. Compared with a national expenditure during this year of $2.25 million for professional librarians, the amounts designated for electronics are not insignificant. *Hypothetically*, noting the above caveats, a loss of two or three professional staff at $70,000 per annum could have beneficial effects for the electronics budget. Looking at the data for electronics support also provides some details or inconsistencies that can further be problematized.

Personal Information on Professional Workers

When the research question was focussed on the labour process components of expertise and power, demographic and personal factors such as age, gender, education, tenure in position, status indicators, and mobility opportunities were introduced. Some of this information was collected as part of an unpublished 1998 downsizing survey of Canadian research librarians by Auster and Taylor with 778 respondents, 71% female and 29% male. It determined that the average respondent is female, between 45 and 54 years old, earning between $60,000 and $69,000, and working over 20 years at the same institution though not necessarily in the same position.[3] Additional key points for professional labour were that one third of the respondents were strong in the expertise category with a master's degree or higher in a subject field outside of librarianship, in addition to their professional degree. Compared with the average librarian's salary of $41,000 reported in the 1996 Census of Canada, the university salary is superior! Salary is the most quantifiable indicator of the value of the work, the value of the credentials, and the strength of the bargaining unit. It may be related to economic strength of the province or region. It is also an indicator of the market value of the work, which is higher for consultants and private industry.

Only 8% of the respondents were under 35 years old, 13% had fewer than five years of service in the institution, and 8% had five years or less of professional experience, supporting interviewee remarks about the need to accommodate younger staff. There are strong implications for the labour market. Within ten years of the survey, at least 25% of the professional academic librarians across Canada will have retired on the basis of age. If the current renewal pattern of under 10% holds, the inflow of librarians will be far smaller than the retirements. This suggests a range of possibilities: retraction, hiring, or re-engineering, depending on the economic or labour climate.

Within the sample, the largest category is reference librarian, and the smallest are systems librarians and administrators. The most surprising finding is the small size, at 15 out of 778 respondents, of the systems category, considering the increasing emphasis in the interviews and observations on information technologies in all spheres of library work. As noted by the principal investigator, systems personnel did not always identify themselves as professional librarians or with the collection and services of the library. Their lack of self-identification or visibility is due to their not always being professional librarians, but computer scientists, analysts, technicians, or clerical workers.

While all demographics are important, and while age and gender have been strong determinants in the statistics of the stability of the staff, expertise has most consistently been identified in the interviews as a measure of various aspects of professional powers. To obtain implications for future labour, I later analyze the hiring trends in the Canadian labour market at the Millennium by tracking position advertisements for university librarians and examining them qualitatively for job content, salary, and requirements.

Professional Benefits and Status

The extent to which professional work is valued may be measured in the amount that the employer pays for it in professional benefits as well as salary. Academic librarians are normally members of unions or staff associations, which, in most cases, are associated with those of faculty, and governed by the general provisions of their contracts.[4] Conditions of work peculiar to librarians are included in separate clauses on professional qualifications, promotion, tenure, merit, job security, and rights and responsibilities. In some universities, professional librarians enjoy sabbatical or study leave, research allowances, and other opportunities for professional growth and output. In others, any leave is closely monitored and gauged in relation to the operational objectives of the library. The questions in this section that are important to labour process are how such benefits reflect the worth of librarians to the institution, and whether any changes in these reflect change to the value of academic library work or the power held by the librarians.

Union contracts are useful for defining things as they formally should be in the scheme of expertise and control, and have certain limitations as data sources. Their language is necessarily general and the clauses are as inclusive as possible, as it is with job descriptions. This is especially problematic in the area of determining authority. Contract clauses relating to autonomy and authority often do not pinpoint the degree of power and control the librarian actually has. They are subject to interpretation by library management, which often results in the limitation of autonomy, and formal grievance procedures are often the only recourse. A further impediment to the use of contract clauses to define the limits of authority is that what is pertinent to faculty may not necessarily be applicable to or analogous for librarians. For example, faculty concerns with the use of technology as a substitute for their labour and expertise, or with the protection of their times, are also of keen interest to librarians but come from a different set of professional expectations. Librarians *serve*; faculty teach and do research! Moreover, the issue might not be covered in the contract at all. In his study of academic unions in United States universities and four-year colleges, Rhoades (1998) noted that academics tend to opt for past practice rather than congeal issues in contract language. Notwithstanding their limitations, collective agreements do provide certain information about authority and control. These relate to monetary issues, professional privileges, opportunities for mobility, and areas of authority or status. As such, they are useful because most of the data sources have provided information about the skill dimension of the professional labour process.

Promotion opportunities and procedures are detailed in collective agreements. Impediments are difficult to identify, but the most visible impediments implied in the interviews are lack of opportunity due to retrenchment, or a lack of specialized expertise in information technologies. Frustrations from lack of mobility are exacerbated by loss of control over time and over work, due to scarce human resources, and result in feelings of alienation (Rinehart, 1996).

With information on rewards, privileges, mobility, and input to governance, union data provide only general indicators of power and control for librarians in university settings. While modeled after the principles of powers and prestige accorded to faculty, the union privileges for librarians are not directly comparable. Nothing is specific and much is open to interpretation. In this regard, librarians have more in common with those of non-tenured academics such as sessional lecturers or lower-level academics such as teaching faculty, for example, in the absence of a research agenda.

Section Summary

This section has provided a snapshot of the basic themes about the labour process situation of professional librarians during the 1990s. Salaries were still the greatest expense for academic libraries. In contrast with categories in the materials budget, the salary component of the operations budget is still relatively sizeable. One would expect, therefore, to see significant reductions in one of the highest paid staff groups, the professional librarians, with the rationale that their work can be de-professionalized. But the proportion of librarians within library staffs remained stable, though the actual numbers decreased with attrition, and salaries began to increase slightly at the end of the decade. While this may be due in part to the intervention of librarians' unions, the information suggests that librarians have enjoyed a degree of stability and recognition during this period. These numbers do not, however, prove that deskilling of the work is not occurring.

The amount spent for electronic materials is increasing, but not as much as would be expected, in comparison with amounts spent on salary. There are also shifts within this broadly based category of electronic expenditures, particularly from software to networking expenses. The costs to the library of these shifts and the impact on staff are not visible in the available statistics. Therefore, it has been virtually impossible to isolate what libraries spend on new information and communication technologies. It must be noted that expenditures for technology do not necessarily conflict with professional labour interests, when software and equipment are needed to improve their work. Apart from measurement limitations such as inconsistencies in collection categories and lack of comparability across time, statistical data of this nature can provide little more than trending information for the institution. More information is required, specifically relational information about the labour dynamics within the institution, such as the quality of work, changes in the diffusion and use of electronic materials, and the nature of professional powers.

Within the institution, librarians are valued enough to be retained as a group, to be paid reasonably, and to allow to control their own hiring. These positive indicators of the value of work and power of librarians are contested by cautious feelings expressed by librarians. Most of these considerations and concerns have been dominated by economic constraints, which affect funding and staff. The following section develops the labour process phenomena that were identified by the workers, *specific to the situation*. It then compares and synthesizes the official and grounded information. It concludes that, with this triangulation of findings from within the institution, we also need information about the forces outside the institution that interact with professional academic library labour, such as the labour market.

IN-DEPTH DATA FROM THE LIBRARIANS: AGREEMENT AND DISAGREEMENT

The grounded problem refinement suggested uncertain feelings in a climate of change, and identified issues in relation to the nature of expertise and power, and the relationship between them. The statistical phase, supplemented by information from collective agreements, showed a declining establishment in which librarians were not as strongly disadvantaged as non-professional staff.

Table 2.   What Librarians Contribute at the Workplace ($n = 15$ female, 5 male).

Professional Expertise or Labour	Total	Fem	Male
Role as players outside the library; not always so viewed			
Electronic products development, with vendors			
Campus involvement, e.g. committees, "schmoozing"; often personal			
initiative required; should be structurally possible			
Campus administrative decisions, especially about library funding	15	10	5
Differing emphases on nature professional skills or expertise			
Service ethic, perceived (by a male) as a "feminine quality"			
Management, coordination, integration; multi-skilled			
Maintenance of control of own work; earning of trust and confidence			
Intellectual freedom vs. "refereeing" Internet use			
Danger of misdirection of skills in clerical or technical work	14	9	5
Awareness of conceptual issues & literacy; responsibility for quality control of information			
"Librarianship not libraries"			
Danger of "button-pushing mentality"; sacrifice of broader knowledge at			
expense of computer literacy; technology is not intellectual			
Inclusion of knowledge of computers and html programming	14	9	5
Teaching, pedagogy, instructional development			
Under-valuation and lack of appreciation by faculty			
Integration of library techniques into courses, collaboration with			
professors			
Primacy of bibliographic instruction, especially in IT, as a library function	8	5	3
Need to stretch, adapt, change; transcend "librarian mentality"			
Changing modes of information seeking, such as access from home			
Inhibiting nature of stereotypical characteristics: "one right answer,"			
Lack of energy for innovation			
Breadth of capabilities should include information technology			
Departure from print reference collection as "core" resource for libraries	8	5	3

To amplify the picture and strengthen the argument, the interview data were mined again for context-specific information about the labour process. The resulting themes are summarized in Table 2.

In this discussion of the data, we see the expertise and control aspects of professional labour begin to interact.

Skill and Expertise Issues

These include: (1) differing emphases on the constitution of critical professional skills or expertise; (2) awareness of conceptual issues, literacy, and quality control of information; and (3) teaching, pedagogy, and instructional development. Views on what constitutes professional work clearly vary among librarians. These conceptual differences may contribute to the lack of a unified voice, hence inhibiting gaining a greater position of power for the group. In the words of one librarian, "Librarians have done it to themselves!" The information literacy and quality control dimensions are frequently highlighted. Regardless of their conventional or radical nature, all librarians share a critical view of information quality. They expand this critical approach to new technologies, and to developments in information provision that are outside their control or input. Here the skill and power issues overlap.

Within a more optimistic interpretation, information technologies represent an important layer of skills added to the complex mix of capabilities that characterizes the contemporary "super librarian." Some librarians believe that many of the negative impacts of technology in the workplace may be temporary roadblocks during a transitional phase and will be removed by the next "generation" of librarian hirings.[5] Where labour is concerned, the stakes involve more than technology. By focussing on the skill dimension of professionalism, respondents lose sight of another important dimension, that of authority or power. At this stage it appears that changes in authority relationships bring the potential consequences of loss of control of one's work, and diminution of its value in favour of the centrality of technology.

The contributions of academic librarians to the instructional process, to use a frequently mentioned function, are numerous. A typical example includes feedback from librarians about students' difficulties in interpreting assignment questions, as well as availability of resources to answer the questions adequately. However, many librarians express disappointment on the degree to which they actually do and could provide such feedback through contribution to the assignment development process. Thus the value of librarians' work is under-appreciated, which is exacerbated if the librarian is not outgoing or the faculty member is protective of his or her teaching "turf." The learning situation is aggravated if the available resources have been reduced or are electronically disorganized to such an extent that the students can not make sense of information gathering and research.

Power and Control Issues

These include insights that: (1) librarians should be players on campus in educational development and administration, but are not always viewed as such; (2) librarians need to stretch, adapt, change; transcend the "librarian mentality"; and (3) differing emphases on what constitutes core professional skills or expertise. From their input to the interviews, the librarians are less definitive about their position of power than the expertise they offer. They are articulate about key skills such as information quality control, their ability to contextualize knowledge, and their engagement with patrons. They are clear about the need to improve their partnerships in campus functions such as educational development, and offer suggestions such as formal committee participation and individual initiative to enhance this interaction. However, few opine *why* this interaction is limited, except that "we are similar but not the same" as faculty. The problem seems to be about the perceptions of clients about the abilities of librarians. They tend to view them as support personnel rather than professionals with unique abilities. This brings the discussion into the area of power based on the authority of their cognitive base, which again shows the convergence of the expertise and power dimensions.

Another power issue involves the deskilling and re-skilling of professional library work, exacerbated by the rationalization of work and the automated of knowledge-based processes. If technologies are mere tools, their increase in value over intellectual capital represents a degradation of professional intellectual work. This would support the views of some respondents that historically the profession has been burdened with too much clerical work, with the trenchant utterance, "We have exchanged one form of clerical work for another!"

Agreement Between Librarians'
Experiences and Official Information

There are three areas of agreement. The first is economic financial stringency. There is no question that academic libraries are indeed being allocated less money for staff, books, and periodicals, and that this impedes the efforts of their staff to provide service. Second, there has been a definite reduction in all levels of staff. Librarians are definitely asked to do "more with less," but have greater job security than the support staff or paraprofessionals. Third, overwork and extended work are happening increasingly, despite the early promises that information technology would save time and working days would shorten (Cordell, 1985). Duxbury and Higgins' (2002) research on the worsening pressures on work due to technology, downsizing, and family pressures more accurately reflects the present picture, though my interviewees never mentioned work-family stress. Burnout and information overload are common, however, as seen in my observations and inferred in the interviews, and often associated with the librarians' level of confidence about their knowledge of new information and communication technologies, or with the library's provision of electronic services to its patrons. They may be associated with demographic factors such as age or recency of credentialling. The contention that librarians have more work than they can effectively handle is supported by statistics showing smaller staff establishments and larger university enrollments. The labour situations evoked by these three factors are not unique to university librarians.

Contradictions Between Librarians' Voices and Official Information

There are three areas where labour process information from working librarians was inconsistent with formal empirical data on the same aspect. First, there is no agreement on what constitutes individual autonomy for librarians. Some interviewees saw a promising future for librarians as information managers. Others saw the erosion of control. Yet others commented that librarians have never had any power. There was even disagreement on what was professional work! As seen above, autonomy is difficult to verify in the structural data. The second issue concerns gender balance and mobility. Both men and women interviewees were silent about gender. The statistics showed that males still constituted a minority of between 20 and 30%. There is no concrete evidence from the interviews, statistics, or library schools about males being more comfortable with or better skilled in using information technologies or computers. Males may have been more comfortable with technology when it was first introduced (Turkle, 1984), but technology is now so widely diffused and user interfaces have so greatly improved that this may no longer be the case (Turkle, 1995).

The third area of contention is the debate between deskilling, proletarianization, and re-professionalization, where there is severe disagreement, especially about causes. The solution inheres in *how skilling is defined*, which I mined from the interviews and develop in the section on professional credentialling. More important, sources of control are shifting to external agencies, which some librarians are loath to admit.[6] Such shifts might include the increasing monopolistic control by corporate publishers of library resources such as scholarly journals and periodical indexes, as they migrate from print-based to electronic resources. Because these commercial products are often under corporate monopoly, there is impact on library control of internal decisions and, thus, the autonomy and freedom of its experts, the librarians. Electronic library resources are also increasingly shared and networked among other universities, which signals that libraries can no longer operate as entities within the university enclave. This shift of power reflects a decline of professional labour powers, and suggests that the movement may be driven by social trends outside the library. The dynamics of this shift are more evident when the analysis is expanded to include other social factors.

Research Directions: Branching Outside the Institution

Working librarians provided specific problem information as well as details on their labouring experience. General labour trending was assessed from institutional and survey data. For a comprehensive analysis of the professional labour process, the triangulation of many sources is necessary. A strong measure of the value and power of librarians is the supply and demand for their labour, which is available in the next section on the professional library labour market. In the words of one respondent, librarians must get "outside of the shoe box of the library!"

THE PROFESSIONAL LABOUR MARKET: CREDENTIALLING INFORMATION PROFESSIONALS

An important component of labour process theory is the availability of practitioners in the labour market and the opportunities available to them (Littler, 1982; Wardell, 1999). The value of professional work and the strength of the labour of librarians may be operationalized using labour market factors, and assessed qualitatively as well as quantitatively. The generation of a supply of professional workers comes from the credentialing of graduates, and the demand may be assessed in the job market.

As the sole designator of the professionalism of librarians, the educational credential is central to the analysis of the expertise component. In Canada, as in the United States, librarians are credentialed by the two-year master's degree in information studies from an ALA-accredited institution.[7] The absence of certification, compulsory professional association membership, self-monitoring practices, and governing legislation or regulation puts most of the emphasis on professional education, not only for definition of the knowledge base but also for labour process factors and for socialization. In the context of professionalism, therefore, credentialling enables, maintains, or alters the value of the labour of librarians or the power it accords.

The acquisition of a knowledge base through credentialling was operationalized by analyzing changes in education over time. The analysis includes the stability of the core strengths of the programs, the development of new fields, and the prominence of socially relevant areas such as intellectual property and freedom of

Table 3.   Cultural and Professional Foundations Courses in 7 Canadian Schools (Mean).

	1971/72	1975/76	1980/81	1985/86	1990/91	1995/96	2000/01
Required	1.8	1	<1	<1	<1	1.1	1.4
All	5	6.7	9.4	6	5.6	4.9	5.1

Source: Canadian university library and information studies calendars, analyzed by J. Carson.

expression. They were empirically examined using data from the credentialling institutions. The calendars of all seven Canadian graduate schools of information studies[8] were analyzed in five-year increments over the thirty years that constitute the "information society" (1971–2001) for course content relevant to information studies. The data provide both summary and qualitative aspects. The statistics give the numbers of courses, concentrations, and change over time. The qualitative information gives topical areas such as entrepreneurship, suggests new specializations such as data mining, and offers new modes of looking at classical functions such as the substitution of information organization for cataloguing.

The first phase of the analysis involved classification and summary counts. Six functional areas were identified: professional and cultural foundations, reference and information services, collection development, information organization and cataloguing, and automation and systems, and administration. While some universities offer courses on academic librarianship, not enough were available for a consistent pattern. Required courses were noted, to represent a minimum level of basic knowledge. Elective courses were also noted, to give an idea of the intellectual breadth and depth of the field. The consistencies and change in required and elective courses were itemized in the Tables 3–8. It is interesting to note that course emphases on professional and cultural foundations and on information services have been relatively constant over the years. Courses in the organization of information and collection development have been reduced. Systems and automation courses were the only concentration that had clearly increased. Courses in administration and management followed a bimodal pattern, with the number of required courses being relatively constant over the years, and

Table 4.   Organization of Information Courses in 7 Canadian Schools (Mean).

	1971/72	1975/76	1980/81	1985/86	1990/91	1995/96	2000/01
Required	1.8	1.9	1.4	1.6	1.6	1.7	1.1
All	5	5.3	5.6	6	5.4	5.1	4.6

Source: Canadian university library and information studies calendars, analyzed by J. Carson.

Table 5.   Reference and Information Services Courses in 7 Canadian Schools
(Mean).

	1971/72	1975/76	1980/81	1985/86	1990/91	1995/96	2000/01
Required	1.7	1.6	1.6	1.3	1.9	1.7	1.7
All	6.5	5.9	7.3	6.9	7	6.1	5.6

Source: Canadian university library and information studies calendars, analyzed by J. Carson.

Table 6.   Library Systems and Automation Courses in 7 Canadian Schools
(Mean).

	1971/72	1975/76	1980/81	1985/86	1990/91	1995/96	2000/01
Required	<1	1	1	1.1	1.4	1.7	2.1
All	3.1	5.6	5.9	6.4	6.4	7.9	7.7

Source: Canadian university library and information studies calendars, analyzed by J. Carson.

Table 7.   Library Administration and Management Courses in 7 Canadian
Schools (Mean).

	1971/72	1975/76	1980/81	1985/86	1990/91	1995/96	2000/01
Required	1.2	<1	<1	<1	1	1	1
All	3	2.6	3.1	3.7	4	3.4	5.1

Source: Canadian university library and information studies calendars, analyzed by J. Carson.

elective courses increasing. This numeric phase provides a baseline for shifts in
expertise acquisition.

   The second phase involved analysis of the qualitative information embedded
in these brief course descriptions. They provided not only changes in emphasis
in establishing course concentrations, for example, from public lending right to
Internet filtering in the professional issues area. They also gave changes in critical
areas where librarians could exercise more power in civil society on the basis of
either their expertise or their role as gatekeepers.

Table 8.   Collections Development & Maintenance Courses in 7 Canadian
Schools (Mean).

	1971/72	1975/76	1980/81	1985/86	1990/91	1995/96	2000/01
Required	1.3	1.1	<1	<1	<1	<1	<1
All	2.3	2.3	2	2	2.4	2.3	1.3

Source: Canadian university library and information studies calendars, analyzed by J. Carson.

Cultural and Professional Foundations

This area includes principles of librarianship, professionalization, and comparative librarianship. It also covers librarianship's traditions, the history of the book, literacy, and communications. An important component of this category is current issues and problem areas, where sensitivity to the changing social context and the continuity of fundamental principles may diverge.

The core and total number of courses that inculcate professional and cultural foundations is constant at about 1 and 5 respectively.[9] Historical, political, professional, and social processes have been constant throughout the years, although political issues have changed with the times. There was an increasing focus on the privacy and access issues exacerbated by the convergence of computers and telecommunications. Strong grounding in cultural and professional foundations ideally enables a critical or proactive social orientation for librarians in their career.

Organization of Information

This curricular concentration includes classification, cataloguing, and indexing. The main shifts throughout the years have been to eliminate the word "cataloguing" in favour of "organization of information" or "bibliographic control," to include all formats of material, and to teach electronic systems.

Cataloguing and classification courses[10] show very small fluctuations until a drop in 2000 by about half a required course and by one course in total. Substantive changes over time include reduced emphasis on mechanics, given the current trend to outsourcing of cataloguing services or the bundling of web-based catalogues with integrated systems such as that offered by Innovative Interfaces, Inc. Many librarians do not reinforce their cataloguing knowledge at the workplace, and are increasingly less equipped to assess changes in the organization of information that are provided from outside sources.

Reference and Information Services

In addition to the knowledge of reference sources and information service, this function includes bibliographic instruction in all formats, and the analysis of user needs and information seeking behaviour in the calendar descriptions. The interview comments suggested that decentralized electronic information service was changing the mode of professional interventions, which would be reflected in the education.

Over three decades, the average number of core reference service courses has remained the same, and total reference offerings tended to diminish by a course on average, after peaking in the 1980s.[11] Many of these focused on disciplinary areas such as science and technology or the social sciences. Increasingly, electronic resources were taught. From the descriptions and the consistencies therein, the core philosophy of reference services appeared to be the same throughout the years. In university libraries, the expanding use of distance communication for information questions and access does not appear to be reflected, nor do the advantages and disadvantages of each. This and other issues, such as the wider diversity of users and public Internet access, appear to be learned on the job or incorporated into "issues" courses.

Library Automation and Systems

This specialization includes systems analysis, programming, information retrieval, database design, and management of information technology in the calendars. The popular expectation, as implied in the interviews, is a notable increase in these courses, such that any graduate can "hit the ground running" in an electronic environment, and have sufficient authority in the area among colleagues, managers, or the computer specialists.

As expected, courses in library automation and systems show steady increases, and more than doubled in three decades. There are variations among the schools, as some caught up with early course innovators such as Western.[12] Coverage in the electives extends into the domains of management, indexing, linguistics, and the online information industry. The core courses, however, cover the standard fundamentals such as systems analysis and database management. Thus, while comfortable with technology, not all graduates are necessarily broadly based, and must learn on the job along with librarians of long tenure. This refutes the myth that recent graduates are the only competent ones with technology. Nor can their expertise in automation and technology be expected to answer labour problems related to technological anxiety, rate of diffusion, or shortage of staff.

Library Administration and Management

This specialization includes management theory, administration of functions, personnel, marketing, public relations, and entrepreneurship. Of interest is whether librarians are sensitive to the increasing commodification of information and labour, and if the growing curricular emphasis on entrepreneurship has a critical component.

In the areas of management, there was no apparent change in the number of core courses, although, during the decades, institutions with high counts (Western, University of Toronto) go down, and those with no required courses in the field go up.[13] There is a significant increase in all schools in 2000 and 2001, due to the focus on entrepreneurship. Montréal shows a major increase in courses oriented to the market applications of professional information services after it undertook a program of revitalization in 1999 that considered labour market requirements as well as student placement after graduation. Recent courses in all programs emphasize marketing of services, which is a form of commodification of labour, but most applications tend to be in corporate libraries and consulting firms rather than at universities.

Collections Development and Management

This function includes acquisitions principles and practice, publishing, the book trade, and preservation of materials. The courses were expected to provide solid grounding for today's challenges of de-selection, resource sharing, and cooperative ventures.

The number of core courses in collections has decreased from about one to one half after the mid-1980s. The total courses have been relatively constant at just over 2, except at the Millennium where they drop substantially.[14] Apart from Dalhousie, collections development is no longer a core course in current programs. In view of economic, technological, and pedagogical challenges facing contemporary academic libraries, this is a serious oversight. These are times when staff must de-select materials through weeding and serials cancellations, select more carefully (which takes greater skill than buying liberally), and judiciously commit large sums of money on electronic purchases. They are also obliged to accept administrative requirements to consolidate purchasing and to undertake cooperative arrangements for economic survival, which may or may not be to the advantage of the researchers and students in the universities.

Critical Aspects of Professional
Education for Information Studies

To pursue the unanswered questions about expertise, technology, and social change in the academic library, I re-examine the textual data in the calendars of all seven institutions over the seven time periods for content related to cultural policy or critical topics. Within the six course groupings, seven topics oriented to cultural issues or social critique emerge. They centre on: (1) professionalization; (2) current issues in the field, such as resource sharing; (3) policy, political, and ethical topics, such as Internet governance; (4) economics of information and marketing; (5) communication and culture; (6) user needs and behaviour; and (7) unions. These social interests peaked between the 1990s and the present, and, in 2000 and 2001, the latest year surveyed, focus on economic issues, political/ethical issues, and library problems. There is not always evidence that a socially activist approach was taken in the program, or that students have even taken these courses. Nevertheless, the assumption can be made that most librarians are minimally equipped with the foundation for appreciating their professional traditions or critically understanding the work they are doing.

From the course breakdown and thematic breakdown, three general themes emerged, centring on continuity, myth, and critical approach. Continuity was evident in the information about courses tabulated and discussed above. The core of the educational program preparing workers for the profession has remained relatively stable, with reasonable increases in expertise related to automation and small decreases in areas that related to organization of information and collections development. The most perceptible disjunction in the data is the featuring of entrepreneurship in elective courses over the past five years in some of the seven institutions. This emerges even in courses that were not really about marketing, such as the structural aspects of management. This contradicts the feedback from the interviews that the primary educational focus was electronic information service, although electronic information service and marketing are interrelated.

Myth-making suggests characterizations such as the electronically-oriented "super-librarian" who will dominate the field of information studies. The credentialling data dispel the myth by showing that this is not the only kind of recent graduate that has been produced. This image of the omnipotent electronic librarian undermines the profile of long-term librarians by labelling them as competent but responsive rather than initiatory, and diminishing their valuable work as members of the cultural work force.

The third theme from the analysis of the generation of expertise is the critical approach to information service on a range of issues where the minimum acceptable level of performance is contested. It can be exercised in varying contexts, from the local sphere in the performance of daily work to larger arenas in the social world. At the working level, a critical approach to library service may involve insistence on quality information service in a world whose resources, such as Internet sources, are increasingly outside professional control and subject to critical assessment. The interview data suggested that librarians were committed to quality control in information provision (though not always appreciated and "invisible"), and the educational data support this concern for excellence. Outside the library institution, as again reflected in the interviews, a critical approach may take the form of social activism in issues that involve the university or the government. Most academic librarians do not have the reputation or experience as social activists, although the educational data show that they are exposed to current issues, and this is continued in their socialization in the workplace. Many librarians are involved with or even president of their unions or staff associations, as was shown in the interviews, and emergent issues involve recognition of the value of librarians' work. Some have made representation to federal and provincial governments about issues related to electronic information access and privacy. At the local institutional level for the majority, however, a critical approach to the work involves a concern for information service issues, and does not generally take the form of visible public action.

In summary, the predominant changes in the acquisition of expertise reflect the digitization of information, the de-concentration of functions, and the systematization of library work. The main disjunction as evidenced in changes in the knowledge base is the *acknowledgement of market forces*. It signifies that the commodification of information is a reality, however inconsistent with the principle of information access in the public sphere of the academy, which is another course or theme. More profoundly for labour, the acknowledgement of market forces implicitly accepts the separation of conception from execution at the point of production that characterizes the *commodification of labour*. This acceptance is implicit, because it is generally not as clear at the educational stage as at the workplace, which is the source of the grounded interview data. The commodification of professional work and strategic expertise separates the contemporary workplace of librarians from the classic view of the profession. Thus professional library work is an excellent example of the contradictions of "post-industrial labour" as exemplified by tensions between the entrepreneurial and the cultural perspectives.

THE PROFESSIONAL LABOUR MARKET: THE DEMAND FOR EXPERTISE

Background and Rationale

As shown in the previous section, professional education for information studies has remained relatively constant in terms of core concentrations over the past three decades, with more focus on systems and less on cataloguing and collection development. The predominant changes in the acquisition of expertise reflect the digitization of information, deconcentration of functions, and further systematization of work. There is a relationship between the development of library expertise through formal education and the demands of the labour market, of which universities are a part. This relationship has many dimensions. The presence of qualified but unemployed graduates mentioned in the interviews, and the disaffection or underemployment of other graduates seen in the observations and heard in the interviews, suggest that there are more professional information workers than available positions. This will change when the "boomers" retire. It is clear that many librarians are beginning to retire, but new librarians represented under 10% of the current staff in 1998. On the demand side, academic libraries may require combinations of skills, for example, in management or systems development, that are hard to find in the available pool of librarians. We must also determine whether the profession tries to monopolize the market for information service workers. For a fuller understanding of the value of the academic labour or professional power, its marketplace needs to be examined.

This is represented by job ads. Ads for positions in academic libraries show the job requirements as indicated through formal requests for new staff as represented through a somewhat stylized form of text. They provide comparative and relatively standardized information about the external labour market, including labour opportunities, desired candidate qualities, and trending. The work represented by these ads encapsulates the two dominant aspects of the professional labour process: the importance of particular areas of expertise, and degrees of autonomy expected. It also highlights areas of congruence and contradiction between the profession depicted at the educational stage and that presented at recruitment. This methodology does not capture the internal labour market, or internal mobility within the library, because those ads are not distributed externally, unless simultaneous internal and external advertising is permitted in collective agreement provisions.

Research Strategy

Notwithstanding these considerations, it is feasible to represent the external labour market because there is a volume of position ads that evidences movement and rejuvenation in academic libraries. In Canada, most external ads are circulated electronically through a list-serve among the 27 chief librarians of the Canadian Association of Research Libraries,[15] who then inform professional staff. This method of dissemination is limited to university library job offerings, and is thus a comprehensive source of external labour market information for this community. Since the list has not been in existence long enough for long-term comparative information, it is informative to analyze the job ads concurrent with the last interval of the credentialling data, 2000 and 2001. As with the credentialling data, both summary and qualitative information were highly informative. The summary data provided the number and level of jobs, and thus support trending information. The qualitative data provided the amount of skill (value) and power entailed in the job, and contributed to the totality of critical information about labour process and professionalism.

The analysis has four phases: (1) the objective picture in terms of numbers and distributions by specialization; (2) aspects of skill reflected in the jobs; (3) aspects of authority in these positions; and (4) discussion and relationship to credentialling. The first phase represents the external job market, and links those ads to changes in jobs and to concentrations in academic libraries. It also links it with professional education and areas of concentration. The second phase represents the labour process component of skills, and how that is changing with new information and communication technologies. The third represents the control aspects of jobs, and is more problematic because relations of authority are hard to encapsulate in descriptive data. Further, while the institutional representations of the jobs try to stress their authority aspects, authority is actually eroding due to economic and other power-based forces external to the academic library. The fourth phase makes thematic social observations.

Findings and Trends

According to the position ad data, there were 44 vacancies in 2000 and 68 in 2001. They are classified into academic library functions in Table 9, then analyzed in terms of professional labour in the academic library workplace.

The ads showed interesting trends, which were normally consistent with emphases in professional education. The greatest proportion of vacancies for both years, at an average of 45% of the ads, was for public service librarians.

Table 9.   Professional Position Ads for Canadian Academic Libraries: Two Year Profile.

Year	Total	University Librarian	Associate Librarian	Dep't Head	Systems	Public Services	Collections	Technical Services	Other
2000	44	2	4	8	4	16	4	2	4
2001	68	2	4	10	14	31	[1]	3	4
Total	112	4	8	18	18	47	4	5	8

Source: Carl-l listserv, compiled by J. Carson.

This confirms implications from the credentialling data that the function remains strong. The next highest representation was for systems heads and librarians, averaging between 15 and 20% over both years. This figure is probably lower than the number of systems specialists actually hired in libraries, as systems personnel may be technical, computer, or even management specialists rather than librarians. About 15% of the labour market vacancies were jobs as department heads,[16] and 10% for senior administrators, either chief or assistant librarians. Only 5% of the librarians in demand were sought to perform collections functions, and five out of 112 librarians were being sought to do technical services functions related to cataloguing or acquisitions. The small proportion of collections and cataloguing librarians is consistent with diminished emphasis at the educational stage. Other individual vacancies include four archivists and three directors of regional consortia of academic libraries such as the BC Electronic Library Network. About 10% of all the ads were for contract, term, or replacement positions. The strongest trends include the reduction of technical services jobs due to outsourcing, and the move toward hiring systems and management staff.

Disjunctions with the past are evident in the hiring of library systems staff, and should be followed. It shows that recruiters are searching outside the library for this expertise, as these positions are not being filled internally. It further shows that even externally advertised positions may reach outside the profession in the acquisition of expert systems labour. For example, one notice was re-advertised with a change in the credentials desired to read, "a computer science degree *and preferably an MLIS*," whereas all of the other ads in the study stipulated the MLS/MLIS/MIS or equivalent degree.[17] For professionals, this scarcely perceptible shift shows that the boundaries between librarians and cognate professions are blurring, as recognized in the research of Abbott (1988) and DiPrete (1988), and that librarians are losing their market monopoly, as in the research of Larson (1977) and Freidson (1986). Pragmatically, it suggests that decisive electronic expertise is not easily found in the market, or that institutions are asking the impossible due to their own changing needs for a combination of abilities. This echoes one of the interview comments that we now need in libraries a "super librarian" who is equally a specialist, manager, and communicator, and combines these roles with other abilities.

The emphasis on public services hiring reflects increases in client services in database searching, web-based instruction, and new catalogue formats. The subject specialization component of that function involves the growing, however demoralizing, area of de-selection and includes the consultation process skills that are necessary for buying anything. For the increasingly important document delivery function, there are no ads for interlibrary loans librarians, except for those relating to a head of access services of which interlibrary loans is often a part. The area of interlibrary loans and document delivery has grown because all libraries need to capitalize on resources outside the library, and provide access rather than holdings.

Administrators represent about 10% of new hiring, which is not out of proportion at face value. If combined with department heads, for a complement of middle management, it amounts to about 25% over 2 years, or 30 out of 112 positions, perhaps to replace retiring staff. This high proportion of ads suggests that libraries may be actively looking *outside* for new staff with the appropriate qualifications and expertise to handle change. Thus, the labour market, as represented by externally-distributed ads, is seeking negotiators and decision makers. This suggests the phenomenon of skill bifurcation and a "declining middle," where work is moving either upward to middle management or downward to support staff (Menzies, 1996).

Labour Process Implications: Expertise Factors

From the finite aspects of the labour market, the discussion proceeds to an analysis of labour process implications in the ads. Aspects of expertise and control from the ads suggest the "optimal" picture presented by the hiring institutions. I assess the degree to which these skill and authority indicators are congruent with professional labour process at the point of production.

The job ads included much detail about the comprehensive cognitive base, degree of complexity, service ethic, level of esteem, and rewards mechanisms components of professional expertise. The analysis affirms the conclusion from the interviews that skill is regarded as the most dominant aspect of labour process.

Knowledge Base

In the context of the labour market, the information studies knowledge base is represented objectively by educational credentials, and situationally by work experience. The ads are consistent in stipulating the need for formal credentials as represented by a post-graduate degree in library and information studies from an accredited institution.[18] Masters degrees in a subject area are often desirable for associate librarians, sometimes for department heads, and occasionally by specific institutions. There is an emergent pattern for professional library positions with highly specialized disciplinary orientations, particularly in schools of law or education, to be further specialized by subject qualifications beyond their information studies credentials. If credentials were the only criteria for designating professional closure, evidence from the external job market shows that labour in libraries is being up-skilled!

In the complementary area of professional experience, requirements range from no mandatory experience for an entry-level position to about ten years of experience for a chief librarian. Most working level jobs, however, require from two to five years of work experience in the area, and major supervisory and management jobs from five to eight years. In one case, to avoid overqualified candidates and inflated expectations, a library advised that, "Because of budgetary constraints, applications from external candidates are limited to those with no more than five years of experience."

Stipulated skill requirements also provide data about changing areas of specialization. The most dominant areas are the digitization of information, the commercialization of the university, and the convergence of library with other university services. Trends in the digitization of information are seen in ads for librarians working with technology, whether they are labelled systems or electronic resources librarians, or need technological expertise as part of their labour. Systems positions regularly stipulate either a computer science degree or significant experience *in addition to* the MIS/MLIS. Trends in the increasingly commercialized university are seen in a joint position for chief librarian and research director, and in the need for administrative librarians to have fund-raising experience. With threats such as budget cuts or mergers with other campus departments, library administrators are required more than ever to account for policy decisions, as helped by statistical analysis and program evaluation competencies. The blurring of boundaries around librarianship and the merging of services are characteristic of the convergence of labour and the extension of capabilities in contemporary professional work. Joint positions normally bring positive benefits for the incumbent. Librarians are asked for instructional skills, not only for the established reference function of bibliographic instruction, but also to collaborate with teaching and learning units. It is clear that, where the knowledge base is concerned, the qualifications requirement is indeed complex.

Complexity

Knowledge base is not a complete indicator of skill, and needs to be complemented by a more composite set of characteristics in the appeal to the labour market. Beginning with the functional experience for the job and the personal qualifications of the candidates, most ads require written, oral, and interpersonal skills; team skills; electronic and web knowledge; and leadership, organizational, and planning abilities. Additionally, candidates should be committed to academic librarianship and to the teaching and research needs of the university. They are asked to be imaginative, creative, and innovative, with "the flexibility to enjoy a changing environment of practice," or "the temperament to thrive in a creative environment with a demanding workload." As seen in the interviews and reinforced by recent studies in labour and organizational behaviour (Burris, 1998; Meiksins, 1994; Smith, V., 1997; Smith & Thompson, 1998), flexibility, multi-layering, and the constancy of change are characteristic of workers in all spheres of the post-industrial university environment.

The suite of required traditional abilities is expanded to include those in cognate areas on university campuses. In the general area of communication of information, librarians need to have a strong understanding of scholarly communication and the research process, because bibliographic, editorial, and publishing systems are converging electronically. In another area of electronic convergence, librarians are expected to also possess knowledge of non-print resources such as geo-spatial and numerical data in addition to textual information, as this is increasingly available on the internet or in CD-ROM format. In the area of pedagogy, many candidates in reference service positions are asked for knowledge of instructional principles, particularly in relation to information literacy, and for capabilities in the development of curricular materials. This is due to the integration of the teaching of research skills with teaching transferable or generic skills, such as defining a research topic. In the legal area, managers and electronic resources candidates are required to know copyright and licensing issues and practices, so they can undertake liaison and negotiation with vendors, and so they can comply with the law when providing access to and disseminating electronic information through library channels. In the administrative area, managers should have the ability to raise funds, especially with the kind of decline in resources from the university, alluded to in the previous chapter. They should be able to manage in a unionized environment, where there are at least two unions, professional and non-professional staff, whose concerns centre on salary and job security.

Library systems and electronic services jobs provide a good example of increasing complexity. They are not just for programmers and analysts. The technical skills now include facility with web page design, the Internet, course instructional systems, and electronic publishing. Many have a strong component of training other staff, some almost exclusively. Others involve the administrative and human relations skills of liaison with the campus computer centre or project management. Electronic resources librarians in public service roles may be required to participate on internal, campus, or inter-university committees in relation to the dissemination of electronic resources.

In addition to conventional library jobs with increasing complexity, the library market is seeing new work combinations. The professional academic library labour market in Canada at the turn of the millennium includes a librarian for "emerging services," an information literacy and cataloguing librarian, and a combined law reference specialist and systems analyst. Thus the traditional jobs are layered with additional subject expertise, skills, and ancillary academic functions, and thus can be said to meet easily the complexity aspect of the skill component of library professionalism. Analytically, the important thing about these changes in complexity is their statements about the social environment. The implications for labour of new electronic technologies, the digitization of information, retrenchment in the academy, and the blurring of boundaries between functional areas in the university are numerous.

Service Ethic

In the interviews, librarians are highly conscious of their professional responsibilities to their clients and their craft, and reflect strong social responsibility in the classical tradition (Durkheim, 1957; Parsons, 1939). In the position ads, however, the only articulation of conventional service refers to a commitment to academic librarianship and to library service in general. There is more emphasis on commitment to electronic librarianship, and to flexibility and change, as mentioned in the above section on complexity, than on principles.

Esteem

In the language of the ads, esteem is inherent in the incumbent's relation to other constituencies on campus and to responsibilities of authority within the library. Some jobs involve committee membership or project assignments. Outside the library, some jobs require campus liaison with areas such as the computer centre and campus committees. The interviews showed that collegiality with faculty and collaborative work are particularly valued as means of esteem as well as professional challenge, whereas working within the library hierarchy requires them to be more responsive and detracts from their professional stature. Aspects that make their labour distinctive and worthy of esteem among clients and colleagues are not addressed. As esteem is related not only to skill but also to authority, this is further explored in the section on the power-based factors of professionalism in the external labour market.

Rewards

In the job ads, rewards for library labour are both honorific and monetary. Honorific rewards inhere in the assigned rank in the organization. Most Canadian libraries have systems that rank the person rather than the position, with four categories roughly corresponding to those of academic faculty.[19] Ranks are based on personal qualifications and experience in addition to the requirements of the job, and thus integrate the skill factors of knowledge base and complexity. With this flexibility in the ranking schemes, library management can factor in budgetary strictures or the desire to refresh library staff when assigning (or limiting) rewards. The evidence in the ads about advertised ranks shows variation in the labour market demands. About 10% specified Librarian I, others Librarian I or II, and others Librarian I, II, or III, commensurate with experience and qualifications. The labour market evidence suggests, therefore, that there are opportunities in the labour market for recent graduates. Salaries are covered by collective agreements. The salaries in the ads correlate not only with rank, experience, and longevity, but also with the generosity of the institution. Most libraries offer an administrative stipend from $3,000 to $5,000. While rank and salary offerings nominally signify the skill component of jobs, they indicate more interesting phenomena at the larger social level. They reflect the recruitment strategies of the institutions and the qualitative and quantitative value they place on professional expertise. Rank may not strictly reflect vacancies in the libraries, but, more correctly, levels and costs at which the libraries are prepared to hire new candidates.[20]

Professional Activity
Compared with service ethic or with rewards, professional activity is strongly emphasized in the ads in the professional labour market. Workers at all position levels are informed that they are expected to engage in professional activity and contribute to the profession. In the data, this takes the form of participation in professional and academic organizations, developing their professional knowledge on a continuing basis, or undertaking scholarship and research. In some cases, the expectations are loosely worded, with "involved with." In other cases, the expectations are stronger, to "contribute actively to law librarianship, information science, and legal scholarship" or "undertake scholarship, research, and professional activity." Only one library advertised release time for professional activity. The reality, as reported by many interviewees, is that they have no time for professional activity, and advancement to higher ranks in university libraries is based only partially on professional activity and mostly on performance at the point of production. Only the promotion to senior librarian, normally Librarian IV, really scrutinizes the professional achievement of the candidate. Professional activity, therefore, is a formal expectation in ads in the labour market as well as in collective agreements. For most librarians, it is seldom fully actualized, or it is done in a fashion that is not as consequential as that applied to other academics.

Summary of Skill Characteristics of the External Labour Market
As formal modes of outreach to academic librarians, the ads in the labour market demand many skill aspects such as disciplinary expertise, work-related experience, and electronic information technologies, and concur with the need

for personal qualities to handle variety, adaptability, and change. There is unchallenged acceptance of this as a reality in today's academy. They invoke "progress." For the most part, they neglect specifics about the university clientele. They appeal to professionalism with statements of expectations of activity, involvement, and creativity. This sounds progressive, but the interviewees suggest that the workplace is more prosaic. Actual rewards such as salary are not specified in many cases, because they are candidate-dependent. The challenges of working in an increasingly entrepreneurial environment are not highlighted, nor are critical perspectives on working with technological convergence. Little is specified about the clout that librarians or libraries should have in the information resources system or network of publishers, database producers, software developers, library consortia, and vendors. Interaction and influence with the commercial agencies with which librarians deal is an important aspect of the power and control component of the labour process. Following up this question provides an entry point for the second part of this external labour market analysis, an examination of the power and control aspects of information studies jobs in the labour market.

Labour Process Implications: Control Factors

These include the three general areas of control: control over one's job, control over professional areas in the library, and control gained from the demographic and personal characteristics that interact with power factors.

Control Over the Job
Within the control dimension of the labour process in the academic library, operational control refers to control over work, library acquisitions, and staff. It is nominally represented by line authority, which involves reporting directly to a department or division head, branch director, associate librarian, university librarian, or academic vice-president of the university. Such employees are normally expected to work with a reasonable degree of independence, but always within a hierarchical institution. Exceptions to direct authority as advertised in professional library jobs are few. They include split jobs at the working level, where candidates report to separate department heads. While outside relationships, such as committee membership, do not bring true "power," they remove librarians from line authority and allow the expression of professional skills outside the immediate environment. Because the digitization of resources and convergence of information systems have an impact on the entire library operation, systems librarians, unlike their other professional colleagues, tend to be accountable "upwards"

to senior management, and "outwards" to agencies outside the library, rather than to other library staff or the demands of the public. Departures from conventional library practices, such as positions split between the library and another campus group, appear to be the privilege of higher staff levels rather than to librarians who are newer or more intimately acquainted with needs of the clientele. They involve allegiance to forces outside the library rather than to professional principles, and may result in a reduction of accountability to the rest of the library in decisions about library service.

Control over acquisitions was not specified in the labour market ads, except for the inclusion of the collections function in the positions of subject specialists or liaison librarians. There were only three jobs exclusively for collections development, which confirms the findings in the professional education data that collections development is being diminished as a library function. Individual control over acquisitions may range from the selection of an individual book title, to negotiation with library colleagues for purchase of an expensive electronic database, to individual contribution to a collective library recommendation for purchase of an expensive electronic title by a university consortium. The importance of such work in an age of constricted funding and increasing interlibrary collaboration is not highlighted to the degree of other labour aspects such as electronic expertise. Control over acquisitions is an area where a greater critical approach may be stressed. Incumbents do discover this at the point of production, as evidenced in the interviews, but the importance of collections management is not visible in representations to the labour market.

Control over staff involves supervisory responsibilities, but there tend to be fewer and fewer subordinates to manage, due to both the flattening of the organization, the loss of support staff, or their up-skilling. As part of the control aspect of the job, ads for department heads and up state the number of staff to be managed. The emphasis on staff level to be supervised is a statement of the power inherent in the position, which could be exercised in different ways, depending on the number and nature of staff. In most cases, the greater the number of professionals, the higher level of expectations and challenge among staff. The greater number of paraprofessionals, the more likelihood of in-house training needs, resentment toward professionals, and union issues involving the allocation of work. Authority over staff may thus be exercised differentially.

The areas of operational authority in labour market ads relate to the situation of positions within the library structure. They include personal autonomy and responsibility for staff. They also show that, despite emphases on change and flexibility seen in the discussion on skills, librarians are working within hierarchical structures. Their power is measured by number and level of staff, and by vaguely specified functional connections outside the department.

Control Over the Situation

This control dimension of the labour process relates to the level of professional status or power that librarians hold in the institution of the library and its environment of the university. In the labour market ads, as in the interviews, this is expressed as control of quality, innovation, and conditions of work. Librarians' responsibility for control over quality, which is part of their classic social responsibility, is implicit in the required qualifications, experience, and nature of the job as summarized. Quality control applies to the provision of information service, the organization of information, the quest for information literacy, and the acquisition of materials alike. A critical approach is part of quality control, but critical in this context really means "discerning," and is addressed to the selection of vendors and resources, the determination of information needs, and the assurance of information literacy, rather than to critical analysis of the library in its social context.

As with quality control, control over innovation relates to the interaction of librarians with outside agencies such as vendors, dealers, or other information providers for new services for document delivery or comprehensive library systems. Their commercial nature requires not only judgment but also leverage and negotiation from librarians who select them and who work to customize them to meet local needs.[21] On campus, quality control is a management concern for library applications and for compatibility with their campus electronic systems. Control over innovations is part of implementing change within a flexible environment of practice, and change and adaptability were seen in the skill section above to be desirable characteristics of many jobs across the spectrum. This being the workplace reality, innovation is *occasionally* seen to be important enough to be in the job title, such as in the job title Emerging Services Librarian or Information Literacy Librarian. While the job ads suggest that responsiveness to innovation is desirable, it is left to the librarian to discover the limitation of choices in that area.

The control of conditions of work includes control over time, and it is implicit in the jobs. The ads state that there are many demands on the work of librarians, which forewarn, as in the interviews, that librarians have little control of their time and are subject to outside pressures. There appears to be little change in control from the responsive nature of librarians of the past, in spite of increased expertise and information literacy. Information technology only increases the volume of their work, as noted in the narratives, partially because it increases with the expanding diversity of the information needs of their clients.

Personal Authority

In the labour process, socio-demographic factors interact with other factors. For example, youth and immigrants provide a certain resource pool that might accommodate non-unionized or unskilled work due to their age or language abilities, respectively. The most prominent demographic factor in a female-intensive profession is gender. About 75% of Canadian academic librarians are female, and this imbalance has continued over the three decades under investigation. Many ads have the requisite statement under provincial equity legislation that the position is open to men and women, but employment equity legislation does not appear to have alleviated the gender imbalance in academic libraries. Age is the other demographic variable of importance in libraries. While age cannot legally be stipulated in the ads, being contrary to the 1982 Canadian Charter of Rights and Freedoms, tenure and experience are proxies of age. The above examples of recommended years of experience are an attempt to attract professional applicants at an early stage in their career. The ads for 2001, in particular, reflect an increase in available positions to accommodate the slow exit of the "boomers."

Summary of Authority Aspects of the External Professional Labour Market
The material in the labour market ads shows that control factors are less frequently referred to than expertise factors, or less precisely stipulated because specific criteria are difficult. This lesser emphasis on control factors is consistent with emphases in professional education, and indeed in the historical experience of the librarians in the interviews.

The Labour Market and Professional Education: Critical Issues

The position ads provide quantitative evidence that hiring is clearly on the rise in 2000 and 2001, and foreshadow the end of an entrenched staffing situation. On a qualitative level, the textual documentation about the labour market is more nuanced. It validates the emphasis of skill over authority, which is consistent with the labour process information elicited in the interviews, and with institutional data about libraries. The ads also show that, in the requirement of the formal information studies credentials, professional closure is still enforced.

The characteristics of professional education that sharpen our understanding of the labour process of librarians were categorized into six functional areas of academic library expertise: cultural and professional foundations, the organization of information, reference and information services, library systems and automation, library administration and management, and collections development. They were matched with labour market needs, and found to be relatively congruent. When assessed from a critical labour-oriented perspective, however, the educators of professional information workers emphasize more socially significant areas in post-industrial society than the agencies that hire them. Such critical areas as information policy have been highlighted in the analysis of educational data above.

In the area of the professionalization of information workers, the labour market language appeals to the strong sense of professional commitment of prospective applicants. Education and the job world are consistent. Unlike the educators, the ads give no direct reference to political and ethical issues such as the filtering of pornographic materials on the Internet, or the larger question of the competing freedoms of access and privacy. In ads for the organization of information, emphasis is directed on expertise, with some reference to integrating new systems into the library. Educators place considerable emphasis on expertise and systems, including their evaluation, and address to a lesser extent techniques of dealing with vendors.

The labour market emphasizes two functional areas of librarianship in particular, reference services and electronic systems development, which are often interrelated. In reference services, the ads emphasize skills and qualifications associated with information services, particularly the increase in electronic resources and concomitant need for virtual libraries and remote services. In keeping with professional training, there is a strong commitment to meeting "user needs," although in the real world of libraries these initiatives may be framed by library imperatives as well as patron requirements. No mention in the ads is made of the increasing diversity among university clientele that presents an increasing challenge. The shift in clientele and their use patterns is beginning to rival, in impact on professional service providers, the technological revolution. In the area of systems development and electronic information services, the labour market ads emphasize – once again – the technologies, their increasingly sophisticated requirements, and competencies in their use. This affirms what was said about changes in library service in the interviews.

Ads for library administration and management do refer to problems associated with the economics of information and the convergence of information services with other related campus services. Some refer to the management of unionized staff as an area of competency, but the more frequent references to unions lie in the benefits accorded to prospective staff for salary, leave, and professional development. In the ads for managers, authority factors are closely bundled with skill factors such as analysis of services and program evaluation. Ads in the labour market stress pragmatically what needs to be done, whereas education stresses what should be done. The collections development components of the ads deal more with subject bibliographic expertise than with the challenge of diminishing resources, except for a headship position which highlights electronic publishing issues and joint ventures.

In conclusion, the critical issues that are addressed in the labour market, as represented by ads seeking labour, are change, flexibility, multiple demands, and resource sharing among universities. These are presented as progressive aspects of the university library operation which require complementary personal attributes and experience from prospective staff. The negative aspects of "the constancy of change" are not highlighted, such as pressures on libraries to buy arrays of electronic products and services from vendors that increasingly monopolize the whole chain of information provision and dissemination[22], and to responsiveness to user needs in an increasingly expanding information environment. The external labour market tends to emphasize the expertise and commitment of professional workers in information studies, by stressing a professional knowledge base at the expense of the maintenance of authority. Professional academic librarians increasingly need to assert power in areas of governance within the university and with the province, and in dealing with the corporate providers of information resources and systems. With little formal authority, they have to exploit their strong complement of expertise.

PROFESSIONAL LABOUR: CONTINUITIES OR CHANGES FOR LIBRARIANS?

The research on the professional labour process was designed to resolve competing claims about the potential and the limitations of academic librarianship in a workplace characterized by increasing information technologies, economic constraints, and global information production. The problem for this specific expert group was grounded in the experience of a case of working librarians across Canada as heard in their narratives, and interpreted within the framework of professionalism and the labour process. Data were gathered and triangulated from interviews, administrative statistics, a survey, credentialling institutions, and the job market. Central to the results of the research was the relationship between the expertise and control factors of labour. As expected for a knowledge-based profession, the skill factors dominated. More illuminating to the findings, and to theorizing professional labour in general, was that the expectations about the importance of expertise were inflated. Information from librarians at the point of production, particularly from the interviews, showed that the professional powers attained through expertise were changing. Historically, librarians have always lacked control due to their semi-professional status as employees, working within hierarchies and bureaucratic structures and responding to the requirements of others (Harris, 1992). Predictions about the post-industrial workplace (Bell, 1973; Gouldner, 1979; Hirschhorn, 1984; Zuboff, 1988) had advanced that the "new class" of knowledge workers, of which librarians are a part, would use their skill or intellectual capital to compensate for a lack of authority. The qualitative data have shown that, in spite of skill enrichment, librarians continued to feel a lack of control and, in some cases, this was getting worse, or "intensified."

Given the continuities that were found in the credentialling process, labour market expectations, and the objective stability of librarians in the institution, the source of the disjunction had to be identified as a new factor. Librarians attributed workplace changes chiefly to the transformative force of new information and telecommunications technologies. Since technology is not a force but interacts with other social processes (e.g. Noble, 1995), the analysis highlighted these areas of interaction in the three levels of analysis of the interviews (the social environment, the components of professional labour, and labour process issues), the credentialling process, and the job market. The major change inhered in the movement *outside the institution* of the actors in the labour process, due to the increasing prominence of commercial information providers, such as publishers, database producers, vendors, and other intermediaries. Agencies such as the Institute for Scientific Information or Reed Elsevier increasingly monopolize the information marketplace by vertically integrating publishing, database production, comprehensive library systems, and specialized intelligence services. One of the outcomes is an increasing lack of choice for libraries. They have worked to overcome this by forming consortia (e.g. The Canadian National Site Licensing Project) that negotiate the cooperative acquisition of databases and full-text serials with the corporate suppliers, and exercise some control. Other initiatives include the participation of librarians and/or faculty in the publishing process (e.g. The Public Library of Science) to escape the profit motive of corporate publishers and increase the input of the scholarly community.

The increasing corporate sector interaction in professional information service affects the labour process. Expert labour, such as catalogue production or materials selection, formerly done by librarians socialized in quality control and the service ethic, has been commodified by commercial agencies driven by the profit motive. This gradual shift in the locus of professional labour contributes to the proletarianization of that labour, because small and large decisions in the workplace are increasingly made by others. While the original definition of proletarianization referred to the limitation of authority by managers (Murphy, 1990), new technologies and the commodification of expertise have facilitated the increasing subordination of workplace decisions to outside agencies, be they institutions or contractors. This changes the locus of control of librarians, and is advanced as an explanation for the numerous reflections in the narratives about increasing pressures and intensified workload.

The research provides an important insight into the labour process. In the contemporary workplace, a complete picture involves the relationship among the economic, social, political, and even symbolic aspects of professionalism and the labour process, within a critical political economic framework. In the research, the original question about library changes and continuities generated three themes – technological, economic, and social factors – that contributed to the final analysis (Table 1). The expertise and power components of professionalism provided theoretical areas of intersection and methodological input to their analysis. The detailed information about professional labour in Table 2 contributed to a relational analysis and understanding of the convergence of skill and control. Much of the data about academic librarians and the robustness of their libraries were economically based, and many of the forces that impacted on professional library work were shown to be economically driven. Yet in the realm of the professional who is still being socialized to have social responsibility, factors such as status and intrinsic rewards still enabled a sense of esteem in spite of the lack of true workplace authority, upward mobility, or large monetary increases. Technology interacts with the factors of skill, authority, and economics, while, at the same time, it transforms the professional knowledge base. In the case researched, information technologies have enabled the deskilling of professional work by taking energy from intellectual activities; the deconcentration of information services by providing a venue for commodified labour; and the proletarianization of librarians by enabling others to decide goals for librarians.

Underlying most changes in professional library work was the digitization and telecommunications revolution, because information technology is embedded in both the product and the means of production. The research clarified its bureaucratizing and disempowering effects in the work life of librarians, though some of this relational evidence had to be inferred from various sources of qualitative information. In the larger sphere, its integration with national and international state and commercial entities ultimately affected the nature of the product, the work with the product, and the cultural capital. *At the point of production, information technology is constituted as an aspect of skill; yet in terms of interactions outside the institution, information technology is associated with power and control.* Thus, in the bureaucratizing aspect and in the external control aspect, information technology has helped reproduce power inequalities for librarians in the academy.

The attribution in the narratives to the "agency" of information technology to enable or retard change in academic libraries was intuitively correct, but needed situation. Through a detailed examination of many aspects of the professional labour process, and their triangulation, the research has shown how change is being experienced at a specific workplace. It also shows through the interconnections among the forms of data how local experiences embody major structural changes and social relationships related to new modes of information production within the global economy.

NOTES

1. Survey information on the gender of academic library managers is not easily available, but it is estimated that, among the librarians of the 27 Canadian Research universities, from one half to two thirds are male.

2. It is important to note that support staff duties vary widely across libraries. Some have university degrees, learn on the job, and enjoy work in reference services and cataloguing that is equivalent to that of professionals. Some even advance to do the work of library administrators, particularly in budget and personnel. Others perform clerical, technical, or support work, and some of these may also have degrees! Many non-professional staff have worked in academic libraries for many years, and have experienced up-skilling in their jobs.

3. Transcribed from the researchers' presentation at the Canadian Library Association Conference in Toronto in June 1999.

4. University collective agreements and handbooks are held online by the Canadian Association of University Teachers at www.caut.ca.

5. There will be more hirings when the present "bulge" of librarians retire.

6. When they address this topic, library educators emphatically affirm that information studies graduates have a strong and promising future. A faculty member from the University of Toronto spoke of future projections of staff and budgetary increases. One from the Université de Montréal took the proactive approach of modifying his education program to meet market demands. Another from the University of Western Ontario spoke of positive job placements. Satisfactory professional placements and fulfillment of market demands do not, however, remove the threat of external control.

7. While graduate programs in information studies are sometimes combined with cognate programs, such as journalism, communication, management, or even law, the degree still designates professional inclusion.

8. The seven institutions were Dalhousie University in Halifax, Nova Scotia; McGill University and the French Université de Montréal in Montreal, Quebec; University of Toronto in Toronto and the University of Western Ontario in London, Ontario; University of Alberta in Edmonton, Alberta; and the University of British Columbia in Vancouver, British Columbia.

9. Typical required courses include McGill's *Introduction to the Information Environment* in 1980 and 1981, which includes "theoretical framework for professional practices"; "sense of professional identity"; "knowledge of historical, social, and economic aspects of information services and of its critical developments and problems," and UBC's *Foundations of Information-based Organizations* in 2000 and 2001, which offers "theories and principles"; "intellectual property"; "intellectual freedom access questions with electronic and physical documents"; "information policy"; "role of the profession and the institution in information access."

10. Typical required courses include Montréal's *Traitement et analyse documentaire I et II* in 1985 and 1986 and Alberta's *Organization of Knowledge and Information* in 2000 and 2001.

11. Typical courses include Dalhousie's *User Services*, which has been offered from 1971 and 1972 to the present and has consistently emphasized user needs, social roles, communications, and in recent years bibliographic instruction.

12. Required courses range from McGill's *Introduction to Data Processing* in 1971 and 1972 to Toronto's *Introduction to Information Technology* in 2000 and 2001 featuring

"conceptual knowledge of information technology and its usage" and "computers, software, systems, and telecommunications systems."

13. An early core course is Alberta's *Administration and Management* in 1971 and 1972 and recent examples include Montréal's *Marketing des services d'information* and *Entrepreneurship et information* in 2000 and 2001.

14. Typical required courses include UBC's *Publishing and the Book Trade* in 1971 and 1972, Western's *Collection Development* in 1995 and 1996, and Dalhousie's *Collections Management* in 2000 and 2001.

15. The CARL libraries are a sub-set of the 50 university libraries that offer doctoral or research programs.

16. "Heads" and "directors" in Canadian libraries may be unionized staff, who are reference staff with some supervisory responsibilities, or management exclusions or union-exempt staff, who do a lot of decision making and little day-to-day work with the public.

17. The sole exceptions were for two university archivists.

18. In Canada, there remain librarians who hold a Bachelor of Library Science or less, awarded before the early 1970s, when the Master's degree became the standard. All should have retired within ten years.

19. Ranking schemes for librarians are fully detailed in union contracts or handbooks, which are publicly available (http://www.caut.ca), whereas only limited information exists in the job ads.

20. Without extensive qualitative research in each institution to compare job description content, organization charts, and gleanings from interviews about staffing changes, the practice of understaffing cannot easily be asserted.

21. Using commercial library vendors is similar to trusting drug companies. On the one hand, they are governed by the profit motive and exert control on regulators and professional bodies, but on the other hand they have better resources than the non-profit sector and the "infrastructure" to engage in the development of a quality product.

22. Elsevier, for example, controls important periodicals, databases, and software, and has taken over a major integrated library cataloguing-acquisitions-serials-circulation system.

REFERENCES

Abbott, A. (1988). *The system of professions: An essay on the division of expert labor*. Chicago: University of Chicago Press.

Bell, D. (1973). *The coming of post-industrial society: A venture in social forecasting*. New York: Basic Books.

Braverman, H. (1974). *Labor and monopoly capital: The degradation of work in the twentieth century*. New York: Monthly Review Press.

Brewer, L. (1996). Bureaucratic organization of professional labor. *Australian and New Zealand Journal of Sociology, 32*, 21–38.

Burris, B. H. (1998). Computerization of the workplace. *Annual Review of Sociology, 24*, 141–157.

Buschman, J. (Ed.) (1993). Critical approaches to information technology in Librarianship: Foundations and applications. Westport, CN: Greenwood Press.

Carson, J. (2002). *The professional labour process in the academic library: A political economic analysis*. [Dissertation] Ottawa: Carleton University.

Clement, W., & Myles, J. (1994). *Relations of ruling: Class and gender in postindustrial societies.* Montreal: McGill-Queen's University Press.

Collins, R. (1979). *The credential society: An historical sociology of education and stratification.* New York: Academic Press.

Cordell, A. (1985). *The uneasy eighties.* Ottawa: Science Council of Canada.

Crawford, W. (1999). *Being analog: Creating tomorrow's libraries.* Chicago: American Library Association.

DiPrete, T. A. (1988). The upgrading and downgrading of occupations: Status redefinition vs. deskilling as alternative theories of change. *Social forces, 66,* 725–746.

Durkheim, E. (1957). *Professional ethics and civic morals.* C. Brookfield (Trans). London: Routledge & Kegan Paul.

Duxbury, L., & Higgins, C. (2002). Work-life balance in the new millennium: Where are we? Where do we need to go? Ottawa: Canadian Policy Research Networks (CPRN Discussion Paper, No. W/12).

Ehrenreich, B., & Ehrenreich, J. (1979). The professional-managerial class. In: P. Walker (Ed.), *Between Labour and Capital* (pp. 5–45). Sussex: Harvester Press.

Emory, C. D. (1999). *CARL Statistics 1991–1992 to 1996–1997: Analyses, trends and tabulations.* Ottawa: Canadian Association of Research Libraries.

Freidson, E. (1986). *Professional powers: A study of the institutionalization of formal knowledge.* Chicago: University of Chicago Press.

Gorman, M. (1994). The treason of the learned: The real agenda of those who would destroy libraries and books. *Library Journal, 111*(February 15), 130–131.

Gouldner, A. W. (1979). *The future of intellectuals and the rise of the new class.* New York: Seabury Press.

Harris, R. M. (1992). *Librarianship: The erosion of a woman's profession.* Norwood, NJ: Ablex.

Harris, M. H., & Hannah, S. A. (1996). The treason of the librarians: Core communication technologies and opportunity costs in the information era. *Journal of academic librarianship, 22*(1), 3–10.

Harris, M. H., Hannah, S. A., & Harris, P. C. (1998). *Into the future: Foundation of library and information services in the post-industrial era* (2nd ed.). Greenwich, CT: Ablex.

Hirschhorn, L. (1984). *Beyond mechanization: Work and technology in a postindustrial age.* Cambridge, MA: MIT Press.

Krause, E. A. (1996). *Death of the guilds: Professions, states, and the advance of capitalism, 1930 to the present.* New Haven, CT: Yale University Press.

Larson, M. S. (1977). *The rise of professionalism: A sociological analysis.* Berkeley: University of California Press.

Littler, C. (1982). *The development of the labour process in capitalist societies: A comparative study of the transformation of work organization in Britain, Japan and the U.S.A.* London: Heinemann Educational Books.

Macdonald, D. (1995). The role of proletarianization in physical education teacher attrition. *Research Quarterly for Exercise and Sport, 66,* 129–141.

McDonald, K. M. (1995). *The sociology of the professions.* London: Sage.

Meiksins, P. (1994). Labor and monopoly capital for the 1990s: A review and critique of the labor process debate. *Monthly Review* (November), 45–59.

Menzies, H. (1996). *Whose brave new world?: The information highway and the new economy.* Toronto: Between the Lines.

Murphy, R. (1988). *Social closure: The theory of monopolization and exclusion.* Oxford: Clarendon Press.

Murphy, R. (1990). Proletarianization or bureaucratization: The fall of the professional? In: R. Torstendahl & M. Burrage (Eds), *The Formation of Professions: Knowledge, State, and Strategy* (pp. 71–96). London: Sage.

Noble, D. (1995). *Progress without people: New technology, unemployment, and the message of resistance.* New York: Knopf.

Novek, J. (1998). Clinical or industrial pharmacy? Case studies of hospital automation in Canada and France. *International Journal of Health Services, 28*, 445–465.

Parsons, T. (1939). Professions and social structure. *Social Force, 17*, 457–467.

Perrolle, J. A. (1986). Intellectual assembly lines: The rationalization of managerial, professional, and technical work. *Computers and the Social Sciences, 2*, 111–121.

Rhoades, G. (1998). *Managed professionals: Unionized faculty and restructuring academic labor.* Albany: State University of New York Press.

Rinehart, J. W. (1996). *The tyranny of work: Alienation and the labour process* (3rd ed.). Toronto: Harcourt Brace.

Sinclair, J., Ironside, M., & Siefert, R. (1996). Classroom struggle? Market oriented education reforms and their impact on the teacher labour process. *Work, Employment and Society, 10*, 641–661.

Smart, A. (1975). Women: The 4/5 minority. *Canadian Library Journal, 32*, 14–17.

Smith, C., & Thompson, P. (1998). Re-evaluating the labour process debate. *Economic and Industrial democracy, 19*, 551–577.

Smith, V. (1997). New forms of work organization. *Annual Review of Sociology, 23*, 315–359.

Turkle, S. (1984). *The second self: Computers and the human spirit.* New York: Simon and Shuster.

Turkle, S. (1995). *Life on the screen: Identity in the age of the Internet.* New York: Simon and Shuster.

Vallas, S. P. (1999). Rethinking post-Fordism: The meaning of workplace flexibility. *Sociological Theory, 17*, 68–101.

Wardell, M. (Ed.) (1999). Labor process: Moving beyond Braverman and the deskilling debate. In: M. Wardell, T. L. Steiger & P. Meiksins (Eds), *Rethinking the Labor Process* (pp. 1–15).

Winter, M. (1996, Fall). Specialization, territoriality, and jurisdiction: Librarianship and the political economy of knowledge. *Library Trends, 45*(2), 343–363.

Wright, E. O. (1997). *Class counts: Comparative studies in class analysis.* London: Cambridge.

Zuboff, S. (1988). *In the age of the smart machine: The future of work and power.* New York: Basic Books.

TWO MODELS OF LEADERSHIP FORMATION IN COMMUNITY: A DIALOGUE IN PROFESSIONAL PRACTICE

Richard F. Bowman, Jr. and Edward D. Garten

In contemporary academe, it is often lamented that faculties rarely converse across unit lines. It seems especially rare to secure opportunities to dialogue about models of leadership in praxis. What follows is a professional dialogue between a longtime library dean associated with a Catholic university and a longtime professor of educational foundations associated with a state university. Dialogical colleagues over many years, both share the urgent belief that new models of academic leadership must emerge if the quality of conversation regarding, and response to, cascading change in academe is to occur in meaningful fashion.

At Winona State University, the catalyst for rethinking and renewing faculty leadership, followership, and citizenship roles has been a collective commitment to community as the organizing principle. Leadership exists as part of a duality. Leaders forge and sustain relationships with followers. Exceptional leaders not only view themselves as *life-size* but are equally adept at enabling self-knowledge in others.

Followership implies commitment, but never without conditions. Followers respond to leaders who create three emotional responses: feelings of significance, community, and excitement. Citizenship reflects the collective need to be

Advances in Library Administration and Organization
Advances in Library Administration and Organization, Volume 21, 61–82
Copyright © 2004 by Elsevier Ltd.
ISSN: 0732-0671/doi:10.1016/S0732-0671(04)21002-1

accountable for the well-being of the larger institution. It is accountability that is self-inflicted.

At the University of Dayton, the catalyst for rethinking and renewing library faculty leadership has been the focus on a major dimension within the charisma of the University's founding and sustaining religious order: The formation of servant leaders in community. Servant leadership is more than an option at Dayton; rather, it has become an altogether different way of framing the purpose of leadership, the true role of the leader, and the potential of those being led. The servant leader at Dayton sees leadership not primarily as a vehicle for accomplishing the organization's objectives, but as an opportunity to serve others who share those objectives. Leadership at Dayton is modeled not as position, recognition, status or prestige; nor is it about controlling people. Importantly, it is about freeing people to meet their full potential in community. Because leadership is all encompassing, it becomes the responsibility of everyone within the University of Dayton libraries.

WINONA: EVOLVING FACULTY ROLES OF LEADERSHIP, FOLLOWSHIP AND CITIZENSHIP

In an interview in 1991, the Nobel Prize-winning author Laurens Van der Post proclaimed that the era of leaders is over (Block, 1998). A decade later, the topic of breakthrough leadership was the subject of the first special issue in the *Harvard Business Review's* seventy-nine year history. Leadership has endured as a consuming issue in both personal and organizational life since Niccolo Machiavelli's *The Prince* was written in 1513. In truth, however, leadership exists as part of a duality: Leaders forge and sustain relationships with followers (Goffee & Jones, 2001). Strikingly, Hitler sensed this duality. In a speech to his personal guard corps, he exclaimed: "All that you are, you are through me; all that I am, I am through you alone" (Kellerman, 2001, p. 21).

Citizenship defines followers' capacity to create for themselves what they have traditionally expected their leaders to accomplish. Moreover, it is the "agreement to receive rights and privileges from the community" in return for living within certain boundaries and "acting in the interest of the whole" (Block, 1998, p. 90). Henry Rosovksy, former dean of the faculty of arts and sciences at Harvard University, declared that "when it concerns our most important obligations – faculty citizenship – neither rule nor custom is any longer compelling" (Braskamp & Ory, 1994, p. 10). Relatedly, he intimated that perhaps it is time for faculty members to rethink their association with the academy. At Winona State University, the impetus for rethinking and renewing faculty leadership, followship, and citizenship roles has been a collective commitment to "community as the organizing principle" (Bowman, 1999, p. 24).

What is a leader, anyway? What is it that impactful leaders do? What are their most important tasks? How do leaders win the respect and allegiance of followers? If there are established principles of leadership, are there also acknowledged principles of followership? Specifically, what is it that followers want and need from leaders? And how does one create a culture of citizenship dedicated to caring for the well-being of the larger institution? Does rediscovering citizenship begin, for example, with paying special attention to the way we come together – the way that we convene? Finally, does the workplace have the "potential to be the place where community is revived and common purpose is reawakened?" (Block, 1998, p. 92).

Elements of Leadership

Anthropologist Lionel Tiger ("All in a day's work," 2001) has observed that "all primate groups create – cannot exist without – leaders" (p. 57). Without a leader, the "group's energy is spent on internal jockeying for dominance," (p. 57) with real work left undone. In *Group Psychology and the Analysis of the Ego*, Freud "suggests that groups of any kind depend on a leader, even one weak and flawed, for their identity and sense of purpose" (Kellerman, 2001, p. 17). As leaders, the character traits of those who have occupied the Oval Office have truly been a deck of cards. Whether Washington, Lincoln, Nixon, Clinton, or Bush, we still tend to organize our perceptions of the country's interests and business around those individuals, "even though we may judge them ineffectual or unworthy" (Kellerman, p. 17).

Fundamentally, leadership is personal. It is a "personal quest, one that can produce blazing triumphs even as it plunges the leader into the darkest, most mysterious reaches of the self" (Collingwood, 2001, p. 8). One of the legendary titans of American enterprise, George Eastman, the father of mass-market photography, penned a dark suicide note that read: "To my friends: My work is done – why wait?" (Tedlow, 2001, p. 78). Socrates argued that the "unexamined life is not worth living." Exceptional leaders honor that haunting summons to examine what animates one inwardly. Parker Palmer (2001) contended that an inner journey was a prerequisite to authentic leadership. Moreover, he exclaims that the examined life – one rich in inner awareness – is an essential source of leadership strength. Relatedly, he observes that "in our time, we've seen the impact of people like Nelson Mandela, Rosa Parks, and Vaclav Havel, who have found the courage to lead from their own deepest truths" (Palmer, p. 26). Thus, before vision and mission and strategy comes self-knowledge. Exceptional leaders like Martin Luther King, Jr. not only view themselves as life-size but also are equally adept at enabling self-knowledge in others.

During a brainstorming exercise in the Department of Education at Winona State, faculty members identified more than fifty discrete roles and leadership demands central to key aspects of the Department's daily operations (Bowman, 2002). Philosophically, colleagues spoke with one voice: Leadership is everyone's responsibility. In a culture of dispersed leadership, the real work of academic leaders begins with inviting probing questions that uncover problems that can threaten the very existence of the organization. Cross-examining reality, moreover, demands an uncommon courage of both leader and follower. Politically, interrogating reality demands giving voices to colleagues and students by listening to their stories and songs.

Importantly, the real work of faculty leaders involves inviting and orchestrating the very penetrating, perceptive, probing questions that often give rise to the tension, dissent, and constructive stress that are essential to defining reality and creating positive organizational change (Bowman, 1999). Impact leaders recognize the "cost of insights unshared and constructive criticism unspoken" (Heenan & Bennis, 1999, p. 300). Treating constructive conflict as a vital resource for organizational learning circumscribes the real work of faculty leaders in a culture of restless self-renewal.

Academic chairs function as leaders when they focus relentlessly on key aspects of organizational culture: mission, vision, engagement, and adaptability (Bowman, 2002). Mission pinpoints the department's purpose and direction, its *reason* for existence. Vision represents what a department strives to be, its aspirations, its ambitions. Adaptability mirrors colleagues' ability to embrace "common purpose" in responding to changing workplace demands. There is, however, a distinctive difference between being a department with a vision and a mission and being a visionary organization. That difference lies in creating alignment. The real work of academic leaders centers on creating and sustaining an alignment that preserves an organization's values, reinforces its mission, stimulates progress toward it aspirations, and invites and affirms colleagues' engaged contributions in pursuit of mission and vision (Collins & Porras, 1997).

In my daily work with student teachers, there is a heightened fascination with the construct of *teacher as leader*. Initially, student teachers experience intrusive thoughts and infectious anxieties related to "managing student behavior." Within a few weeks, however, developing student teachers shifts focus from managing students' behavior to "managing students' instructional interactions." As the end of the student teaching draws near, one or more of the student teachers will wondrously begin to "amplify student interactions." The tipping point occurs when "learning replaces instruction, participation replaces presentation, and questions become more important than answers" (Block, p. 88). As *teacher as leader*, the commitment is no longer that of controlling energy in others or even in managing energy in others but rather releasing creative, combustible energy in others.

Finally, peeling the leadership onion reveals that leadership is a "multifaceted and nuanced capability," much of which appears "hardwired in people before they reach their early or mid-twenties" (Sorcher & Brant, 2002, p. 83). Admittedly, there is far more interest in leadership than there is agreement upon just what it is. In fact, what strikes preeminent leadership scholars like Warren Bennis is how difficult it is to describe anyone's leadership. Pointedly, Bennis (2002) contends that "leadership is not a science. It's not a recipe. It's not the five rules about this or the six effective habits of that. It is an art, and as Georges Braque wrote, 'The only thing that matters in art is the part that can't be explained' " (p. 98). In the deepest sense, leadership represents our collective best efforts to understand and respond to the inexplicable in our midst.

Elements of Followership

It is axiomatic that one cannot be a leader without followers. Like leadership, followership is deeply personal. The sociological and psychological literature on the follower's experience "tells us that people seek, admire, and respect – that is, they follow – leaders who produce within them three emotional responses" (Goffee & Jones, 2002, p. 148).

The first emotional response is a feeling of significance. Colleagues seek to be appreciated and affirmed for a job well done, not just through formal recognition programs but also informally through little things like hand-written notes, positive voice-mail, and e-mail messages. In truth, every communication offers a chance to recognize and affirm colleagues' value to the organization (Nelson, 2002). Recently, the State of Minnesota witnessed the largest state workers' strike in Minnesota history. Dozens of Winona State office workers and maintenance workers walked the picket lines in full ferment. Administrative leaders across the campus ventured out to the picket lines, assuring workers that they understood workers' needs, appreciated their contributions to the University, and had workers' best interests at heart, by not hiring much-needed replacements from outside the union's ranks. Kouzes and Posner (1995) note that while titles are granted, it's your behavior that wins you respect, loyalty, and followership.

The second emotional response that followers want from their leaders is a feeling of community. Goffee and Jones (2001) contend that "community occurs when people feel a unity of purpose around work, and simultaneously, a willingness to relate to each other as human beings" (p. 148). Faculty members in the Winona State Department of Education share a deeply-embedded belief that the defining elements of community are "perceived interdependence" and "generosity" (Pinchot, 1998, p. 44). In fact, those beliefs were implicit in the Department's recent invitation to the University President, Vice-President, and Dean of the College of Education to join faculty members in two hours of "dialogue as inquiry" regarding a perplexing programmatic issue. Briefly, the administration's acceptance and subsequent participation in that dialogue signaled a powerful, public caring about the consequences of colleagues' work. Importantly, that public caring functioned as a "foundation of community" (Pinchot, p. 44). Generosity is another of the defining principles of community. The administration's participation allowed faculty to sense that generosity palpably. When a feeling of community is "successfully engineered, it is so deeply gratifying that followers will call the person who created it their leader" (Goffee & Jones, 2001, p. 148.)

Thirdly, "followers will tell you that a leader is nearby when they get a buzzing feeling" (Goffe & Jones, p. 148). That feeling is triggered by a leader's orientation toward the inexorability of tomorrow ("All in a day," 2001, p. 56). In a phrase, followers respond to the gravitational pull of a department, school system, or university in which the future is actively under construction.

Freud believed that the "primal need to follow grows out of the infant's need for care and protection" and " 'the longing for the father that lives in each of us from our childhood days' " (Kellerman, 2001, p. 20). While followership implies need and commitment, that commitment is never without conditions. The follower demands that the leader create feelings of significance, community, and excitement.

Elements of Citizenship

An exploration of the elements of citizenship unearths the collective need to be accountable for the well being of both the larger institution and society. Too often in the past, accountability was entrusted only to those in positions of authority. Block (1998) asserts that "one reason we seek leadership and lose faith in the principle of self-governing systems is that we live in a culture of entitlement" (p. 90). From the public perspective, there is an aura of narcissistic entitlement in higher education. Faculty members genuflect at the altar of academic freedom, wield their union contracts with religious fervor, pay homage to rank and tenure, and view office hours as something akin to penance. To the uninitiated public, there is scant evidence of a faculty willing to give up territory. Moreover, to the degree that narcissistic entitlement constitutes claiming rights without full payment, it threatens and destroys institutions and community. In contrast, "citizenship is accountability that is chosen" (Block, 1998, p. 90). It is a responsibility for the common good which is self-inflicted.

Block argues compellingly that "citizenship, self-management, and engagement come together when we collectively learn to rethink and redesign the place where we assemble" (p. 94). In the Winona State Department of Education, colleagues are experimenting with a community structure that has been christened "The Faculty Forum" (Bowman, 1999). The bimonthly forum is clearly distinct from regularly scheduled faculty meetings. In important ways, the two structures reveal the characteristics of both traditional and emerging workplaces. The Faculty Forum draws upon community as the organizing metaphor. Implicitly, forums confront colleagues with four questions: "Who am I? What am I a part of? What connects me to the rest of the world? What relationships matter to me?" (Bressler & Grantham, 2000, p. 161). Because Roberts' Rules of Order are not honored formally in The Faculty Forums, colleagues are characteristically able to value tension and manage constructive stress across weeks of dialogue and debate on particularly contentious issues. In those instances, there is a sustained, shared sense of a collective good-faith search for common ground among powerful equals. The attending sensitivities and behaviors of openness, inclusiveness, trust, engagement, and creative collaboration reflect a commitment to common cause, communal success, and faculty citizenship.

Max DePree (1992) has described leadership as "serious meddling in other peoples' lives" (p. 17). If we are committed as faculty to meddling seriously in the lives of students and colleagues in a spirit of servant-leadership, we should do so with the conscious intent that those served become healthier, wiser, freer, and more autonomous (Greenleaf, 1977). Secondly, followership can be tracked along two continua. The first runs from uncritical, dependent thinking to critical, independent thinking. The second runs from passive engagement to active engagement. Those who are at the high end of each scale are exemplary followers. The growing demands of organizational life today require higher and higher levels of critical, independent thinking and active engagement – what Robert Kelly (1998) has defined as *exemplary followership*. Thirdly, citizenship takes form and is lived out in community when colleagues reclaim choice for themselves and others. At its core, citizenship involves creating and sustaining *relationships* around a shared sense of purpose and accountability for the whole. Thus, leadership, followership, and citizenship all involve processes of inner growth followed by outer organizational consequences.

DAYTON: INVITATION TO SERVANT LEADERSHIP

In the late twentieth century, Robert Greenleaf brought renewed attention to the concept of servant leadership. His well known "test" of servant leadership triggered an energized dialogue among modern leadership theorists.

The difference manifests itself in the care taken by the servant-first to make sure that other people's highest priority needs are being served. The best test, and difficult to administer, is: Do those served grow as persons? Do they, *while being served*, become healthier, wiser, freer, more autonomous, more likely themselves to become servants? *And*, what is the effect on the least privileged in society; will they benefit, or, at least, not be further deprived? (1970, p. 7).

Greenleaf became the reference point for leadership writers such as Kouzes and Posner (1995), Wheatley (1994), Heifetz (1994) and Senge (1990) who found in servant leadership a way to create new organizations built on a different leadership model. Senge, for example, stressed that "dynamic learning organizations are built and maintained by servant leaders who lead because they choose to serve" (1997, p. 17).

Dayton's desire to give voice to this model of leadership is not one that is trendy or transient; rather it is rooted in the University's most ethical and moral posture. Students are urged to adopt a servant leader style through their involvement in a vast array of service-learning opportunities off-campus. In faculty reviews – both tenure leading and post-tenure – "service" is truly an equal leg of the three-legged academic milking stool of "service, teaching, and research." Leadership works because it is based on how people should be treated, motivated and led. This is the kind of leadership that administrators and faculty expect at the University of Dayton and the model of leadership intentionally modeled by library staff.

At Dayton, servant leadership is an altogether different way of framing the purpose of leadership, the essential and authentic role of the leader, and the potential of those being led. Because leadership becomes the responsibility of everyone within the Libraries, the faculty and staff are accountable for the ways and manners in which they effect the servant leader disposition during yearly and mid-year Portfolio Review conversations. The Portfolio Review is the peer review model that Dayton library faculty members employ for yearly performance assessment and development of future goals. It is premised on the belief that individual effort must be aligned with library direction and vision. Conversations over prior year's attainments and anticipation of future year objectives concentrate on: (1) Attainment of focus: Broken focus ends in failure but concentrated and well-planned and shared goals end in high performing departments and individual librarians; (2) Alignment of effort with the Libraries' mission: open and trusting relations and communication result in coordinated efforts in moving the Libraries toward their vision and priorities; (3) Individual accountability: What gets measured also gets managed and accomplished; (4) Manner of goal execution: In accomplishing your goals how will you build trust, promote involvement, provide structure, facilitate learning and provide generative thinking, and built a healthy organizational culture that improves morale and reduces conflict and cynicism. Servant leaders at Dayton are specifically asked to use their positions and influence to empower those they lead, working alongside those being led as partners and in community. As Max DePree has so eloquently observed: "The first responsibility of a leader is to define reality, the last is to say thank you, and in between the two, the leader must become a servant and a debtor" (1989, p. 11).

Quite literally, until recent years, the power inherent in the servant leadership model had never been properly researched or made operational. Jim Laub (1999) undertook this task through an extensive research project in which he employed a team of fourteen experts in the field of servant leadership to come to consensus on the essential qualities of the servant leader. Those writers included Jim Kouzes and Barry Posner (1995), Larry Spears (1995), Bill Millard (1995), and Lea Williams (1996). Laub used the results of his study to create an operational definition of servant leadership as well as an expanded servant leadership model. His *Organizational Leadership Assessment* resulted from this study and provided a model by which servant leadership could be studied and measured systematically in organizations. Library faculty at Dayton will soon adapt this model (Fig. 1) to use, as one touchstone for reflection during yearly and mid-year Portfolio Review conversations.

"Leaders are perpetual learners" (Bennis & Nanus, 1985, p. 176). Servant leaders know they don't have all the answers. They know they are still growing and becoming. They are open to input from all levels of the organization because they understand that each person is a necessary, unique, and valuable part of the whole. Servant leaders need people; they need their potential, creativity, knowledge, questions, and ideas. Servant leaders are committed to freeing people to fulfill their potential, thus allowing people to grow individually and to contribute to the shared mission of the organization and its teams.

Personal Authenticity as Essential Element

Leadership is a matter of how to be, not how to do (Hesselbein, 1966, p. 4). Importantly, leadership is about becoming an integrated human being. Such integration includes one's values, talents, personality, and self-image. Leadership excellence requires being in touch with one's mental, emotional, physical, and spiritual aspects (Nahavandi, 2000), including one's gifts, passions (Vicere &

Evolves into an understanding and practice of leadership that places the good of those led over the self-interest of the leader. Servant leadership promotes the valuing and development of people, the building of community, the practice of authenticity, the provision of leadership for the good of those led and the sharing of power and status for the common good of each individual, the total organization and those served by the organization.

The Servant Leader ...	
Values People	• By believing in people • By serving other's needs before his or her own • By listening receptively and non-judgmentally.
Develops People	• By providing opportunities for learning and growth • By modeling appropriate behavior • By building up others through encouragement and affirmation
Builds Community	• By building strong personal relationships • By working collaboratively with others • By valuing the differences of others
Displays Authenticity	• By being open and accountable to others • By a willingness to learn from others • By maintaining integrity and trust
Provides Leadership	• By envisioning the future • By taking initiative • By clarifying goals
Shares Leadership	• By facilitating a shared vision • By sharing power and releasing control • By sharing status and promoting others

At Dayton the Servant Library and Information Organization Becomes One in which the characteristics of servant leadership are displayed through the organizational culture and are valued and practiced by the Libraries faculty and staff.

Adapted from Millard (1995) *Organizational Leadership Assessment*

Fig. 1.   Servant Leadership at Dayton.

Fulmer, 1997), personality, intellect, competencies, personal aspirations, and family and community life (McCauley et al., 1998). Effective leaders understand themselves, learn to set personal goals, and work to achieve those goals through their self-selected plans and abilities (Kouzes & Posner, 1993). This type of self-understanding includes areas such as strengths, weaknesses (Nahavandi, 2000), authenticity (Ruderman & Rogolsky, 2001), and self-leadership (Sims & Manz, 1997). Personal development as a leader is a process that includes discovering who you are, as well as what skills you possess (Bennis, 1989). Bennis (as cited in Kouzes & Posner, 1993) observed that, "Until you truly know yourself, strengths and weaknesses, know what you want to do and why you want to do it, you cannot succeed in any but the most superficial sense of the word" (p. 59). Specifically, Nouwen (1996) indicated that future leaders who embrace a Christian worldview will be most effective when they rediscover their true identities and stand before the world authentically.

That leaders should be authentic, self-aware, and able to act on the basis of that awareness is a key premise of the servant leader model at the University of Dayton libraries. M. N. Ruderman has concretely observed that: "Feeling authentic, living a life that is strongly connected to one's belief system, is energizing and promotes growth, learning, and psychological well-being – all important elements of effective leadership and leadership development. Conversely, inauthenticity can often be recognized by others and become a disruptive, negative force in the organization" (Ruderman & Rogolsky, 2001, p. 86). Authentic leaders are more agile in their behavior, more effective in decision making, clearer about motivations and expectations of others, and more flexible in adjusting to new situations (Lee & King, 2001). Authentic leaders have a deep sense of purpose for their leadership and are true to their core values. They are people of the highest integrity who are committed to building enduring organizations. Authentic leaders see themselves as stewards of the assets they inherit and servants of all their stakeholders (George, 2003, p. 9).

Certain skills are necessary in order to remain authentic as a leader: learning to increase self-awareness, including discernment of things that are important and things that are not, and taking time to reflect on those things; learning to assess and evaluate one's deeply held values; deciding to take action regarding priorities and potential life changes; and learning how to secure support for achieving one's goals (Ruderman & Rogolsky, 2001). The benefits of practicing these skills are that leaders become more effective in working with others, and become more flexible and confident in their approaches to goal achievement (Lee & King, 2001).

Becoming the Learning Organization

To nurture leadership that makes a difference in the lives of others there is a compelling need for visionary leaders to demonstrate: (1) a commitment to build a collaborative culture of trust; (2) a personal mastery of the principles and practices to lead a generative learning organization; and (3) creative, conceptual, and collaborative acumen to implement systems theory within one's unit and throughout the organization. At Dayton, librarians and members of the Dean's Leadership

Team are asked during yearly and mid-term appraisals to describe how they have assisted their colleagues in reframing approaches to leadership to better effect a servant modality and to derive actionable organizational learning.

Organizational learning is an interactive construction that transforms knowledge into informed practices. This occurs in a reflective process when accountability is assigned by the organization. Such learning is complete when it is internalized and acted upon by individuals and teams (Brown & Packman, 1999). The learning organization incorporates the full realm of theory, praxis, and practice in recognition of its norms and values. At the same time, it reflects on the organizational culture to generate further learning to foster self-renewal and self-organization (Argyris et al., 1985; Hodgkinson, 1991; Senge, 1990). Bennis summarizes the function of visionary leadership, within the context of a learning organization culture, by emphasizing the importance of purposes, beliefs, and vision as essential to the continuous improvement of people and programs (1984).

Without question, the work of Peter Senge has advanced the practice of systems thinking substantially. And, Senge (1990, 1994) promoted the building of learning organizations in which people continually expand their capacity to produce optimal results while fostering new and expansive patterns of thinking. In a learning organization, shared vision and collective intelligence are set free, and leaders and employees continually learn how to learn and grow together (1990). Deming believed in the inherent desire of workers to learn, grow, and transform themselves and organizations through directed effort. He outlined his framework for leadership transformation in fourteen points. Two of the fourteen points focused on institutionalizing on-the-job training and a vigorous program of education and self-improvement (Deming, 1986). Senge built on the practice of learning in organizations by advocating the continuous testing of experience through reflective dialogue, and transforming that experience into knowledge accessible to the entire workforce in alignment with the mission, values, and vision of the organization (1994). Kolb (1984) promoted the concept of an individual learning cycle (i.e. reflecting, connecting, deciding, and doing) while Spears (1995) advanced the individual learning cycle. Handy's (1990) concept of the learning wheel transformed into a variation that applied to teams (i.e. public reflection, shared meaning, joint planning, and coordinated action). Senge later incorporated team learning into his five disciplines (i.e. personal mastery, mental models, shared vision, team learning, and systems thinking).

Charan and Tichy (1998) discovered that winning organizations need to go beyond learning organizations and become teaching organizations. In their work with outstanding companies they suggest that teaching organizations are more inventive, agile, and come up with more responsive strategies. Dotlich and Noel (1998) furthered the concept of team learning and the work of Charan and Tichy by institutionalizing the Action Learning framework at Honeywell and General Electric. Action Learning became widely recognized as a collaborative process through which to enable organizations to respond to major business problems and opportunities while developing key employees with the capacity to lead organizations in the desired strategic direction. Finally, Heifetz (1994) asserted that *leadership is the process of influencing workers, units, and organizations to learn to solve their own problems rather than build dependency or co-dependency.* We would suggest that this is the essence of the learning organization.

Receptivity to Innovation and Change

Since organizations are most effective when the members share values, servant leader librarians learn that leaders should view organizational culture as a valuable resource to manage. However, if a leader takes up the difficult and time-consuming challenge to change the organization's existing culture, the task may provoke anxiety because of the deeper levels of cultural assumptions. As students of leadership learn to reveal underlying assumptions within themselves, as well as develop a servant spirit that values the members of the organization (Laub, 1999), they become more adept at creating a culture of trust across their organizations.

An in-depth understanding of the dynamics of innovation and change is critical to understanding the very nature of leadership. The ability to be servant leaders who bring about informed and positive change in the world lies at the very core of the University of Dayton Mission Statement. Kotter (1996) contended that this ability to achieve positive change is essential to any kind of effective leadership, concluding that "leadership is a set of processes that creates organizations in the first place or adapts them to significantly changing circumstances." Faculty and staff passion to become change agents, however, must come from a strong sense of value and purpose. Tellingly, Fullan (2001) proposed that moral purposes and noble crusades will lead to nothing more than martyrdom without an understanding of the dynamics of change.

Advisedly, any solid study of change theory must inform the astute servant leader. A review of the literature associated with Lewin's (1951) unfreezing, movement, refreezing approach is helpful; but more critically, today's focus must be on more modern approaches that would include Wheatley's (1999) look at the new sciences, Senge's (1990 and 1999) learning organization approach to change, and much earlier, Koesler's (1967) landmark exploration of chaos theory. Additionally, Hord et al. (1987) stressed the need to address concerns in the change process and developed the Concerns Based Adoption Model. Millard (1994) expanded this concept to create the Change Concern Cycle, proposing that this process is constantly cyclical because each previous cycle ends with the introduction of revisions and new ideas, which automatically initiates the process all over again. Understanding the role and relationship between individuals and organizations is critical in the change process. Critically, Black and Gergersen (2002) observed that most approaches are backward, trying to change all layers of an organization in hopes that the individuals will follow. They concluded that lasting change occurs when individuals are changed first, with the organization following.

One of the most important components in developing a servant leader may be his or her dexterity in the application of ethical principles that must necessarily govern and administer the organization. Such principles are, unfortunately, rarely surfaced and brought to the conversation table. Pointedly, they need to be. Librarians at Dayton are urged to reflect on the organizational culture by attending to the details of organizational structure, organizational relationships, and the clarification of roles.

Such analysis includes not only structures and roles, but also operational processes and systems design. Moorhead and Griffin (1995) suggest that one of the most critical roles of understanding governance is "the structural policies that affect operations and prescribe or restrict how employees behave in their organizational structure" (p. 391). As library leaders grow to understand structural models, they likely will apply them to the servant leadership and collegial models (Laub, 1999). Each member of the Dean's Leadership Team has attended, over recent years, the ACRL/Harvard Leadership Institute and, accordingly, is able to apply at learning experience's focus on the Bolman and Deal (1997) frames of leadership (the political, human resource frame, symbolic, and structural frames) through which to assist them with leading through governance issues.

The management of any organization must take place within an ethical framework. As a Catholic and Marianist university, the University of Dayton holds that the ethical context of an organization is central to its effective functioning. Greenleaf (1991) suggested that the ethical component is always a part of the servant leader mentality – a moral principle to be trusted. Library and information service professionals at Dayton are urged to evaluate ethical dilemmas in organizational leadership and suggest concrete means through which to resolve such dilemmas.

THE AUTHORS DIALOGUE

We have explored two different, yet mutually-reinforcing models of organizational commitment to the formation of the learning organization: One grounded in important notions of leadership, followership, and citizenship and the other steeped in theory that underpins a servant style of leadership.

Richard: In their breakthrough study, *Geeks and Geezers*, Bennis and Thomas (2002) probed the powerful processes through which leaders of any era emerge. Specifically, they focused upon how era and values shaped those leaders who grew up in the shadows of the Depression and World War II versus those who matured in the phosphorescent glow of computer screens. In a essence, their research findings suggested that true leaders of any age share a cluster of critical qualities: adaptive capacity, the ability to engage others in shared meaning, a distinctive and compelling voice, and a sense of integrity. But, what of the perceived negative reaction some might have to the phrase "servant leader," especially given the religious connotations sometimes laid upon that phrase?

Edward: I'm aware of the limitations that phrase often evokes because servant leadership remains a misunderstood concept. In a recent paper Bill Millard (2001) has noted this fairly commonplace reaction, one that some have not found captivating or up-to-date. He found this attitude to be one shared by quite a few others in the field of leadership and, subsequently, has been puzzled by that attitude. Pointedly, however, he goes on to suggest that the power of servant leadership has never really been derived from terminology but, rather, from principle. He notes that persons who are compelled by mission to be servant leaders, as is the case with the library staff at Dayton, do so because *they believe that it to be the right way to lead.* Servant leadership as a theme or an idea has a lineage as old as the scriptures and perhaps even Hammurabi. What appears to have slowed the development of servant-leadership literature in organizational science has been the sense of unease among scholars of ideas that have a religious salience. Yet the principles that ground servant leadership mirror a universal ethic: honesty, humility, trust, healing, empathy, community, and service. The playwright Arthur Miller observed that we know an era has ended when its basic allusions have been exhausted. What are the historical illusions about leaders and organizations that now appear shattered?

Richard: Taylorism, the scientific management of work, focused on the improvement of the efficiency of the worker. In its broadest application, life was viewed mechanistically. The task of organizational leadership was to create a better functioning machine. Moreover, workers were "viewed as machines and controlled to perform with the same efficiency and predictability" (Wheatley, 1998, p. 342). That engineering image of people led to organizational lives that ignored the deep realities of human existence. It allowed leaders to ignore that individuals carry spiritual questions and quests into their work that individuals need affirmation and love, and that emotions are an integral part of individuals' work lives (Wheatley, 1998). Servant-leadership, in contrast, invites individuals and groups to pause and question their fundamental beliefs about each other, the nature of their work, and their capacity for self-awareness, self-creation, and self-organization. Pointedly, the exhausted illusions of Taylor's mechanistic story have yielded to an emergent, deeper and richer image of who followers and leaders are. Servant-leadership, at its core, is an expression of the need to push back against a story that excludes spirit, love, meaning, purpose, and legacy from the workplace. In a word, servant-leadership is about deep identity; it invites persons to lives closer to the human spirit. Compellingly, servant-leadership poses the question: "What might our organizations accomplish if they trusted and called on the human spirit? (Wheatley, 1998, p. 350). Recently, a Minnesota State University received a five million dollar grant to launch a mentoring program pairing student teachers and veteran cooperating teachers. Implicitly, the grant forces a fundamental question: Is the role of mentoring essentially helping a student teacher learn how to "be" as opposed to persuading a student teacher "what to do." Greenleaf once described George Wythe's house as the "place where Thomas Jefferson was born" because so much of what Jefferson was to become "as an intellectual force stemmed from Wythe's example and Wythe's person" (McCollum, 1998, p. 336). At the height of Taylorism, mentoring had a machine and parental dimension to it. Servant-leadership, in contrast, attaches a more spiritual quality to mentoring. For mentees, the focus would be on how to "be," as opposed to how to "do." The student teacher would learn how to "be" in the classroom and "be" in professional relationships, and "be" in society. Critical issues like classroom management, for example, would be viewed fundamentally as a matter of character, as opposed to merely a matter of technique.

Edward: Perhaps it was only a subliminal desire to maintain continuity with my Southern Appalachian roots, but recently one morning I found myself softly singing the words to an old hymn that includes the phrase: "*Like a sheep he was humbled to His Father's will.*" That then got me to thinking about what animal we might think of when we reflect on servant leadership . . . and why? Does such an overt religious-laden image create problems in our secular organizations? Only a few days back I was skimming an unsolicited theological school newsletter that comes to my office and happened upon a dialogue by two seminarians, both of whom are also real life shepherdesses, one in Indiana and one in Wyoming. Dialogically in the article, these two women speak about the nature and characteristics of the sheep they tend and how, over time, they have come to be closely attuned to those over whom they watch. One of the women observed:

> Sometimes on cold nights in the fall I would wake up at 1:00 a.m. and hear the coyotes howling. My flock was still out there in the late pasture. There wasn't much I could do, but I did the one

thing I needed to do. I got up, got in the pickup, and drove out into the darkness to where the flock was sleeping. And I shined a light out into the darkness as I drove. I could catch pairs of eyes in the beam of my light, and the howling would stop. The coyotes would slink off into the darkness, over the ridge, to seek other prey. You could hear their calls fade into the distance as they went their way. That is all we are called to do as shepherds: To care for the flock, and to shine a light in the darkness (Moore, 2003, p. 16).

Richard, if we squarely face the uncomfortable truths of organizational life today and add in the sometimes haunting awareness of the snares that seem to be around every corner (some of them quite evil); perhaps the only correct and morally responsible leadership posture we can assume is that of the servant leader. It seems we increasingly work in one wilderness or another, and some can be quite dark. Perhaps all we are called to do as servant leaders is to care deeply in love for those whom we serve and, then, to shine lights into the darkness to ward off that which would undermine or destroy the rich learning communities we wish to create.

Richard: While all leaders have imperfections and shortcomings, servant-leaders resist the seductive tendency to deny them or cover them up by shining a bright light on their acknowledged weaknesses to under them better and to avoid falling prey to the dynamics of leader recklessness and folly that so dot the organizational landscape today. In truth, Greenleaf acknowledged that the idea of *servant* is rooted in our Judeo-Christian heritage. Clearly the words servant, serve, and service punctuate the pages of Holy Scripture. Historians tell us that Jesus was a leader. The Gospel writers tell us that Jesus was also a servant: "If anyone wants to be first, he must be the very last, and the servant of all" (Mark, pp. 9, 35). In both contemporary religious and secular organizations, however, servant-leadership has emerged as a guiding moral principle. The test of that moral principle in an organizational setting today is Greenleaf's: Do those served grow as persons? Do they, while being served, become healthier, wiser, freer, more autonomous, and more likely themselves to become servants? At Winona State University, there is compelling evidence of the change in attitude and practice required to achieve Greenleaf's ideals of servant leadership. The social architecture of the campus honors the deepest realities of human existence by promoting community, connection, interdependency, and the sharing of power in decision making. Today, fifty-five colorful banners fly high over the campus proclaiming "A Community of Learners Dedicated to Improving our World." In concert, four faculty teams are currently engaged dialogically in designing a "new university" in which colleagues will intentionally explore a collective vision of organization as servant, with a deep desire to help others.

Edward: The more we dialogue about the critical elements of leadership, followership, servanthood and indeed, citizenship within community, another old gospel song rambles in my mind; a tune brought home to me this past year given its place in the fabric of the love story that was Johnny and June Carter Cash. Both musical geniuses in their own right, June was known to take the servant position to John in family and community matters; much less to mention her central role as healer in John's long and finally overcome addictions. Toward the end of both of their lives they sang this almost prescient metaphor of heaven:

> I'll be waiting on the far side banks of Jordan.
> I'll be sitting drawing pictures in the sand.
> And when I see you coming, I will rise up with a shout
> And come running through the shallow waters; reaching for your hand.

What are great leaders but those who work and wait in patience to invite persons into full citizenship in community (alert welcoming), that when fully realized, dazzles beyond our imaginations? Not only do servant leaders wait in patient concern, they welcome the opportunity to "rise up with a shout" in both hospitality and encouragement and to embody within themselves those characteristics that make for full entry and participation into earthy organizational forms. Moreover, in true servant fashion, they wade out into the waters (they are courageous), reaching for the hands (the talents and the creative impulses) of those who can – and, indeed, will – make flesh rich learning communities that ultimately embody the eternal qualities of humility, reflection, truth-telling, and action for the sake of others. As guiding metaphors, citizenship in community and servant-hood in community mirror one another; indeed, they simply may be lens through which to address the simple but powerful questions that you raised earlier: "Who am I? What am I a part of? What connects me to the rest of the world? What relationships matter to me?" Richard, to restate what you suggested earlier, citizenship (and I believe servant leadership) both take form and are lived out in community when colleagues reclaim choice for themselves and others and act in humane and caring ways on behalf of the whole community. Both citizenship and servant leadership involve creating and sustaining *relationships* around a shared sense of purpose and accountability for this whole community, whether that be a university, a hospital, a group of believers within a faith tradition, or *any* organization whose mission is to serve the higher needs of others. Ego, as much as it can be, is left behind and humility and encouragement to task begin to rule. As you have observed, leadership, followership, and citizenship all involve processes of inner growth followed by outer organizational consequences. As I continue to reflect on our discussion here regarding those elements that might better anchor us in, as you term it in your context "leadership, followership, and citizenship," and as I term it in my context "servant leadership" its apparent that we are both drawing upon intermingled and mutually supportive literatures and laying the groundwork for further dialogue on our respective campuses.

The Authors Conclude: The social philosopher, Charles Handy, observed that in many ways the twentieth century was the Organization Century. It was clearly an age in which much of a worker's identity came from the organization or enterprise that one worked for. Individuals in those organizations were often "plugged into predetermined slots or roles" and were known more by their job titles than their names (Handy, 2003, p. 90). Many workers were often slaves to the moment, moving from task to task, in a machine-like process. Relatedly, management styles were often exploitative and authoritarian.

Robert Greenleaf spent his first career of forty years at AT&T probing issues of power and authority. He searched for ways in which individuals could relate to others in less coercive and more creatively supporting ways. And he championed the belief that becoming a servant-leader begins with the natural feeling that one truly wants to serve – to serve first, then lead. Thus, servant-first and leader-first remained polarities for Greenleaf. In practical terms, Greenleaf's vision foreshadowed a twenty-first century in which workers would matter more than their roles; worker discretion would matter more than dutiful compliance; and shared purpose would matter more than efficiency. In life, the most profound truths are often deceptively simple, yet almost impossible to apply in practice. Sustaining a university in which the authority of ideas, as opposed to the idea of authority, reigns supreme is admittedly problematic (Summers, 2003). The acknowledged difficulty in applying Greenleaf's philosophy of servant-leadership in contemporary organizations, therefore, does not invalidate that philosophy. Nor does it invalidate Greenleaf's test of servant-leadership: Do those served grow as persons? Do they, while being served, become healthier, wiser, freer, more autonomous, and more likely themselves to become servants?

At two different institutions – one a state university and the other a private one sustained by a faith tradition – we have chronicled complimentary and necessary forms of both community building and approaches to the establishment of the learning organization. In truth, however, communities and learning organizations are not created by deans or department chairs, but rather by visionary servant-leaders at all levels who risk stepping forward one by one. The strategy of those hopeful servant-leaders is captured disarmingly in a bit of verse from Edwin Markham's "Outwitted":

> They drew a circle that shut me out,
> Heretic, rebel, a thing to flout.
> But love and I had the wit to win.
> We drew a circle that took them in (Markham, 2000, p. 1224).

Servant leadership captures the markers of productive leadership with grace. Servant leadership invites leaders at all levels to view their accomplishments and foibles with the detachment and discernment of one who is in service to others and to the organization. Servant leadership exhorts leaders at all levels to focus on what truly matters in life, as a way of developing and sustaining the humility required of the servant leader. Because servant leaders are intimately connected to the lives of others in their quest to "give something back," they avoid the very dangers of becoming isolated and insulated from the realities of organizational life that have triggered the lapses in judgment and personal conduct that have stalked so many of today's fallen leaders. In daily practice, servant leadership reminds leaders at all levels that no one, including President Bush, Cardinal Law, Ken Lay, and Martha Stewart, is exempt from the rules that govern other people's behavior. And, in daily practice, servant leadership exhorts leaders at all levels to confront their self-enhancing illusions regarding their bloated sense of importance in organizational life, coupled with their exaggerated sense of entitlement to organizational resources. In the ultimate sense, servant leadership is accountability that is self-inflicted in the service of others.

REFERENCES

All in a day's work (2001). *Harvard Business Review, 79*(11), 54–66.
Argyris, C., Putnam, R., & Smith, D. (1985). *Action science: Concepts, methods, skills for research and intervention.* San Francisco: Jossey-Bass.
Bennis, W. (1984). Transformative power and leadership. In: T. J. Sergiovannie & J. E. Corbally (Eds), *Leadership and Organizational Culture* (pp. 64–71). Urbana, IL: University of Illinois Press.
Bennis, W. (1989). *On becoming a leader.* Reading, MA: Addison-Wesley.
Bennis, W. (2002). Will the legacy live on? *Harvard Business Review, 80*(2), 95–99.
Bennis, W., & Nanus, B. (1985). *Leaders: The strategies for taking charge.* New York: Harper & Row.
Bennis, W., & Thomas, R. J. (2002). *Geeks & geezers: How era, values, and defining moments shape leaders.* Boston: Harvard Business School Press.
Black. J. S., & Gergersen, H. B. (2002). *Leading strategic change: Breaking through the brain barrier.* Upper Saddle River, NJ: Prentice-Hall.
Block, P. (1998). From leadership to citizenship. In: L. C. Spears (Ed.), *Insights on Leadership* (pp. 87–95). New York: Wiley.
Bolman, L. G., & Deal, T. E. (1997). *Reframing organizations: Artistry, choice and leadership.* San Francisco: Jossey-Bass.
Bowman, R. (1999). Community as the organizing principle. *Catalyst for Change, 28*(3), 23–24.
Bowman, R. (2002). The real work of department chair. *The Clearing House, 75*(3), 158–162.
Braskamp, L., & Ory, J. (1994). *Assessing faculty work.* San Francisco: Jossey-Bass.
Bressler, S. E., & Grantham, Sr., S. E. (2000). *Communities of commerce: Building internet business communities to accelerate growth, minimize risk, and increase customer loyalty.* New York: McGraw Hill.
Brown, M., & Packman, R. (1999). *Organizational learning, critical systems thinking, and systemic learning* (Centre for Systems Studies Research Memorandum 20). Yorkshire, England: University of Hull.

Charan, R., & Tichy, N. M. (1998). *Every business is a growth business: How your company can prosper year after year*. New York: Times Business.

Collingwood, H. (2001). Know thyself. *Harvard Business Review, 79*(11), 8.

Collins, J., & Porras, J. (1997). *Built to last: Successful habits of visionary companies*. New York: Simon & Schuster.

Deming, W. E. (1986). *Out of crises*. Cambridge, MA: MIT Press.

DePree, M. (1989). *Leadership is an art*. New York: Dell Publishing.

DePree, M. (1992). *Leadership jazz*. New York: Doubleday.

Dotlich, D. L., & Noel, J. L. (1998). *Action learning: How the world's top companies are recreating their leaders and themselves*. San Francisco: Jossey-Bass.

Fullan, M. (2001). *Leading in a culture of change*. San Francisco: Jossey-Bass.

George, B. (2003, October). *Harvard Management Update, 8*(10).

Goffee, R., & Jones, G. (2001). Followership: It's personal too. *Harvard Business Review, 79*(11), 148.

Greenleaf, R. K. (1977). *Servant leadership*. New York: Paulist Press.

Greenleaf, R. K. (1991). *The servant as leader*. Indianapolis: The Robert K. Greenleaf Center.

Handy, C. (1990). *The age of unreason*. Boston: Harvard Business School Press.

Handy, C. (2003). Behind the numbers. *Harvard Business Review, 81*(8), 90.

Heenan, D., & Bennis, W. (1999). *Co-leaders: The power of great partnerships*. New York: Wiley.

Heifetz, R. A. (1994). *Leadership without easy answers*. Cambridge, MA: Harvard University Press.

Hesselbein, F. (1966). The "how to be" leader. In: F. Hesselbein, M. Goldsmith & R. Beckhard (Eds). *The Leader of the Future: New Visions, Strategies, and Practices for the Next Era*. San Francisco: Jossey-Bass.

Hodgkinson, C. (1991). *Educational leadership: The moral act*. Albany, NY: State University of New York.

Hord, S. M. et al. (1987). *Taking charge of change*. Alexandria, VA: Association for Supervision and Curriculum Development.

Kellerman, B. (2001). Required reading. *Harvard Business Review, 79*(11), 15–24.

Kelly, R. (1998). Followership in a leadership world. In: L. C. Spears (Ed.), *Insights on Leadership* (pp. 170–184). New York: Wiley.

Koesler, A. (1967). *The ghost in the machine*. London: Hutchinson.

Kolb, D. (1984). *Experiential learning: Experience as the source of learning and development*. Engelwood Cliffs, NJ: Prentice-Hall.

Kotter, J. P. (1996). *Leading change*. Boston: Harvard Business School Press.

Kouzes, J. M., & Posner, B. Z. (1993). *Credibility: How leaders gain and lose it, why people demand it*. San Francisco: Jossey-Bass.

Kouzes, J. M., & Posner, B. Z. (1995). *The leadership challenge: How to keep getting extraordinary things done in organizations*. San Francisco: Jossey-Bass.

Laub, J. A. (1999). *Assessing the servant organization: Development of the organizational leadership assessment (OLA) instrument*. Boca Raton, FL: Dissertation.

Lee, R. J., & King, S. N. (2001). *Discovering the leader in you: A guide to realizing your personal leadership potential*. San Francisco: Jossey-Bass.

Markham, E. (2000). Outwitted. In: C. Nelson (Ed.), *Anthology of Modern American Poetry* (p. 1224). Oxford: Oxford University Press.

McCauley, C. D., Moxley, S. R., & Velsor, E. V. (Eds) (1998). *Handbook of leadership development*. San Francisco: Jossey-Bass.

McCollum, J. (1998). The inside-out proposition: Finding (and keeping) our balance in contemporary organizations. In: L. C. Spears (Ed.), *Insights on Leadership* (pp. 340–351). New York: Wiley.

Millard, B. (1994). *ChangeQuest: A process for modifying your organization.* Ventura, CA: Life Discovery Publications.

Millard, B. (1995). *Servant-leadership – it's right and it works!* Colorado Springs: Life Discovery Publications.

Moore, K. (2003). Like a shepherd leading the flock. *The Mosaic of Louisville Seminary, 10*(3), 13–16.

Nahavandi, A. (2000). *The art and science of leadership.* Upper Saddle River, NJ: Prentice-Hall.

Nelson, B. (2002). The rewards of recognition. *Leader to Leader, 23,* 16–19.

Nouwen, H. J. M. (1996). *In the name of Jesus: Reflections on Christian leadership.* New York: Crossroad.

Palmer, P. (2001). Leadership and the inner journey. *Leader to Leader, 22,* 26–33.

Pinchot, G. (1998). An alternative to hierarchy. *Leader to Leader, 10,* 41–46.

Ruderman, M. N., & Rogolsky, S. (2001). Getting real: How to lead authentically. *Leadership in Action, 21,* 3.

Senge, P. M. (1990). *The fifth discipline: The art and practice of the learning organization.* New York: Currency Doubleday.

Senge, P. M. (1997). Creating learning communities. *Executive Excellence, 14*(3), 17–18.

Sims, H. P., & Manz, C. C. (1997). Company of heroes: Unleashing the power of self leadership. *Long Range Planning, 30*(1), 141.

Sorcher, M., & Brant, J. (2002). Are you picking the right leaders? *Harvard Business Review, 80*(2), 78–85.

Spears, L. C. (Ed.) (1995). *Reflections on leadership: How Robert K. Greenleaf's theory of servant-leadership influenced today's top management thinkers.* New York: Wiley.

Summers, L. (2003). The authority of ideas. *Harvard Business Review, 81*(8), 144.

Tedlow, R. (2001). What titans can teach is. *Harvard Business Review, 79*(11), 70–79.

Vicere, A. A., & Fulmer, R. M. (1997). *Leadership by design.* Boston: Harvard Business School Press.

Wheatley, M. J. (1994). *Leadership and the new science: Learning about organizations from an orderly universe.* San Francisco: Berrett-Koehler.

Wheatley, M. J. (1998). What is our work? In: L. C. Spears (Ed.), *Insights on Leadership* (pp. 326–329). New York: Wiley.

Wheatley, M. J. (1999). *Leadership and the new science: Discovering order in a chaotic world* (2nd ed.). San Francisco: Berrett-Koehler.

Williams, L. E. (1996). *Servants of the people: The 1960s legacy of African-American leadership.* New York: St. Martin's Press.

AN ORGANIZATIONAL CULTURE MODEL TO STIMULATE CREATIVITY AND INNOVATION IN A UNIVERSITY LIBRARY

Ellen Martins, Nico Martins and Fransie Terblanche

Post-industrial organizations today are knowledge-based organizations faced with inevitable change in their environment; developments in innovative technology; and changes in market structures, customers and competitors in the social and political environment. Internal change is reflected in the way they adapt to these changes. An effective reaction to these demands leads not only to changes in individuals and their behavior, but also to innovations in the organization designed to ensure their existence. Their success and survival depend on creativity, innovation, discovery and inventiveness (Read, 1996). It appears that the rate of change is accelerating rapidly, as new knowledge, idea generation and global diffusion increase (Chan Kim & Mauborgne, 1999; Senge et al., 1999).

Universities and university libraries are also faced by changes in their external and internal environment. The role of the university library is subject to changes as a result of the altering academic communication processes and progress in the field of information technology (Pienaar, 1995). University libraries are faced with challenges relating to finance, to continuous technological changes, and to competition from other information services like the internet and changing user needs (Burke, 1994; De Gennaro, 1992; Kong, 1996). The increase in competition has led to the increased necessity for fast, accurate, and relevant information.

Advances in Library Administration and Organization
Advances in Library Administration and Organization, Volume 21, 83–130
© 2004 Published by Elsevier Ltd.
ISSN: 0732-0671/doi:10.1016/S0732-0671(04)21003-3

Globalization has extended to the need for local information to include a need for national and international information as well (Burke, 1994). In most libraries, the focus has shifted from ownership of information sources to customer focused just-in-time access to information (Kong, 1996; Pienaar, 1994).

University libraries are finding themselves in the midst of information technological development and progress and, therefore, are experiencing fast and radical changes. The process that is used to assist organizations in adapting to change is organizational transformation. Not only does transformation make it necessary that library management teams should be able to manage and accept change, but it also means that they should be able to design their own transformation. To be able to adapt and lead in a new era, both library management and personnel should be flexible, creative and innovative (Marchant & England, 1989; Riggs, 1997). The importance of innovation and creativity is emphasized as follows by Zaltman et al. (In: West & Farr, 1990, pp. 3–4): "The importance of new ideas cannot be overstated. Ideas and their manifestations as practices or products are at the core of social change." Today's successful organizations, including university libraries, must foster creativity and innovation and master the art of change or they will become candidates for extinction (Robbins, 1996).

In the midst of change, organizations and leaders are trying to create an institutional framework in which creativity and innovation are accepted as basic cultural norms. To succeed at this, management must create a new reality for employees by stimulating creativity and innovation. According to Martell (1989) the organizational culture is a critical aspect in this context. It has become clear that "the unwritten rules of the game" (the norms of behavior) and shared values influence morale, performance and the application of creativity and innovation in many different ways. There seems to be an urgent need to understand how organizational cultures should be dealt with in order to promote creativity and innovation. This need was already identified by Schuster in 1986. University libraries need a competitive drive in order to manage and adapt to the changes that they are experiencing. According to Martell (1989) an investigation of the organizational culture of university libraries is a tool that can be used to determine whether creativity and innovation is stimulated during this change process. Authors such as Johnson (1996), Judge et al. (1997), Pienaar (1994), Shaughnessy (1988), Tesluk et al. (1997) and Tushman and O'Reilly (1997) all agree that organizational culture is a factor which contributes to the degree to which creativity and innovative behavior is found among employees in an organization. Michela and Burke (2000) argue that quality and innovation in organizations are inextricably intertwined with organizational culture.

RESEARCH PROBLEM

In some organizations action is taken to stimulate creativity and innovation. The right steps may have been taken, such as involving employees in decision making, recruiting and appointing employees who evidence characteristics of creativity, setting standards for work performance and giving regular feedback, yet creativity and innovation are hampered in some way. The culture of an organization may be a factor contributing to the extent to which creativity and innovation occur in an organization (Johnson, 1996; Judge et al., 1997; Pienaar, 1994; Shaughnessy, 1988; Tesluk et al., 1997; Tushman & O'Reilly, 1997 in Martins & Terblanche, 2003). The current organizational culture and the demands of creativity and innovation may lead to a conflict situation.

This leads to the following questions:

- What is the nature of the organizational culture within organizations?
- What is understood by creativity and innovation in organizations?
- What is the relationship between creativity, innovation and organizational culture?
- How does organizational culture stimulate creativity and innovation in organizations?
- What determinants of organizational culture have an influence on creativity and innovation in a university library?

The purpose of this article is to present, by means of a literature-based model, the determinants of organizational culture which influence the degree of creativity and innovation in organizations. Furthermore the purpose is to present, by means of an empirically tested model, the determinants of organizational culture that influence creativity and innovation in a university library.

METHOD

A literature study, which was descriptive in nature, was undertaken. The aim was to describe the phenomena considered in this article as accurately as possible. Literature in the managerial sciences was used to describe organizational culture, creativity and innovation in organizations. The manifestation of organizational culture in university libraries is examined in detail. The demands that creativity and innovation place on the culture of an organization are derived from the study of the literature. Then, in an empirical research study, a university library was tested against these demands so as to determine how organizational culture in a university library promotes creativity and innovation. The empirical study was based on an initial survey process in order to describe the culture of the university library. Existing data was used and further analyzed, and then quantitative data was gathered and processed. Conclusions are drawn about promoting creativity and innovation by means of the organizational culture in the university library.

THE NATURE OF ORGANIZATIONAL CULTURE

Organizational culture is defined in many different ways in the literature. Perhaps the most commonly known definition is "the way we do things around here" (Lundy & Cowling, 1996). In this research, organizational culture is defined as the deeply seated (often subconscious) values and beliefs shared by personnel in an organization. Organizational culture is manifested in the typical characteristics of the organization. It therefore refers to a set of basic assumptions that worked so well in the past that they are accepted as valid assumptions within the organization. These assumptions are maintained in the continuous process of human interaction (which manifests itself in attitudes and behaviour), in other words as the right way in which things are done or problems should be understood in the organization. The components of routine behavior, norms, values, philosophy, rules of the game and feelings all form part of organizational culture (Hellriegel et al., 1998; Smit & Cronje, 1992 in Martins, 2003).

The Origin and Maintenance of Organizational Culture

In the first place, the origin of any organizational culture can be traced back to the founders of the organization. These founders are usually dynamic personalities, with strong values and a clear vision of what the organization should be. The organizational culture develops as a result of the interaction between the founders' preferences and beliefs and what the original employees learn from their own experiences. An example is the Walt Disney company, an organization that continues to focus on Walt Disney's original vision of a company designed to create fantasy entertainment (Robbins, 1997, p. 242). Kilman (cited in Theron, 1996) describes the early stage of organizational culture as follows:

- An enormous stream of energy is released when an organization is founded as employees struggle to make it work.
- An organizational culture forms fairly soon, based on the organization's vision, mission, goals, objectives and requirements for success.

In some cases, the values, preferences and beliefs of the founders become the accepted values, preferences and beliefs in the organization and remain so as long as the founders are around, and even afterwards (Furnham & Gunter, 1993; Robbins, 1997). In others, organizational culture could develop (or change) as a result of the organization's experiences with the external environment. Each organization should create its own image and find its niche in the sector in which it functions. For example, a university library might strive to provide an outstanding quality of service delivery as opposed to reasonable quality and self-service. Since the external environment continuously changes, organizations are pressured to change (Furnham & Gunter, 1993).

A third instance leading to the development of an organizational culture is necessary to support effective working relationships amongst employees in the organization. The nature of the business and the personalities of the type of people employed lead to the development of values and expectations that differ from one organization to another. In one type of library it might be necessary to communicate quickly and openly. This might lead to the valuing of free and open communication and informal working relationships between employees. In contrast, different values and communication processes might develop in other organizations with other types of employees and different goals/purposes (Furnham & Gunter, 1993).

Organizational culture can also develop as a result of the role that key individuals play in an organization, specifically based on the matters on which they focus (for instance, what they say and do in crisis situations, who is appointed and promoted, recognition of status and compensation, role modeling and the types of training provided) (Furnham & Gunter, 1993; Smit & Cronje, 1992; Theron, 1996). The development of norms with regard to critical incidents in an organization could also lead to the development of an organizational culture, especially when mistakes are made. The lessons learned contribute to forming the culture. An example would be when someone completed a task very well on his or her own initiative, but was then reprimanded because no instruction was given to carry out the task (Furnham & Gunter, 1993; Theron, 1996).

Manifestation of Organizational Culture in an Organization

Organizational culture manifests itself in several ways in organizations. Certain work procedures and habits are an indication of the type of culture that exists. These cultural guidelines enable employees to interpret the work situations and form a general understanding of the organizational culture, according to which they then behave. These cultural guidelines are:

- Material Symbols like the architecture of the building, arrangement of offices of management and other levels of staff; material symbols that project status and the degree of elitism in the organization – for instance office space, allocation of parking space, size of desk – corporate image – for instance, a friendly staff member at the information desk projects a different image than obnoxious behavior; physical environment – for instance, artifacts and facilities; clothing – for instance, wearing a uniform in a bank, or white uniforms in a hospital.
  The message transferred by material symbols explains to employees who is important, the degree of formality or informality expected by management and the type of behavior expected (e.g. risk-taking, conservative, authoritarian, participative, individualistic and social) (Coffey et al., 1994; Kreitner & Kinicki, 1992; Robbins, 1996; Robbins et al., 2003; Smit & Cronje, 1992).
- Rites and rituals are repetitive sequences of activities that express and reinforce the key values of the organization, e.g. the annual graduation ceremonies that take place at universities; or meetings in one organization might take place at the same time and place every week, but in another organizations meetings might take place only when necessary (Coffey et al., 1994).
- Language use is an important manifestation of culture. Through learning the "organization's language," members accept the culture and consequently help to maintain it (Robbins, 1997; Smit & Cronje, 1992). In the library profession the use of acronyms is very popular. Examples are ARL (Association of Research Libraries), OCLC (the center in Ohio that does cooperative cataloguing) and OPAC (*Online Patron Accessing Catalogue*) (Robbins, 1996; Robbins et al., 2003). In support of this point several acronyms appear in the article by Roher (1998), e.g. PLUS (*Promoting Larger Units of Service*), SLICD (*Statewide Library Information for Caregivers of the Disabled*) and MAP (*Multi-Media Access Project*). In a university library an example could be the LMC (*Library Management Committee*). These terms are inherent in the library profession, but peculiar to outsiders.
- Legends and stories are often spread in organizations. These stories typically contain a narrative of events about the organization's founders, rule breaking, relocation of employees, reactions to past mistakes, and organizational coping (*CIMA Study Text*, 1996; Deal & Kennedy, 1982; Robbins, 1997). According to Deal and Kennedy (1982), story tellers bring about cohesion and provide guidelines for everyone in the organization to follow. In other words the values of the organization are preserved by communicating the legends and stories to newcomers.
- Interpersonal relationships that develop between management and subordinates, between management, different departments, colleagues, employees and customers inform employees of the "correct" way to behave. Is the

organization, for example, focused on cooperation rather than competition amongst employees (Sathe, 1985)?

- Values, beliefs and moral principles that filter down from top management through memoranda, guidelines and personal and other behavior also influence the organizational culture (Smit & Cronje, 1992). Values and beliefs are subjacent to decision-making and are supported by different rules and procedures with regard to compensation, socializing and acknowledgement as well as by heroic figures and legends. Conflict could arise when management supports different value systems. Some organizations formally document a set of values and what is meant by each value. These values are handed over to new employees to assist them in adapting to the culture of the organization (Kreitner & Kinicki, 1992). It has been found that successful organizations have clear and strong enunciations concerning their organizational values (Smit & Cronje, 1997). Kakabadse (as cited by The Pioneers who put people first, 1995) has noted that there is often a gap between spoken values and what the organization actually does. This could be because management follows different sets of values, which may affect the trust relationship between management and employees negatively. This is why the manifestation of organizational culture as influenced by management is very important.

Three factors contribute to maintaining the organizational culture: leadership, the recruitment process of candidates who might possibly support and fit in with the organization's culture, and the socialization process (e.g. induction training, mentorship) through which employees' attitudes, perceptions and behavior are formed (Robbins, 1996).

It is the senior managers in the organization who establish the norms and cause them to filter through the organization. Examples are: whether risk taking is encouraged, how much freedom subordinates are allowed, what dress is found to be acceptable and which actions are beneficial in terms of compensation, promotion and remuneration (Robbins, 1996; Sathe, 1985). These continuous processes strengthen the organization. One leader will, for example, establish and maintain a culture with an entrepreneurial environment where informality, innovation, risk taking and creativity are promoted. Another leader in an organization might implement bureaucratic control measures where the atmosphere is formal, internal politics and power struggles are the order of the day, and managers "play policeman." Another leader might focus on quality and effective customer service by compensating this type of behavior (Robbins, 1996). In the *CIMA Study Text* (1996) four types of cultural leadership are distinguished that emphasize the influence of leadership on organizational culture. These styles should not be mistaken for leadership styles.

Table 1.   Cultural Leadership.

Type of Cultural Leadership	Role in Maintaining the Culture
Creative leadership	The culture of an organization reflects its founder. It can therefore be assumed that the founder's vision will set the tone of, for example, the creative atmosphere or ethnic style in the organization.
Protective leadership	These leaders maintain the culture. In an organization where customer service is a key value, some leaders will focus strongly on ensuring customer service and subsequently live the value.
Integrative leadership	These leaders try to obtain consensus and flourish in a participative culture. They should, however, guard against political manipulation. The consensus that is obtained should be directed towards striving to enliven the cultural values thought to be valuable in the organization.
Adaptable leadership	These leaders change an existing culture and set new values.

Source: Martins (2000, p. 37).

The interaction between leaders in an organization and organizational culture becomes clear from the examples mentioned above and from the cultural leadership styles in Table 1. Leaders establish a code of conduct that ties people together and creates an awareness of culture. At the same time the culture also has a strong influence on the behavior of leaders and managers. As the culture develops and becomes stronger, everything a manager does, thinks and feels is influenced by the culture. All aspects that managers regard as effective management, for example goal setting, control and performance evaluation, et cetera, permeate an organizational culture, rather like leaven. This implies that the concepts of management and leadership cannot be culture-free.

The purpose of the selection and recruitment process is to identify and employ individuals with the necessary knowledge, skills and potential to carry out tasks. Both interviewers and candidates have the opportunity in this process to determine whether the candidate will fit in with the organization and the way things are done. Consequently the organizational culture is maintained through the selection process, by means of which candidates who might not support the key values of the organization are turned away (Hellriegel et al., 1998; Robbins, 1996). In an organization that supports a team-orientated culture, egoistic people or loners will not be appointed (Robbins, 1996).

The socialization process is the continuous process through which the key elements of organizational culture are transferred to employees. It consists of formal methods (for instance induction training of new employees) and informal methods (for instance role models that act as mentors). Top management decides which methods should be used. These methods help to form employees' attitudes, perceptions and behavior (Furnham & Gunter, 1993; Newstrom & Davis, 1997). The socialization process will take place throughout employees' careers in the organization, which also contributes to maintaining the organizational culture (Robbins, 1996).

The Role of Organizational Culture in an Organization

Organizational culture forms an integral part of the general functioning of an organization. A strong culture provides shared values that ensure that everyone in the organization is on the same track (Robbins, 1996). The role that organizational culture plays in an organization can be divided into the functions of organizational culture and the influence that organizational culture has on the different processes in the organization.

Furnham and Gunter (1993) summarize the functions of organizational culture as internal integration and coordination. Based on a literature study of the functions of organizational culture, internal integration can be described as the socializing of new members in the organization and creating the boundaries of the organization, a feeling of identity among employees and commitment to the organization. The coordinating function refers to creating a competitive edge, making sense of the environment in terms of encouraging acceptable behavior and social system stability (which is the glue that binds the organization together) (Martins, 2000; Martins & Terblanche, 2003).

Organizational culture also offers a shared system of meanings, which forms the basis of communication and mutual understanding. If the organizational culture does not fulfill these functions in a satisfactory way, the culture may significantly reduce the efficiency of an organization (Furnham & Gunter, 1993).

Organizations use different resources and processes to guide behavior and change. Organizational culture complements rational managerial tools by playing an indirect role in influencing behavior. Culture epitomizes the expressive character of organizations: it is communicated through symbolism, feelings, the meaning behind language, behaviors, physical settings and artifacts (as explained in this article under manifestation of organizational culture in organizations). Rational tools and processes such as strategic direction, goals, tasks, technology, structure, communication, decision-making, cooperation and interpersonal relationships are designed to do things while the expressive practice of culture is more a reflection of a way of saying things (Coffey et al., 1994). An example is the role that organizational culture plays in the mission and goal statements. Organizational culture fills the gaps between what is formally announced and what actually takes place. It is the direction indicator that keeps strategy on track (Martins, 2000).

Changing Organizational Culture

Organizational culture has a huge influence on change in organizations because change often encompasses the transformation of basic values and beliefs (Smit & Cronje, 1997). The fact that organizational culture has relatively stable characteristics implies that culture is difficult for management to change. It is difficult to change people's beliefs, values and attitudes (Armstrong, 1995; Hellriegel et al., 1998; Robbins, 1996). Different arguments are found in the literature about whether or not culture can be changed. Arguments against the changing of culture are that:

- Culture is elusive and cannot be completely diagnosed, managed or changed.
- Because of its deep-rooted nature, the culture of the organization is difficult to change, as there is often resistance to giving up something which is valued and has worked well in the past.
- It is not practical because it requires difficult techniques, rare skills and much time to understand culture and it takes additional time to change the culture.
- Culture supports people in difficult times by keeping fear away. One of the ways in which culture succeeds at this is by providing stability and continuity, and, therefore people will resist changing the culture (Ivancevich & Matteson, 1993; Sempane et al., 2002).

Those who argue that cultural change is possible contend that change is a long term process that often takes five to ten years (Hellriegel et al., 1998; Newstrom & Davis, 1997). They contend that certain conditions should be present to bring about cultural change, namely:

- a crisis situation (e.g. dramatic technological breakthrough);
- a new leader (e.g. one who has a different set of values);
- a young organization (culture not deeply seated);
- a weak culture (e.g. culture not supported by all employees – easier to change than deeply seated culture);
- rejection of the viewpoint that power and politics make things happen (e.g. shift to customer satisfaction);
- two cultures that merge (confusion amongst employees about how they should behave);
- devolution of a division or department (whereby a unique and autonomous culture is created) (Coffey et al., 1994; Robbins, 1996).

According to Robbins (1997) there has been a general shift to more flexible, responsive organizational cultures that focus more on customer needs, service and quality. Harvey and Brown (2001) argue that due to the rapid environmental

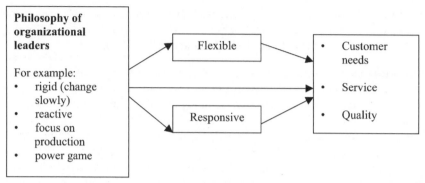

Fig. 1. Shift in Focus in Organizational Cultures in Order to Adapt to Changing Environments. *Source:* Martins (2000, p. 56).

changes a static organizational culture can no longer be effective. Managers must be able to recognize when changes are needed and must possess the necessary skills and competence to implement these changes. This change in focus can be illustrated as in Fig. 1.

Organizations like AT&T and Xerox that have attempted to change their culture have focused on new cultural values that support a shared vision, customer orientation, less management control, increased tolerance with regard to risk taking, conflict, innovation, open communication channels and participation in decision making (Robbins, 1997). Organizations that are considering changing their culture focus on the following:

- Restructuring (organizational structure changes).
- Investigating current rules and regulations.
- Top management acting as positive role models in order to set an example of the type of behavior that is acceptable. Management should also make employees aware of the value of any appropriately changed behavior.
- Communicating the new values to employees by announcements and creation of new stories, symbols and rituals to replace the old ones.
- Selecting, promoting and supporting people that advocate the new values, but considering the pros and cons of losing people with exceptional talent and skills who do not support these values.
- Providing the necessary resources, including funds, staff and materials.
- Redesigning the socialization process to fit in with the new values.
- Changing the reward and remuneration system to encourage acceptance of the new values.
- Breaking current sub-cultures through transfers, job rotation and/or lay-offs.

* Working on gaining peer group consensus through personnel participation and creating a climate with a high level of trust (Galpin, 1996; Harvey & Brown, 2001; Ivancevich & Matteson, 1993; Robbins, 1996, 1997).

Newstrom and Davis (1997) argue that communication of support of new values by management, training of employees, formulating value statements and rewarding behavior have the greatest impact on changing the culture of an organization.

It should be realized that organizational culture changes have an impact on the organization as well as the emotions of people within the organization. It is therefore important to involve employees in the change process (e.g. collective clarification of values) so as to bring about their understanding and acceptance of the changes being introduced (Harvey & Brown, 2001; Macaulay & Blakely, 1995).

Manifestation and Change of Organizational Culture in University Libraries

It is difficult to simplify the concept of organizational culture and apply it to university libraries in general. Two university libraries in the same geographical area, with similar values and organizational structures, can be two totally different places in which to work. The question can be asked: what causes organizations to differ from each other? The concept of organizational culture is useful in explaining how organizations differ from one another and enables one to gain a better understanding of a specific organization (Hellriegel et al., 1998).

Shaughnessy (1988) asked that, if it is true that each library has its own special organizational culture, is there a possibility that there are certain components of culture that will appear in all libraries? In other words, are there corresponding values and beliefs (and perhaps a world view of organizational culture) in libraries in general? The degree to which library training and education institutions socialize members in regard to the information science profession can lead to the conclusion that a corresponding library culture does exist on the macro level. This corresponding culture, if it does exist, is certainly formed and changed to adapt to the culture of the specific library in which employees find themselves (Shaughnessy, 1988).

It appears that very little research has been performed into the manifestation of organizational culture in university libraries. However, some articles about changing organizational culture in university libraries were located during the literature search. Davies et al. (1992) examined the relationship between strategy and organizational culture in a United Kingdom university library. This study formed part of a process to develop a more service-orientated ethos. Culture was defined as the general philosophy, official and informal rules according to which employees behaved and worked in carrying out their tasks. These rules were described on the basis of interviews, participant observation and a comprehensive questionnaire. The findings showed that all employees did not share the general philosophy of library management. There were differences between management's preferences (typically included in strategies) and the existing way of behaving and working (organizational culture). An example of the different views of this library's philosophy is that management and senior library workers agreed that the library should demonstrate its effectiveness as an academic department by focusing services on a specific department's needs. Other staff members felt that the library should be a community resource, although they agreed that the view of the library as a public service was not a strong supposition within the system. It was concluded that describing organizational culture as in this particular study was very time-consuming, but provided an effective way of bringing the norms and rules that could interfere with strategy implementation to light. This type of analysis can provide useful inputs in the planning phase of change (Davies et al., 1992).

The article by Barker (1995) explains how constructive change was planned and brought about by managing the organizational culture at the University of California Libraries in Berkeley. The model that was used was based on strategic planning documents, making use of two columns to indicate the current situation and the proposed vision. The strategic model was adapted to indicate the current culture and proposed change. It included some of the library's strategies as text in order to expand on parts of their vision. An example of the model is displayed in Table 2.

Barker (1995) comes to the following conclusions based on the experiment at Berkeley:

- it is possible to manage organizational culture;
- it is possible to transform it into a powerful, constructive driving force;
- the success of such a process is dependent on the support of library staff as well as of top management for an organizational culture change;
- organizational culture change takes time, as people need time to understand the concepts and to realize that culture change is actually allowed. It also takes time for older-generation management and personnel to shake off cynicism;
- organizational culture is not a wonder cure for everything, but a useful tool for an organization that would like to renew itself and keep pace with changing times.

Lee and Clack (1996) wrote an article about the continuous transformation process that started in 1990 at the Harvard College Library, Cambridge, Massachusetts.

Table 2.   Example of Culture Change.

Move Away from . . .	Move Toward . . . Proposed Vision and Strategy to Get There
Make organizational structure flatter Hierarchical organization	The library culture task team visualizes the organizational structure as "flat." • Move toward a flatter structure with only absolutely essential middle management levels.
Everyone's goal is to offer one stop services Employees (staff) are not empowered to take decisions that they are actually able to take. They are also not supplied with all the information and training needed to refer clients.	Managers on higher levels are trained to give permission to solve problems, tolerate risk taking, take responsibility to train others to be successful and to use accountability systems instead of pre-controlling devices.

Source: Adapted from Barker (1995).

The organizational culture there was analyzed by focusing solely on cultural aspects that were important in the library for effectiveness and culture change. It was found that the university library had a strong culture. One of the most noticeable characteristics of the larger university culture was decentralization. Autonomy in each unit and its effect on the service requirements of each unit was regarded as valuable. The advantages of decentralization are that it helps to focus individual efforts, enables local reaction to local problems, promotes stronger cohesion within each unit and keeps each unit's mission strongly in the foreground. The disadvantages are that it leads to a duplication of efforts, competition for resources and personnel and close identification with the employees' own unit. This prevents cooperation, integration and flexibility. The challenge was to find ways to change certain elements of the organizational culture. The first step was to identify the existing culture and determine which elements would prevent future adaptation and change (Lee & Clack, 1996).

The university library also went through a process of determining its values by using focus groups consisting of library employees to compile value statements. The focus was on changing to participation and openness, unity, integration, cooperation, expanded compensation, trust, a learning culture on all levels, a flatter organizational structure, shared problem solving, cross-functional team work, innovation and change (as our organizational value) (Lee & Clack, 1996).

It was decided that, in order to enable the university library to focus on the vision as a whole, the existing bureaucratic culture of functional units, characterized by infighting and finger-pointing, had to change. An environment that encouraged initiative, follow-up and ownership of problems had to be created. The main purpose of the organizational development strategy that was followed was to work to develop a shared understanding of the vision, mission and values and move toward a cooperative environment where people felt as follows: "We're in this together: get help, give help, and have fun working together." Since Harvard College intended to change continuously in the light of the demands of the new era, the next phase was to develop a strategy that took individual and organizational needs and goals (that were based on planned change and that encouraged participation amongst all members of the library) into consideration (Lee & Clack, 1996). According to Lee and Clack (1996) the model used at Harvard offered an approach through which organizational development strategies were applied to change the organizational culture after the organizational culture had been diagnosed.

The only study conducted in a South African university library that could be located was at the University of Pretoria library (Gerryts, 1991). The culture change that was attempted in this university library formed part of the organizational development process. It was attempted to change the existing organizational culture (over a period of ± 15 years) to a customer-centered, market-oriented service delivery culture. During this process organizational changes were introduced to cause the library to function, and be acknowledged, as an academic unit of the university, for example:

• the Director of the university library obtained full academic status;
• salaries were made the same as for academic staff and different from those of administrative staff;
• a centralized instead of decentralized system was introduced (Gerryts, 1991).

The next phase was computerization of systems followed by a shift from a focus on literature to a focus on information services, after which the organizational structure change process was initiated. The purpose was to change the collection-centered, functional structure to a market-orientated matrix structure (Gerryts, 1991). The matrix structure is based on a multi-support system in which some employees report to two managers instead of one, among other things (Hellriegel et al., 1998). Two forms of departmentalism were combined, namely function and product (Robbins, 1996). An example is the marketing unit that took responsibility for market research as well as customer training (Gerryts, 1991).

As far as organizational culture as such was concerned, it was decided at Pretoria at a workshop on strategic organizational development to promote a culture that would support innovation (Gerryts, 1991). In a telephonic interview with Professor Gerryts (Academic Information Service, University of Pretoria, 2000) it was mentioned that major organizational culture changes had taken place over the previous nine years. Some examples of these changes were the implementation

of service units that took ownership of the full process of delivering services
to customers; changing the name of the university library to the Academic
Information Service; abolishing the hierarchical structure and, consequently,
empowering staff members; the promotion of team cooperation and the delegation
of decision-making to work teams (for example teams would decide on the
competencies a new person would need when a vacancy occurred). In addition, an
effort was made to promote the same vision and value system among all employees. The manifestation of this change in the organizational culture brought about
the promotion of innovation in the Academic Information Service. For example, it
became part of the culture that teams continuously generated new ideas about how
processes could be improved to address and accomplish the goals and objectives
taken up in the strategy of the Information Service. An organizational culture
survey was also undertaken to establish the degree to which the vision and values
were internalized.

On account of the above studies, it can be concluded that the three studies in
the United States and United Kingdom attempted to diagnose the organizational
culture. The studies then determined which stumbling blocks were in the way of
strategic change and what moves had to be made in order to develop and establish
the vision, mission and values that would enable the organization to continuously
renew itself. The change process in the South African university library was approached from an organizational development perspective, with concern for the
organizational culture underlying this process.

MODELS USED TO DESCRIBE ORGANIZATIONAL CULTURE IN ORGANIZATIONS

Theoretically based and empirically valid research about organizational culture
and its impact has not yet been adequately carried out. Methods used to evaluate culture and the ways in which conceptual changes take place have not yet
evolved. Although studies about organizational culture had already appeared in
the seventies, it was only in the eighties that authors such as Deal and Kennedy
(1982), Hofstede (1980), Ouchi (1981) and Sathe (1985) cited in Hatch (1993)
attempted research in this field. Schein is thought to be the person who made the
biggest contribution. According to Hatch (1993), Schein's model was regarded as a
classic study which guided empirical research and assisted researchers to develop
theories through the nineties. Hellriegel et al. (1998) were still using Schein's
model to describe organizational culture in 1998.

Several models have been developed to describe the relationships between the
phenomena and variables of organizational culture. Some examples are the model

of organizational culture as a part of an organization's reality, developed by Sathe (1985), which focuses on the influence of leadership, organization systems and personnel on the actual and expected behavior patterns, the effectiveness thereof for the organization, and the level of personnel satisfaction brought about by these behavior patterns. A criticism of this model is that it does not examine the influence of external factors on the organizational culture. Schein's (1985) model depicts the levels of organizational culture, namely artifacts, values and basic assumptions, and their interaction. Schein's model is criticized for not addressing the active role of assumptions and beliefs in forming and changing organizational culture (Hatch, 1993).

Some researchers see organizational culture in organizations against the background of the systems theory developed by Ludwig von Bertalanffy (1950) and adapted by several authors such as Katz and Kahn, who initially applied the systems theory to organizations in 1966 (as cited in French & Bell, 1995), Kast and Rosenzweig (1985) and Kreitner and Kinicki (1995) for application in the organizational development field. The systems approach offers a holistic approach, while emphasizing the interdependence between the different sub-systems and elements in an organization, which is regarded as an open system (French & Bell, 1995). The organizational system model explains the interaction between the organizational sub-systems (goals, structure, management, technology and psycho-sociology). This complex interaction, which takes place on different levels between individuals and groups within the organization, and with other organizations and the external environment, can be seen as the primary determinant of behavior in the work place. The patterns of interaction between people, roles, technology and the external environment represent a complex environment which influences behavior in organizations.

Against this background and the work of Schein (1985), Martins (1989) developed a model to describe organizational culture based on the typical ideal organization, and also the importance of leadership in creating an ideal organizational culture as shown in Fig. 2.

Martins's model is based on the interaction between the organizational sub-systems (goals and values, structural, managerial, technological and psycho-sociological sub-systems); the two survival functions, namely the external environment (social, industrial and corporate culture) and the internal systems (artifacts, values and basic assumptions); and the dimensions of culture. These dimensions encompass the following (Martins, 1989, 1997):

• *Mission and vision* (determines employees' understanding of the vision, mission and values of the organization and how these can be transformed into measurable individual and team goals and objectives).

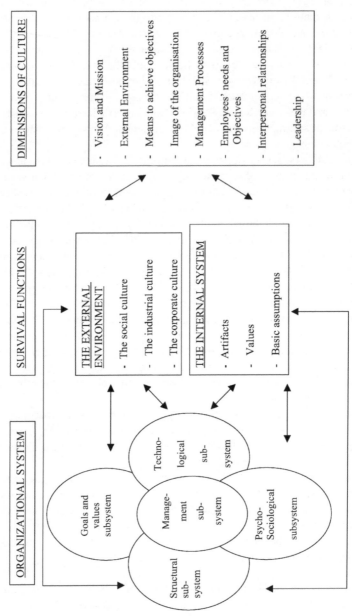

Fig. 2. A Model of Organizational Culture. *Source:* Adapted from Martins (1989, p. 92, 1997).

- *External environment* (determines the degree of focus on external and internal customers and also employees' perceptions of the effectiveness of community involvement).
- *Means to achieve objectives* (determines the way in which organizational structure and support mechanisms contribute to the effectiveness of the organization).
- *Image of the organization* (focuses on the image of the organization to the outside world and on whether it is a sought-after employer).
- *Management processes* (focuses on the way in which management processes take place in the organization such processes include aspects such as decision-making, formulating goals, innovation processes, control processes and communication.
- *Employee needs and objectives* (focuses on the integration of employees' needs and objectives with those of the organization as perceived by employees).
- *Interpersonal relationships* (focuses on the relationship between managers and personnel and on the management of conflict).
- *Leadership* (focuses on specific areas that strengthen leadership, as perceived by employees).

This model is a comprehensive one that encompasses all the aspects of an organization upon which organizational culture could have an influence, and vice versa. This model can therefore be used to describe organizational culture in an organization and thus be used as background in order to determine which determinants of organizational culture influence the degree of creativity and innovation in organizations.

CREATIVITY AND INNOVATION DEFINED

The concepts of *creativity* and *innovation* are often used interchangeably in the literature. Consequently, it is important to analyze these concepts in the context of this research. Some definitions of creativity focus on the nature of the thought processes and intellectual activity used to generate new insights or solutions to problems. Other definitions focus on the personal characteristics and intellectual abilities of individuals, and still others focus on the product with regard to the different qualities and outcomes of creative attempts (Arad et al., 1997; Udwadia, 1990).

Creativity as a context-specific evaluation can vary from one group, one organization and one culture to another and can also change over time. Evaluating creativity should therefore be considered at the level of the individual, organization, industry, and profession, and wider still (Ford, 1995). In the research under discussion the context of creativity is at the level of the organization, and the concept of *creativity* can be defined as the generation of new and useful/valuable ideas for products, services, processes and procedures by individuals or groups in a specific organizational context.

Definitions of *innovation* found in the literature vary according to the level of analysis that is used. The more macro the approach (e.g. social, cultural), the more varied the definitions seem to be (West & Farr, 1990). Some definitions are general and broad, while others focus on specific innovations like the implementation of an idea for a new product or service. In an organizational environment, examples of innovation are the implementation of ideas for restructuring, or saving of costs, improved communication, new technology for production processes, new organizational structures and new personnel plans or programs (Kanter, 1983 in Robbins, 1996; West & Farr, 1990).

West and Farr (1990, p. 9) define innovation as follows: "the intentional introduction and application within a role, group or organization of ideas, processes, products or procedures, new to the relevant unit of adoption, designed to significantly benefit the individual, the group, organization or wider society." It appears that the context in which a new idea, product, service or activity is implemented determines whether it can be regarded as an innovation within that specific context (Martins, 2000; Martins & Terblanche, 2003).

Innovation is often associated with change (Drucker, 1985 in Hellriegel et al., 1998; Robbins, 1996; West & Farr, 1990). Innovation is regarded as something new that leads to change. However, change cannot always be regarded as innovation since it does not always involve new ideas nor does it always lead to improvement in an organization (*CIMA Study Text*, 1996; West & Farr, 1990). An example of change that cannot be regarded as an innovation is changing office hours in an exceptionally hot summer season.

In the research under discussion *innovation* can be defined as the implementation of a new and possibly problem-solving idea, practice or material artifact (e.g. a product) which is regarded as new by the relevant unit of adoption and through which change is brought about (Martins, 2000; Martins & Terblanche, 2003).

The concepts of creativity and innovation in the context of this research (determining which determinants of organizational culture influences creativity and innovation) can be illustrated as in Fig. 3.

According to Fig. 3 creativity and innovation can be regarded as overlapping constructs between two stages of the creative process, namely idea generating and implementation (Martins, 2000; Martins & Terblanche, 2003).

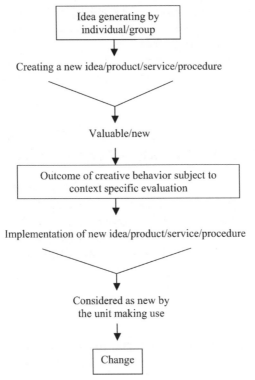

Fig. 3.   Defining Creativity and Innovation.

Creativity and Innovation Process

Researchers have different opinions about how the creativity and innovation process takes place. Schroeder et al. (cited by King, 1990) describes the process as the succession of activities that take place in the development and implementation of new ideas. The classic model of Wallis (cited by King, 1990; Kreitner & Kinicki, 1992; Pienaar, 1994) has had a continuous influence on the models of creativity, creative problem solving and individual creativity and innovation since its development in 1926. Other authors who have developed models of the creativity and innovation process are Amabile (1983), Basadur (1982), Van de Ven (1986) and Zaltman et al. (1973) (cited in King, 1990; Kreitner & Kinicki, 1992; Pienaar, 1994; Schoenfeldt & Jansen, 1997). Based on a study of these models it appears that the creativity and innovation process mainly consists of four essential components, namely conceptualization (cognitive process of idea generation), testing the innovation, and approval of it and its implementation. According to Brodtrick (1997) the creativity and innovation process is a dynamic, continuous and never ending process.

Several factors (internally and externally) can influence this process in an organization. One of these factors is a culture in an organization that could promote or counteract creativity and innovation. This relationship is now discussed.

RELATIONSHIP OF CREATIVITY AND INNOVATION TO ORGANIZATIONAL CULTURE

Organizational culture seems to be a critical factor in the success of any organization. Successful organizations have the capacity to absorb innovation into the organizational culture and management processes (Syrett & Lammiman, 1997; Tushman & O'Reilly, 1997). According to Tushman and O'Reilly (1997), organizational culture lies at the heart of organization innovation.

The Influence of Basic Elements of Organizational Culture on Creativity and Innovation

The basic elements of organizational culture (the shared values, beliefs and behavior expected of members of an organization) influence creativity and innovation in two ways:

(1) Through the socialization processes in organizations, individuals learn what behavior is acceptable and how activities should function. Norms develop and are accepted and shared by individuals. In accordance with these shared norms, individuals will make assumptions about whether creative and innovative behavior forms part of the way in which the organization operates (Chatman, 1991; Louis, 1980 in Tesluk et al., 1997).

(2) The basic values, assumptions and beliefs become enacted in established forms of behaviors and activity and are reflected as structures, policy, practices, management practices and procedures. These structures and other factors impact directly on creativity in the workplace, for example, by providing resource support to pursue the development of new ideas (Tesluk et al., 1997). In this way individuals in organizations come to perceive what is considered valuable and how they should act in the workplace.

Organizational culture affects the extent to which creative solutions are encouraged, supported and implemented. A culture supportive of creativity encourages innovative ways of representing problems and finding solutions, regards creativity as both desirable and normal, and favors innovators as models to be emulated (Lock & Kirkpatrick, 1995).

Influence of Organizational Culture on Creativity and Innovation in Organizations as Open Systems

Against the background of the systems approach, which sees organizations as open systems consisting of different sub-systems interacting with each other, Martins (2000) and Martins and Terblanche (2003) explain the relationship between organizational culture, creativity and innovation. In their view, certain environmental circumstances, strategic approaches, the values and actions of top management, organizational structure and technological cycles can be associated in the following ways with organizational cultures that support creativity and innovation:

- *External environment* (e.g. economy and competitiveness encourage continual changes in products, technology and customer preferences) (Kanter, 1988 in Tesluk et al., 1997).
- Reaction to critical incidents outside and within the organization, which is reflected in the *strategy* (e.g. innovation strategy) of the organization (Robbins, 1997; Schein, 1990a, b in Tesluk et al., 1997).
- *Managers'* values and beliefs (e.g. free exchange of information, open questioning, support for change, diversity of beliefs) (Amabile, 1988; Kanter, 1988; King & Anderson, 1990; Woodman et al., 1993 in Tesluk et al., 1997).
- The *structure* of the organization, which in turn allows management to reach organizational goals (e.g. flexible structure characterized by decentralization, shared decision making, low to moderate use of formal rules and regulations, broadly defined job responsibilities and flexible authority structure with fewer levels in the hierarchy) (Hellriegel et al., 1998).
- *Technology*, which includes the knowledge possessed by individuals and the availability of facilities (e.g. computers, internet) to support the creative and innovative process (Shattow, 1996).

The assumptions of personnel in the organization about how to act and behave within the sub-systems context, as explained above, will have an impact on the amount of creativity and innovation present in the organization (Martins, 2000; Martins & Terblanche, 2003).

Based on the explanation of the relationship between organizational culture, creativity and innovation, the question now arises as to which specific determinants of organizational culture have an influence on the degree to which creativity and innovation are encouraged and stimulated in an organization.

DETERMINANTS OF ORGANIZATIONAL CULTURE THAT SUPPORT CREATIVITY AND INNOVATION

A literature study for this research found that there is little agreement on the type of organizational culture needed to improve creativity and innovation. There also seems to be a paradox in the sense that organizational culture can stimulate or hinder creativity and innovation (Glor, 1997; Tushman & O'Reilly, 1997). Several researchers (Ahmed, 1998; Filipczak, 1997; Judge et al., 1997; Nÿstrom, 1990; O'Reilly, 1989; Pinchot & Pinchot, 1996; Tesluk et al., 1997) have worked on identifying the values, norms and assumptions involved in promoting and implementing creativity and innovation. Very few empirical research quantitative studies seem to have been performed to support the findings of researchers, but several values, norms and beliefs have been identified such as Judge et al. (1997), Nÿstrom (1990) and O'Reilly (1989) through their research.

In order to synthesize the cultural values and norms that influence creativity and innovation, as found in the literature, an integrated interactive model was created (Martins, 2000; Martins & Terblanche, 2003) (Fig. 4).

In studying the influence of organizational culture on creativity and innovation, it became clear that the dimensions of Martins's model of organizational culture (1989, 1997) have direct bearing on the influence of organizational culture on creativity and innovation. Consequently this model was used as a starting point in developing a model of the determinants of organizational culture that influence creativity and innovation. Although the newly developed model may illustrate only part of the phenomenon, it offers a starting point for improved understanding.

The model (Fig. 4) shows that the dimensions that describe organizational culture have an influence on the degree to which creativity and innovation take place in the organization. This influence can be divided into five determinants of organizational culture. Each of these determinants is discussed briefly to describe their influence in promoting or hindering creativity and innovation.

Strategy

An innovation strategy is a strategy that promotes the development and implementation of new products and services (Robbins, 1996). Covey (1993) claims that the origin of creativity and innovation lies in a shared vision and mission,

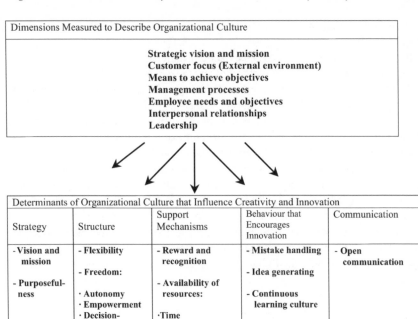

Dimensions Measured to Describe Organizational Culture
Strategic vision and mission **Customer focus (External environment)** **Means to achieve objectives** **Management processes** **Employee needs and objectives** **Interpersonal relationships** **Leadership**

Determinants of Organizational Culture that Influence Creativity and Innovation				
Strategy	Structure	Support Mechanisms	Behaviour that Encourages Innovation	Communication
- Vision and mission - Purposeful-ness	- Flexibility - Freedom: · Autonomy · Empowerment · Decision-making - Cooperative teams and group interaction	- Reward and recognition - Availability of resources: ·Time · Information technology · Creative people	- Mistake handling - Idea generating - Continuous learning culture - Risk taking - Competitiveness - Support for change - Conflict handling	- Open communication

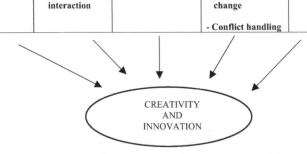

Fig. 4. Influence of Organizational Culture on Creativity and Innovation (Preliminary Model). *Source:* Martins (2000, p. 171), Martins and Terblanche (2003, p. 70).

which are focused on the future. Furthermore, the vision and mission of a creative and innovative organization are also customer and market-oriented, focusing on solving customers' problems among other things (*CIMA Study Text*, 1996).

An example of a vision that emphasizes creative and innovative behavior is: "Our company will innovate endlessly to create new and valuable products and services and to improve our methods of producing them" (Lock & Kirkpatrick, 1995, p. 119).

It is also important that employees should understand the vision and mission (which support creativity and innovation) and the gap between the current situation and the vision and mission in order for them to be able to act creatively and innovatively. Judge et al. (1997) describe successful innovation as chaos within guidelines: in other words top management prescribes a set of strategic goals, but allows personnel great freedom within the context of the goals.

Organizational goals and objectives reflect the priorities and values of organizations, and, as a result, they may promote or hinder innovation (Arad et al., 1997). Hall (in Arad et al., 1997) found that personal and organizational goals that emphasize quality rather than effectiveness improve the levels of innovation. It appears that reflecting the value of purposefulness in the goals and objectives of organizations also has an influence on creativity and innovation. Arad et al. (1997) mention that, apart from a few research studies, the effects of organizational and individual goals and objectives have not yet been sufficiently researched.

Structure

Organizational culture has an influence on the organizational structure and operational systems in an organization (Armstrong, 1995). Such a structure seems to emphasize certain values that have an influence on the promotion or restriction of creativity and innovation in organizations.

In the innovation literature, much has been written about the structural characteristics of organizations, and according to Arad et al. (1997) and the *CIMA Study Text* (1996), the contention is that a flat (non-hierarchical) structure, autonomy and work teams will promote innovation, whereas specialization, formalization, standardization and centralization will inhibit innovation.

As regards the influence of organizational culture on a structure that supports creativity and innovation, values such as flexibility, freedom and cooperative teamwork will promote creativity and innovation. On the other hand values such as rigidity, control, predictability, stability and order (mostly associated with hierarchical structures) will hinder creativity and innovation (Arad et al., 1997). It is especially the values of flexibility as opposed to rigidity, and freedom as opposed to control, that are emphasized in the literature. A high level of responsibility and adaptability also accompanies an organizational structure that allows for flexibility. Examples of flexibility in organizations are: to make use of a job rotation program, or to do away with formal and rigid job descriptions.

Freedom as a core value in stimulating creativity and innovation is manifested in autonomy, empowerment and decision-making. This implies that personnel are free to achieve their goals in an autonomous and creative way within guidelines (described as "chaos within guidelines" by Judge et al., 1997). Employees therefore have the freedom to do their work and determine procedures as they see fit within the guidelines provided. Management should also believe in employees and encourage them to be more creative by allowing them more freedom, in other words empowering them instead of controlling them (Judge et al., 1997).

The literature study revealed that the degree to which employees have freedom and authority to participate in decision-making and in solving problems determines the level of empowerment, which is positively related to the level of creativity and innovation in an organization (Arad et al., 1997).

The speed of decision-making can also promote or inhibit creativity and innovation. Tushman and O'Reilly (1997) claim that cultural norms which lead to quick decision-making (e.g. that speed is important and that the work rate is rapid) should promote the implementation of innovation.

Co-operative teams are identified by some authors as having an influence on the degree to which creativity and innovation take place in organizations. Well-established work teams which allow for diversity and individual talents that complement each other should promote creativity and innovation (Arad et al., 1997; Mumford et al., 1997). Cross-functional teams which encourage social and technical interaction between developers and implementers can improve and promote creativity and innovation. Another important aspect is that team members should be able to trust and respect one another, understand other's perspectives and style of functioning, solve differences of opinion, communicate effectively, be open to new ideas and question new ideas. Such effective teamwork is partly based on team members' skills and abilities and partly on the shared values within the group (e.g. values about shared trust and solving differences) (Shattow, 1996; Tushman & O'Reilly, 1997).

Support Mechanisms

Support mechanisms should be present in the culture of an organization in order to create an environment that will promote creativity and innovation. The literature study revealed that rewards and recognition, and making available resources, namely time, information technology and creative people, support this role. Behavior that is *rewarded* reflects the values of an organization. If creative behavior is rewarded, it will become the general, dominant way of behaving (Arad et al., 1997). The problem is that many organizations hope that employees will think more creatively and take risks, while actually rewarding well-proven, trusted methods and fault-free work. Employees should also be rewarded for risk-taking, experimenting, and generating ideas if change is to be encouraged. Intrinsic rewards like increased autonomy and improved opportunities for personal and professional growth may support the innovation process (Amabile & Gryskiewicz, 1987; Kanter, 1983 in Arad et al., 1997; Shattow, 1996). It is also important to reward individuals as well as teams (Tushman & O'Reilly, 1997). Management should be sensitive to which methods of reward and recognition will inspire employees in their specific organization to be more creative and innovative (Tushman & O'Reilly, 1997).

An organizational culture that promotes creativity and innovation should allow employees time to think creatively and experiment (Shattow, 1996). In organizations where creativity and innovation are encouraged, employees are, for example, allowed to spend 15% of their time on generating new ideas and working on their favorite projects. An emphasis on productivity and downsizing, which leads to more pressure on employees to work harder, is not conducive to creativity and innovation in organizations (Filipczak, 1997).

Information technology as a support mechanism is an important resource for successful innovation (Shattow, 1996). In organizations where it is part of the culture to use aspects of computer technology such as the internet and intranet to communicate and exchange ideas, the chances that creativity and innovation will take place are improved (Bresnahan, 1997; Khalil, 1996).

Recruitment, selection and appointment and keeping employees are an important part of promoting a culture of creativity and innovation in an organization. The values and beliefs of management are reflected in the types of people that are appointed. Apart from personality traits such as intelligence, knowledge, risk-taking, inquisitiveness and energy, a value such as diversity is of utmost importance in the appointment of creative and innovative people. Appointing people of diverse backgrounds should lead to a richer mix of ideas and processes that should in turn stimulate creativity and innovation (Bresnahan, 1997; Gardenswartz & Rowe, 1998).

Behavior that Encourages Innovation

Values and norms that encourage innovation manifest themselves in specific behavioral forms that promote or inhibit creativity and innovation. The way in which mistakes are handled in organizations will determine whether employees feel free to act creatively and innovatively. Mistakes can be ignored, covered up, used to punish someone or perceived as a learning opportunity (Brodtrick,

1997). Tolerance of mistakes is an essential element in the development of an organizational culture that promotes creativity and innovation. Successful organizations reward success and acknowledge or celebrate failures, for example, by creating opportunities to openly discuss and learn from mistakes (Ryan, 1996; Tushman & O'Reilly, 1997). An organizational culture in which employees are encouraged to generate new ideas without being harmed, and where the focus is on what is supported instead of on what is not viable should encourage creativity and innovation (Filipczak, 1997). A fair evaluation of ideas will also support and encourage creativity (Amabile, 1995). Several authors (Arad et al., 1997; Lock & Kirkpatrick, 1995; Samaha, 1996) indicate that an organizational culture that supports a continuous learning orientation should also encourage creativity and in-novation. By focusing on being inquisitive, encouraging employees to talk to each other (e.g. to clients within and outside the organization so as to learn from them), keeping knowledge and skills up to date and learning creative thinking skills, a learning culture can be created and maintained.

Taking risks and experimenting are behaviors that are associated with creativity and innovation. A culture in which too many management controls are applied will inhibit risk-taking, and, consequently, will retard creativity and innovation (Judge et al., 1997). According to Robbins et al. (2003), innovative organizations tend to have similar cultures. They encourage experimentation, and they reward both successes and failures. The assumption that risks may be taken as long as they do not harm the organization will not encourage employees to be creative and innovative by experimenting and taking risks (Filipczak, 1997), and, as a result, it is important that a balance be reached in the degree to which risk-taking is allowed. This equilibrium can be achieved by spelling out expected results, assigning the responsibility of monitoring and measuring risk-taking to someone in the organization, creating a tolerant atmosphere in which mistakes are accepted as part of taking initiative, regarding mistakes as learning experiences, and assuming that there is a fair chance of risks being successful.

Research by Nÿstrom (1990) indicates that the most creative and innovative departments in an organization regard competitiveness as an important aspect of their culture. According to Read (1996) competitiveness in organizations has shifted to the creation and assimilation of knowledge. In creating a culture of competitiveness, managers should reach out to internal and external knowledge, encourage debating of ideas, create an environment in which constructive conflict will lead to information flow, support projects based on information flow and actively manage the choice of organizational design.

Support for change is a value that will influence creativity and innovation pos-itively (Arad et al., 1997; Eyton, 1996; Glor, 1997; Johnson, 1996; Tushman & O'Reilly, 1997). Managers can create a culture that supports change by looking for new and improved ways of working, creating a vision that emphasizes change and revealing a positive attitude towards change (Arad et al., 1997; Tushman & O'Reilly, 1997). An example of an organization whose culture supports change is one that expects employees, when stating their annual objectives for the year, to indicate how they intend to change their work methods.

Tolerance of conflict and handling conflict constructively are values that support creative and innovative behavior in organizations (Judge et al., 1997; Mumford et al., 1997; Robbins, 1997). When there is conflict between different ideas, perceptions and ways in which information is processed and evaluated, the process of handling conflict should be handled constructively in order to promote creativity and innovation. Understanding different individual thinking styles, and training employees in the process of constructive confrontation, will create a culture supportive of creativity and innovation.

Communication

An organizational culture that supports open and transparent communication, based on trust, will have a positive influence on promoting creativity and innovation (Barret, 1997; Robbins, 1996). Teaching employees that disagreement is acceptable since it offers the opportunity to expose paradoxes, conflict and dilemmas can promote openness in communication. At the same time employees must feel emotionally safe enough to be able to act creatively and innovatively and should therefore be able to trust one another, which in turn is promoted by open communication. An open-door communication policy, including open communication between individuals, teams and departments to gain new perspectives, is therefore necessary to create a culture supportive of creativity and innovation (Filipczak, 1997; Frohman & Pascarella, 1990; Samaha, 1996).

Findings Regarding the Model of the Influence of Organizational Culture on Creativity and Innovation

It appears that creativity and innovation will flourish only under the right circumstances in an organization. The values, norms and beliefs that play a role in creativity and innovation in organizations can either support or inhibit creativity and innovation, depending on how they influence the behavior of individuals and groups. The model highlights the determinants that play a role in promoting creativity and innovation. The way in which these determinants (namely strategy, organizational structure, support mechanisms, behavior that encourages innovation and communication) operate will either support or inhibit creativity and innovation. It is clear that these determinants overlap and interact with one another, which supports the open systems approach that was followed.

EMPIRICAL RESEARCH

The purpose of this research was to determine empirically, through quantitative research, the determinants that influence creativity and innovation in a university library from a cultural perspective and to compare the findings with the theoretical model. In a previous section, the way in which change is dictated in organizations (and specifically in university libraries) was discussed. It was mentioned that creativity and innovation play an important role in the change process and that the degree to which change is found in organizations is influenced by organizational culture among other things. Against this background, it was decided to carry out an empirical study in a university library that was involved in transformation and change processes. It was also decided to perform the study in only one university library, as the organizational culture could differ from one university library to another (Hellriegel et al., 1998; Shaughnessy, 1988).

A survey was conducted in the particular university library in 1997 to describe the organizational culture of the library as part of the transformation and change process. The focus of the survey was to determine, against the background of typical ideal organizations, the perceptions of employees in the university library regarding the organizational culture. The questionnaire used in the university library was developed by Martins in 1989 and adapted for this study in 1997. It was based on the organizational culture model that was referred to in the previous section (see Fig. 2). It follows a holistic approach that covers all the facets of an organization that could influence organizational culture. Since the organizational culture of the particular university library was already quantitatively described, it was decided to use the existing data in this current research with a specific focus on the influence of organizational culture on creativity and innovation. The research design is subsequently discussed by describing the population, the measuring instrument, method of investigation and statistical analyses. Rational decisions taken to eliminate negative impacts on the study are also mentioned.

Population

The total population of 286 employees received questionnaires and 188 (70.1%) questionnaires were returned and analyzed. Saunders et al. (1997) report different authors' opinions about the number of respondents to questionnaires in general, namely:

• for paper questionnaires that are posted to respondents, a response rate of 30% is reasonable (Owens & Jones, 1990).
• in 1978 Dillman found that response rates of between 50 and 90% were reported.
• more recent studies indicate that response rates of as low as 15–20% for postal surveys have been reported. Some authors claim that this can be attributed to "questionnaire exhaustion."
• in this researcher's consultancy firm it is reported that the response rate to paper surveys handed out to employees in organizations varies between 50 and 75%.

In light of the above, it appears that 70% is an acceptable response rate for one to be able to draw conclusions based on the data. The largest group of participants was female (73.8%), while 26.2% were male. Afrikaans-speaking participants were the largest group (57.7%) followed by English-speakers (21.4%), speakers of African languages (19.7%) and speakers of other languages (1.2%). Most respondents (46.8%) had longer than 10 years of service with the organization, 42.5% had between 4 and 10 years of service, 8.6% between 1 and 3 years and 2.2% less than one year of service.

Measuring Instrument

The instrument developed by Martins (1989, 1997) to describe organizational culture was used, since it follows a holistic approach that covers all the facets of an organization that could influence the culture. Fundamental to the development of the questionnaire was the belief that organizational culture can be defined in terms of a set of uniform dimensions or characteristics. This approach falls firmly within the positivistic approach to culture (Denison, 1996). A factor analysis previously carried out on this instrument indicated a reliability (Cronbach Alpha) of 0.933. The internal consistency of the dimensions was between 0.655 and 0.932. In order to describe the organizational culture of the university library, the questionnaire was also tested for face validity so as to determine whether the questions measured the concepts that they were supposed to measure (Hussey & Hussey, 1997; Sekaran, 1992). The questionnaire was discussed with the project team appointed in the library to investigate the culture of the library. Concepts and terminology were clarified and a couple of questions were added, which came to 95 questions in total.

Method of Investigation

Existing data from the previous survey administered to describe the organizational culture, as part of the transformation and change process, was used. Based on the theoretical model (Fig. 2) and the literature study, variables that might influence the degree to which creativity and innovation occur in an organization were selected. Of the original 95 questions, 46 were identified as variables. According to Hair et al. (1995) the sample should include at least 100 subjects. The general rule is that there should be at least five times more observations than the number of variables that are analyzed. The highest observation per variable will ensure that the factors obtained from the analysis are not sample-specific and, therefore, ungeneralizable. Although there were more than 100 respondents in this research, the proportion was four-to-one (188 respondents and 46 variables).

Statistical Analysis

The statistical calculations of the study/investigation were carried out by the researcher, using Hintze's (1997) Number Cruncher Statistical System (NCSS). An explorative approach (where no prior restriction or estimate of the number of components to be extracted from the data is set) was followed in order to do a factor analysis (Nunnally, 1978). The purpose of the factor analysis was to determine which variables (questions identified at face value) strongly correlate with each other in order to determine a pattern of correlations between variables (Kervin, 1992). The factor analysis allowed the researcher to determine the construct validity of the items (i.e. do the items measure what they are supposed to measure?) (Mouton & Marais, 1990). It was decided to use the component factor analysis method, where the total variance is taken into account and the factors that are postulated contain small proportions of unique (specific) variance (Huysamen cited by Odendaal, 1997). This component factor analysis method is mostly used when the purpose is to summarize most of the original information (variance) in a minimum number of factors for forecasting purposes, whereas the factor analysis method is mainly used to reflect, in the underlying factors of dimensions, what the variables have in common (Hair et al., 1995).

An item analysis using the Cronbach Alpha coefficient was used to determine the internal reliability of the items in the "newly discovered" factors. The purpose was to determine how accurately the items measured the factors and, consequently, whether they could be regarded as reliable – that is whether they would produce the same results when the measurement was repeated (Sekaran, 1992).

Statistical Analysis

The first proof analysis of the component factor analysis, with the factor selection method set as an eigen value of 100 as the cut-off point, did not produce a satisfactory factor structure. The variables were divided into 13 factors with only three or four questions each, which made interpretation difficult. A second proof analysis of the component factor analysis was done using percentage of eigen value as the criterion for factor selection. The best factor structure was obtained when 50% of the variance was met. According to Hintze's *NCSS User's Guide II* (1997) and Hair et al. (1995), the factors should correspond with at least 50% of the variance. The results of the number of factors are displayed in Fig. 5.

For factor selection, an eigen value greater than one was used. Only seven factors were postulated and within reason those with an eigen value close to one were eliminated. Cartell's scree test, which is a rough indication of how many factors should be retained (Hintze, 1997), also indicated that there is a drastic decline in eigen values (see x in Fig. 5) after the seventh factor, which consequently confirms

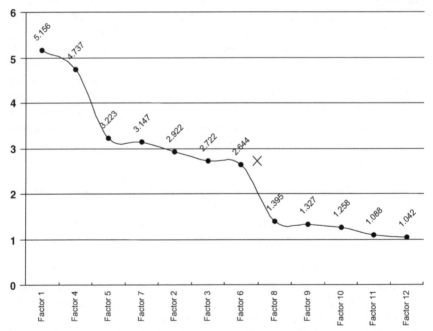

Fig. 5. Eigen Values of Factors for Factor Selection (After Varimax Rotation). *Source:* Martins (2000, p. 210), Martins and Martins (2002, p. 60).

Table 3. Percentages of Eigen Values After Varimax Rotation.

Factor	Eigen Value	Percentage of Eigen Value	Cumulative Percentage
1	5.156	10.97	10.97
2	2.922	6.22	17.19
3	2.722	5.79	22.98
4	4.373	9.30	32.28
5	3.223	6.86	39.14
6	2.644	5.63	44.77
7	3.147	6.70	51.46
8	1.395	2.97	54.43
9	1.327	2.82	57.25
10	1.258	2.68	59.93
11	1.088	2.31	62.25
12	1.042	2.22	64.46

Source: Martins (2000, p. 211), Martins and Martins (2002, p. 60).

that seven factors are an acceptable postulation. The percentages of eigen values for the first 12 factors after VARIMAX rotation are displayed in Table 3.

It appears that the first seven factors measure up to 50% of the variance. The Number Cruncher Statistical System summarized the factor structure after VARI-MAX rotation and only seven factors were postulated, which once again confirms that this is an acceptable postulation. It will be noted that the factors are not ranked from highest to lowest eigen value. The reason for this is that the results of rotated factors are postulated, which produces a clearer factor interpretation than the initial factor postulation (Martins & Martins, 2002).

Conceptual Naming of Factors

Conceptual naming of the different factors produced the names as displayed in Table 4.

The factor analysis was done with the selected items and 0.40 was used as the cut-off point for factor loading per item. A total of five items had a loading of lower than 0.40, and it was decided to eliminate them, as these variables appeared weakly represented. Six items loaded high on two different factors, and it was decided to include the item in the factor to which it was conceptually best suited. The items that were used to identify the influence of culture on creativity and innovation explain 14.196% of the total variance of the total measuring instrument, which is satisfactory. This percentage is the total communality of all the factors together (Martins & Martins, 2002).

Table 4.   Naming of Factors.

Factor	Naming
Factor 1	Strategy
Factor 2	Purposefulness
Factor 3	Trust relationship
Factor 4	Behavior that encourages innovation
Factor 5	Working environment
Factor 6	Customer orientation
Factor 7	Management support

Source: Martins (2000, p. 213), Martins and Martins (2003, p. 61).

Item Analysis with Cronbach Alpha

The internal reliability of the factors is displayed in Table 5.

The reliability coefficient varies between 0.643 and 0.863. These measurements may be regarded as acceptable (reliable) since they are all above 0.6. Two of the measurements are above 0.8, which can be regarded as good (very reliable) (Martins & Martins, 2002).

Discussion of Results

The empirical study indicated that a new model can be developed to explain the influence of organizational culture on creativity and innovation in this university library. The model appears in Fig. 6.

The results of the factor analysis showed that seven factors were postulated that would promote creativity and innovation in this university library. Each factor will be discussed briefly with reference to the literature-based model (Martins & Martins, 2002) (Fig. 4).

Table 5.   Results of Reliability of Factors.

Factor	Cronbach Alpha
Factor 1 Strategy	0.863246
Factor 2 Purposefulness	0.703082
Factor 3 Trust relationship	0.680553
Factor 4 Behavior that encourages innovation	0.838808
Factor 5 Working environment	0.770422
Factor 6 Customer orientation	0.700476
Factor 7 Management support	0.642976

Source: Martins (2000, p. 221), Martins and Martins (2002, p. 61).

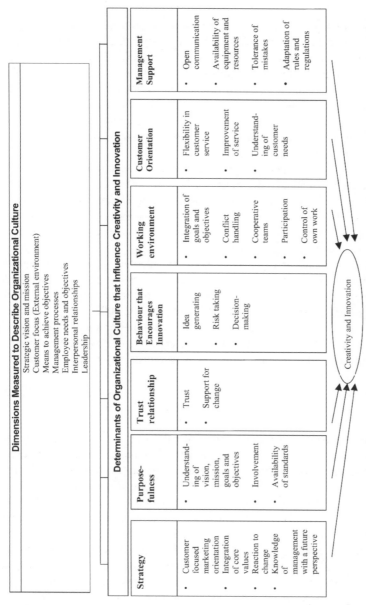

Fig. 6. Model of the Influence of Organizational Culture on Creativity and Innovation. *Source:* Martins (2000, p. 223), Martins and Martins (2002, p. 62).

Strategy

The factor "strategy" postulated in the empirical research supports the preliminary theoretical model to a large extent, in that a strategy that leads to creativity and innovation in an organization is described in the vision and mission statements as a customer-focused marketing orientation. In the literature it is pointed out that a library culture that supports a service orientation and focuses on customer-oriented vision has become established in university libraries (Barker, 1995; Davies et al., 1992). This orientation also includes active research into the needs of existing and potential customers with a view to promoting creativity and innovation (Martins, 2000; Martins & Martins, 2002).

The core values should be integrated with activities and results and employees should be informed about these values through the vision and mission statements of an organization. An example of a vision that focuses on creativity and innovation would be the following: "Our company will innovate endlessly to create new and valuable products and services and to improve our methods of producing them" (Lock & Kirkpatrick, 1995, p. 119).

Reaction to change and management's knowledge in leading the organization into the future did not form part of the determinant "strategy" in the preliminary model, but can be interpreted as offering support to the strategy followed in this university library (Martins, 2000; Martins & Martins, 2002). This is supported by Shin and McClomb (1998), who claim that the types of top management who are most inclined to make innovation happen are those who have a clear vision of future direction and of the operation of organizational change and creativity.

Purposefulness

Although purposefulness formed part of the determinant "strategy" in the preliminary model, it was postulated as a separate determinant for an organizational culture that supports creativity and innovation (Martins, 2000; Martins & Martins, 2002). The employees' understanding of the vision and mission should have an influence on the implementation thereof (Lock & Kirkpatrick, 1995). The extent to which creativity and innovation occur in an organization can only be determined if the vision and mission statements mention these factors. In other words the question regarding employees' understanding of the vision and mission does not make it possible to determine the extent to which creativity and innovation occur in the organization; only that an understanding of the vision and mission will influence their implementation (Martins, 2000; Martins & Martins, 2002).

Employees' involvement in identifying outputs and participating in reaching goals and objectives will also influence the extent to which creativity and innovation take place, and this is supported by Terblanche (1990) (Martins, 2000; Martins & Martins, 2002).

The availability of measurable standards for the results that need to be achieved by individuals also seems to play a role in purposefulness and the promotion of creativity and innovation. Lock and Kirkpatrick (1995) claim that it is necessary to state specific quantitative and time-related objectives for creative services and products.

Stating *"stretch objectives"* such as generating 30% of all income from products that are younger than four years, and measuring results against set standards, should lead to improved creativity and innovation (Filipczak, 1997; Martins, 2000; Martins & Martins, 2002). Senge et al. (1999) state that stretch goals are one of the key-lessons that force employees to let go of existing conventional wisdom and become creative and innovative as they design new approaches.

Trust Relationship

In the preliminary model the trust relationship between management and employees and between employees was discussed under open communication, with the focus on "openness." In the empirical research the focus seems to have moved to "trust." This new focus is supported by Barret (1997, p. 15) who claims that an organizational culture that is based on trust that manifests itself in openness and sincerity is one that supports creativity and innovation. Many researchers argue that trust is crucial to an organization's success in an increasingly complex and rapidly changing environment (Dunford, 1999; Martins, 1999). The trust relationship in an organization will be strengthened when management and employees act openly toward each other. People will feel emotionally safe, and this should lead to an atmosphere in which creativity and innovation can flourish (Filipczak, 1997; Frohman & Pascarella, 1990). Management should also trust the process of innovation from lower to higher levels by taking note of the potential of innovative projects. In contrast, employees should also trust managers when they intervene (Shaw, 1997). In other words, a high degree of innovation can be achieved if the organizational culture created by management promotes a high degree of trust (Martins, 2000; Martins & Martins, 2002).

Support for change formed part of behavior that encourages innovation in the preliminary model. Glor (1997) argues that resistance to change is a stumbling block in the way of innovation in an organization. The degree of support or resistance will influence the degree to which innovation is implemented in the university library. The willingness of employees to adapt to change (new ways of doing things) formed part of the value of "flexibility" as part of the structure. The factor postulation in the empirical research included these aspects in the trust relationship factor. This creates the impression that it will be easier for people to adapt to change and to new ways of doing things if there is a good trust relationship amongst employees (including management). This statement is supported by Shaw (1997), who claims that trust amongst employees should increase the probability of successful change, in other words that employees will replace old practices with new practices. It appears that support for change and trust are related to each other and that both will influence the degree to which creativity and innovation are stimulated and promoted in an organization.

Behavior that Encourages Innovation

In the preliminary model, idea generating and risk taking also formed part of the determinant "behavior that encourages innovation," which corresponds to the empirically postulated factor of behavior that encourages innovation. Idea generating involves aspects such as encouragement to generate ideas, selling good ideas, management giving credit for ideas, encouragement to take initiative and to find new ways of solving problems.

Management should create values that support risk taking and should demonstrate through their actions that risk taking and experimenting are acceptable behavior (Arad et al., 1997; Khalil, 1996; Robbins, 1996). At the same time it is important that risk taking should be calculated and balanced to allow employees freedom in taking risks, but also to increase the possibility of success by creating a culture that allows for moderate risk taking. Management should realize that innovative employees are largely motivated by the possibility of success rather than the results of success (Aber, 1996; Frohman & Pascarella, 1990).

Decision-making formed part of the determinant "structure" under the value "freedom" in the preliminary model. Shattow's (1996) claim that participation in decision-making could lead to (among other things) more ideas being generated, quicker decisions being made and ideas being converted into outputs, possibly explains why this item forms part of this newly postulated factor, namely behavior that encourages innovation.

Working Environment

The determinant "working environment" focuses on employees in the organization and the way in which work takes place in the working environment as part of the organizational culture. When compared with the preliminary model, it becomes clear that the items were extracted from three different determinants, namely strategy, innovation behavior and organizational structure (freedom of decision-making and empowerment, team cooperation and group interaction).

The actualization of personal goals and objectives in pursuing organizational goals and objectives seems to relate to creativity and innovation. This corresponds to Terblanche's (1990) statement that the integration of personal and organizational goals creates a culture conductive to creativity. The effects of organizational and personal goals on creativity and innovation have not yet been researched adequately (Hall & Quin cited by Arad et al., 1997) and could not be measured in this research with the available items.

Conflict handling in the working environment should be handled constructively to promote creativity and innovation (O'Reilly, 1989). According to Robbins (1997) some conflict is absolutely necessary for a group to perform effectively.

Another factor that has an influence on the degree to which creativity and innovation take place in an organization is the existence of cooperative teams. This is supported by Arad et al. (1997), Covey (1993) and Tushman and O'Reilly (1997). The degree to which cooperative teams are regarded as an important characteristic in the university library will influence the degree to which creativity and innovation are promoted and stimulated.

The degree to which the working environment can be described as participative forms part of this new determinant, while in the preliminary model (Fig. 2) it formed part of decision-making and empowerment. One can conclude that, if the environment is participative, employees will probably have the freedom to generate new ideas and participate in decision-making, which forms part of empowerment (Martins, 2000; Martins & Martins, 2002). According to Tarlton (1996) a feeling of having control over one's own work is necessary to promote creativity.

Developing better work methods formed part of the support for change in the preliminary model, since such development would indirectly imply changes taking place. In the new postulation, developing better work methods seems to fit in well with the working environment in which employees find themselves. The action of developing such methods would promote creativity and innovation.

Customer Orientation

This factor focuses on understanding the needs of internal and external customers, on improving customer service and on flexibility in customer service. For many organizations, fostering creativity and innovation is essential to their ability to offer high quality products and services (Hellriegel et al., 2001). It is interesting to note that the factor postulation clearly distinguishes between a market-orientated strategy (as discussed under strategy) and this factor, which focuses on a customer orientation on the operational level. Although Nÿstrom (1990) did not emphasize customer orientation as a core value of the most innovative department in his research, this factor supports his finding that reaction to customer needs should be flexible.

Management Support

In the preliminary model the role of management was emphasized in each of the determinants. However, in the new postulation of the empirical study, it appears that management has a specific supporting role in promoting creativity and innovation. Open communication between employees, management and different departments as a determinant of organizational culture that would support creativity and innovation is supported by authors like Filipczak (1997), Lock and Kirkpatrick (1995) and Shattow (1996). Bresnahan (1997) emphasizes the role of management by pointing out that "open doors" foster innovation. Furthermore, Ahmed (1998) points out that face to face communication promotes innovation.

Availability of equipment and resources is dependent on management's support. The degree to which equipment and resources are available or not available improves or detracts from the likelihood of there being creativity and innovation. This issue is supported by authors such as Khalil (1996) and Bresnahan (1997).

The degree to which employees are blamed for mistakes is an indication of managers' tolerance of mistakes made. This role of managers in promoting or hindering creativity and innovation by tolerance or otherwise is emphasized by Tushman and O'Reilly (1997). The supporting role of managers in adapting rules and regulations is related to their role in supporting change which will have an influence on creativity and innovation. In other words, the degree to which managers support the adaptation of rules and regulations to keep up with change will have an influence on creativity and innovation.

CONCLUSIONS

In attempting to create a culture supportive of creativity and innovation, it has been found that one of the best approaches to describe organizational culture is based on an open systems approach. This conclusion is based on the fact that this approach offers a holistic perspective that allows for the investigation of the interdependence, interaction and interrelationship of the different sub-systems and elements of organizational culture in an organization. The patterns of interaction between people, roles, technology and the external environment represent a very complex situation. Under these circumstances creativity and innovation can be influenced by several variables. It appears that creativity and innovation will only flourish under the right circumstances in an organization. The values, norms and beliefs that play a role in creativity and innovation in organizations can either support or inhibit creativity and innovation, depending on how they influence the behaviour of individuals and groups.

The model designed in this research highlights the determinants that play a role in promoting creativity and innovation. The way in which these determinants, namely strategy, organizational structure, support mechanisms and behavior that encourages innovation and communication operate will either support or inhibit creativity and innovation. It is clear that these determinants overlap and interact with each other, which supports the open systems approach that was followed.

The results of the comparisons between the preliminary model and the model that evolved from the empirical study have indicated interesting similarities, differences and new perspectives. Strategy and behavior that encourage innovation were identified as determinants in both models. The factors called trust relationship, working environment, management support and customer orientation on an operational level were interesting shifts in emphasis in the new model. Although the role of management was emphasized in each determinant in the preliminary model, a specific management support role in terms of communication, tolerance of mistakes, flexibility in adapting rules and regulations and support in availability of equipment and resources emerged.

Although the new model cannot be regarded as an ideology, it helps shed light on the determinants of culture that influence creativity and innovation. The model is applicable to one organization (specifically a university library) only and will have to be tested in other organizations to claim generalizability of the model.

Furthermore, it was not possible in the study to test (measure) all the determinants that were identified in the literature study. However, this is a possibility for further research and would be a step in the direction of a complete model. Areas that need to be addressed are certain aspects of *purposefulness* (e.g. values that support quality rather than effectiveness, freedom of employees to achieve goals at their own discretion, the effect of personal and organizational goals and objectives on creativity and innovation, goals that focus on innovation, promotion of creativity and innovation as an outcome of the understanding of the vision and mission), *cooperative teams* (the way in which groups and teams interact with each other and the impact on creativity and innovation of effective functioning of teams), *support mechanisms* (availability of time to be creative and innovative, recruitment, selection and keeping of creative people, rewards and recognition), *behavior that encourages innovation* (learning culture, competitiveness), speed of decision-making, and values such as flexibility, freedom and autonomy.

In conclusion, it appears that compiling an instrument that specifically measures a creative and innovative organizational culture shows great promise especially if all the aspects that could not be tested in this research are included. This will enable organizations, and especially other libraries, to determine the degree to which the culture of a specific organisation supports creativity and innovation, which is essential in being successful and adapting to changing circumstances.

REFERENCES

Aber, J. W. (1996). Building a risk management culture. *Bankers Magazine, 179*, 36.

Ahmed, P. K. (1998). Culture and climate for innovation. *European Journal of Innovation Management, 1*(1), 30–43.

Amabile, T. M. (1995). Discovering the unknowable, managing the unmanageable. In: C. M. Ford & D. A. Gioia (Eds), *Creative Action in Organizations: Ivory Tower Visions & Real World Voices* (pp. 77–81). London: Sage.

Arad, S., Hanson, M. A., & Schneider, R. J. (1997). A framework for the study of relationships between organizational characteristics and organizational Innovation. *The Journal of Creative Behaviour, 31*(1), 42–58.

Armstrong, M. (1995). *A handbook of personnel management practice* (5th ed.). London: Kogan Page.

Barker, J. W. (1995). Triggering constructive change by managing organizational culture in an academic library. *Library Acquisitions, 19*(1), 9–19.

Barret, R. (1997). Liberating the corporate soul. *HR Focus, 74*(4), 15–16.

Bresnahan, J. (1997). The elusive muse. *CIO, 11*(2), 50–56.

Brodtrick, O. (1997). Innovation as reconciliation of competing values. *Optimum, 27*(2), 1–4.

Burke, M. E. (1994). Creativity circles in information management. *Librarian Career Development, 2*(2), 8–12.

Chan Kim, W., & Mauborgne, R. (1999). Strategy, value innovation, and the knowledge economy. *Sloan Management Review* (Spring), 41–54.

CIMA Study Text (1996). *Organisational management & development, stage 3, paper 11* (3rd ed.). London: BPP Publishing.

Coffey, R. E., Cook, C. W., & Hunsaker, P. L. (1994). *Management and organizational behavior*. Burr Ridge, IL: Irwin.

Covey, S. R. (1993). Innovation at four levels. *Executive Excellence, 10*(9), 3–5.

Davies, A., Kirkpatrick, I., & Oliver, N. (1992). The organisational culture of an academic library: Implications for library strategy. *British Journal of Academic Librarianship, 7*(2), 69–89.

De Gennaro, R. (1992). Paradigm lost: Research libraries in an era of change. In: J. W. Weiss (Ed.), *Innovation for Information: International Contributions to Librarianship: Festschrift in Honour of A. H. Helal* (pp. 67–73). Essen: Universitätsbibliothek.

Deal, T. E., & Kennedy, A. A. (1982). *Corporate cultures: The sites and rituals of corporate life*. Reading, MS: Addison-Wesley.

Denison, D. R. (1996). What is the difference between organizational culture and organizational climate? A native's point of view on a decade of paradigm wars. *Academy of Management Review, 21*, 619–654.

Dunford, R. (1999). If you want loyalty get a dog! In: S. R. Clegg, E. Ibarra-Colorado & R. Bueno (Eds), *Global Management: Universal Theories and Local Realities* (pp. 68–82). London: Sage.

Eyton, R. (1996). Making innovation fly. *Business Quarterly, 61*(1), 59–64.

Filipczak, B. (1997). It takes all kinds: Creativity in the work force. *Training, 34*(5), 32–40.

Ford, C. M. (1995). Creativity is a mystery: Clues from the investigators' notebooks. In: C. M. Ford & D. A. Gioia (Eds), *Creative Action in Organizations: Ivory Tower Visions & Real World Voices* (pp. 12–52). London: Sage.

French, W. L., & Bell, C. H. (1995). *Organizational development: Behavioural science interventions for organizational improvement* (5th ed.). Englewood Cliffs, NJ: Prentice-Hall.

Frohman, M., & Pascarella, P. (1990, March 19). Achieving purpose-driven innovation. *Industry Week, 239*, 20–24.

Furnham, A., & Gunter, B. (1993). *Corporate assessment: Auditing a company's personality*. London: Routledge.

Galpin, T. (1996, March). Connecting culture to organizational change. *HR Magazine, 41*, 84–90.

Gardenswartz, L., & Rowe, A. (1998). Why diversity matters. *HR Focus, 75*(7), S1–S3.

Gerryts, E. D. Head: University of Pretoria Academic Information Service (2000). Telephonic interview, 29 February, Pretoria.

Glor, E. D. (1997). Encouraging public sector innovation. *Optimum, 27*(2), 41–48.

Hair, J. F., Anderson, R. E., Tatham, R. L., & Black, W. C. (1995). *Multivariate data analysis with readings* (4th ed.). Englewood Cliffs, NJ: Prentice-Hall.

Harvey, D., & Brown, P. R. (2001). *An experimental approach to organizational development* (6th ed.). NJ: Prentice-Hall.

Hatch, M. J. (1993). The dynamics of organizational culture. *Academy of Management Review, 18*(4), 657–693.

Hellriegel, D., Slocum, J. W., & Woodman, R. W. (1998). *Organizational behaviour* (8th ed.). Cincinnati, OH: South Western College.

Hellriegel, D., Slocum, J. W., & Woodman, R. W. (2001). *Organizational behavior* (9th ed.). Australia: South-Western College.

Hintze, J. L. (1997). *Number cruncher statistical system user's guide I & II: NCSS 97 statistical system for windows*. Kaysville, UT: Number Cruncher Statistical Systems.

Hussey, J., & Hussey, R. (1997). *Business research: A practical guide for undergraduate and postgraduate students*. Houndmills: Macmillan.

Ivancevich, J. M., & Matteson, M. T. (1993). *Organizational behavior and management* (3rd ed., Instructor's ed.). Homewood, IL: Irwin.

Johnson, M. M. (1996). Finding creativity in a technical organization. *Research Technology Management, 3*(5), 9–11.

Judge, W. Q., Fryxell, G. E., & Dooley, R. S. (1997). The new task of R&D management: Creating goal-directed communities for innovation. *California Management Review, 39*(3), 72–85.

Kast, F. E., & Rosenzweig, J. E. (1985). *Organization and management: A systems and contingency approach* (4th ed.). New York: McGraw-Hill.

Kervin, J. B. (1992). *Methods for business research*. New York: HarperCollins.

Khalil, O. E. M. (1996). Innovative work environments: The role of information technology and systems. *SAM Advanced Management Journal, 61*(3), 32–36.

King, N. (1990). Innovation at work: The research literature. In: M. A. West & J. L. Farr (Eds), *Innovation and Creativity at Work: Psychological and Organizational Strategy* (pp. 15–59). Chichester: Wiley.

Kong, L. M. (1996). Academic reference librarians: Under the microscope. *Reference Librarian, 54*, 21–27.

Kreitner, R., & Kinicki, A. (1992). *Organizational behaviour* (2nd ed.). Homewood, IL: Irwin.

Kreitner, R., & Kinicki, A. (1995). *Organizational behaviour* (3rd ed.). Chicago: Irwin.

Lock, E. A., & Kirkpatrick, S. A. (1995). Promoting creativity in organizations. In: C. M. Ford & D. A. Gioia (Eds), *Creative Action in Organizations: Ivory Tower Visions and Real World Voices* (pp. 115–120). London: Sage.

Lundy, O., & Cowling, A. (1996). *Strategic human resource management*. London: Routledge.

Macaulay, S., & Blakely, C. (1995). Ensuring that big is really better. *People Management, 1*(12), 36–39.

Marchant, M. P., & England, M. M. (1989). Changing management techniques as libraries automate. *Library Trends, 37*(4), 469–483.

Martell, C. (1989). Achieving high performance in library work. *Library Trends, 38*(1), 73–91.

Martins, E. C. (2000). *Die invloed van organisasiekultuur op kreatiwiteit en innovasie in 'n universiteitsbiblioteek/The influence of organisational culture on creativity and innovation in a university library*. Unpublished Master's dissertation, University of South Africa, Pretoria.

Martins, E. C., & Martins, N. (2002). An organisational culture model to promote creativity and innovation. *SA Journal of Industrial Psychology, 8*(4), 58–64.

Martins, E. C., & Terblanche, F. (2003). Building organisational culture that stimulates creativity and innovation. *European Journal of Innovation Management, 6*(1), 64–74.

Martins, N. (1989). *Organisasiekultuur in 'n finansiële instelling/Organisational culture in a financial institution*. Unpublished doctoral dissertation, University of South Africa, Pretoria.

Martins, N. (1997). *Elandsrand goldmine: Organisational culture survey*. Unpublished report, Johannesburg.

Martins, N. (1999). Managing employee trust during transformation. Paper presented at VI European Congress of Psychology, Rome.

Michela, J. L., & Burke, W. W. (2000). Organizational culture and climate in transformations for quality and innovation. In: N. M. Ashkanasy, C. P. P. Wilderom & M. F. Peterson (Eds), *Handbook of Organisational Culture and Climate* (pp. 225–244). California: Sage.

Mouton, J., & Marais, H. C. (1990). *Basiese begrippe: Metodologie van die Geesteswetenskappe/Basic principles: Methodology of the humanities*. Pretoria: Raad vir Geesteswetenskaplike Navorsing/Council for Human Sciences Research.

Mumford, M. D., Whetzel, D. L., & Reiter-Palman, R. (1997). Thinking creatively at work: Organization influences on creative problem solving. *The Journal of Creative Behavior, 31*(1), 7–17.

Newstrom, J. W., & Davis, K. (1997). *Organizational behavior: Human behavior at work* (10th ed.). New York.

Nunnally, J. C. (1978). *Psychometric theory* (2nd ed.). New York: McGraw-Hill (McGraw-Hill series in psychology).

Nÿstrom, H. (1990). Organizational innovation. In: M. A. West & J. L. Farr (Eds), *Innovation and Creativity at Work: Psychological and Organizational Strategies* (pp. 143–161). Chichester: Wiley.

Odendaal, A. (1997). *Deelnemende bestuur en korporatiewe kultuur: Onafhanklike konstrukte?/Participative management and corporate culture: Independent constructs?* Unpublished master's dissertation, Rand Afrikaans University, Johannesburg.

O'Reilly, C. (1989). Corporations, culture and commitment: Motivation and social control in organizations. *California Management Review* (Summer), 9–25.

Pienaar, H. (1994). *Die kreatiewe en innoverende universiteitsbiblioteek/The creative and innovative university library*. Unpublished doctoral dissertation, University of Pretoria, Pretoria.

Pienaar, H. (1995). Kreatiewe en Innoverende Universiteitbiblioteke/Creative and Innovative University Libraries. *South African Journal of Library and Information Science, 63*(3), 107–113.

Pinchot, E., & Pinchot, G. (1996). Five drivers for innovation. *Executive Excellence, 13*(1), 9–10.

The Pioneers Who Put People First (1995, August). *People Management, 10,* 20–25.

Read, W. H. (1996). Managing the knowledge-based organization: Five principles every manager can use. *Technology Analysis and Strategic Management, 8*(3), 223–232.

Riggs, C. E. (1997). What's in store for academic libraries? *Journal of Academic Librarianship, 23*(1), 3–8.

Robbins, S. P. (1996). *Organizational behaviour: Concepts, controversies, applications* (7th ed.). Englewood Cliffs, NJ: Prentice-Hall.

Robbins, S. P. (1997). *Essentials of organizational behavior* (5th ed.). Upper Saddle River, NJ: Prentice-Hall.

Robbins, S. P., Odendaal, A., & Roodt, G. (2003). *Organisational behaviour: Global and Southern African perspectives.* Cape Town: Pearson Education.

Roher, S. (1998). LSCA: A history of innovation and cooperation in Illinois library service. *Illinois Libraries, 80*(3), 117–179.

Ryan, M. J. (1996). Driving out fear. *Healthcare Forum Journal, 39*(4), 28–32.

Samaha, H. E. (1996). Overcoming the TQM barrier to innovation. *HR Magazine, 41*(6), 145–149.

Sathe, V. (1985). *Culture and related corporate realities: Text, cases and readings on organizational entry, establishment, and change.* Homewood, IL: Irwin.

Saunders, M., Lewis, P., & Thornhill, A. (1997). *Research methods for business students.* London: Pitman.

Schein, E. H. (1985). *Organizational culture and leadership.* San Francisco, CA: Jossey-Bass.

Schein, E. H. (1990a). Are you corporate cultured? In: R. Bellingham, B. Cohen, M. R. Edwards & J. Allen (Eds), *The Corporate Culture Sourcebook* (pp. 23–30). Amherst, MA: Human Resources Development Press.

Schein, E. H. (1990b). Organizational culture. *American Psychologist, 45*(2), 109–119.

Schoenfeldt, L. F., & Jansen, K. J. (1997). Methodological requirements for studying creativity in organizations. *The Journal of Creative Behavior, 31*(1), 73–90.

Schuster, F. E. (1986). *The proven connection between people and profits.* New York: Wiley.

Sekaran, U. (1992). *Research methods for business: A skill-building approach* (2nd ed.). New York: Wiley.

Sempane, M. E., Rieger, H. S., & Roodt, G. (2002). Job satisfaction in relation to organisational culture. *South African Journal of Industrial Psychology, 28*(2), 23–30.

Senge, P., Kleiner, A., Roberts, C., Ross, R., Roth, G., & Smith, B. (1999). *The dance of change: The challenges of sustaining momentum in learning organizations.* A fifth discipline resource. London: Nicholas Brealy.

Shattow, M. (1996). Out of the blue. *Electric Perspectives, 21*(3), 44–54.

Shaughnessy, T. W. (1988). Organizational culture in libraries: Some management perspectives. *Journal of Library Administration, 9*(3), 5–10.

Shaw, R. B. (1997). *Trust in the balance: Building successful organizations on results, integrity and concern.* San Francisco: Jossey-Bass (The Jossey-Bass business and management series).

Shin, J., & McClomb, G. E. (1998). Top executive leadership and organizational innovation: An empirical investigation of nonprofit human services organizations (HSOs). *Administration in Social Work, 22*(3), 1–21.

Smit, P. J., & Cronje, G. J. de J. (Eds) (1992). *Management principles.* Kenwyn: Juta.

Smit, P. J., & Cronje, G. J. de J. (Eds) (1997). *Management principles: A contemporary edition for Africa* (2nd ed.). Kenwyn: Juta.

Syrett, M., & Lammiman, J. (1997). The art of conjuring ideas. *Director, 50*(9), 48–54.

Tarlton, M. A. (1996). Only human. *Law Practice Management, 22*(7), 16, 60.

Terblanche, J. (1990). Kreatiwiteit in die organisasie/Creativity in the organisation. *South African Journal of Library and Information Science, 58*(3), 282–286.

Tesluk, P. E., Faar, J. L., & Klein, S. R. (1997). Influences of organizational culture and climate on individual creativity. *The Journal of Creative Behavior, 31*(1), 21–41.

Theron, P. (1996). International competition: What about organisational culture. *Human Resource Management, 12*(4), 19–21.

Tushman, M. L., & O'Reilly, C. A., III (1997). *Winning through innovation: A practical guide to leading organizational change and renewal.* Boston, MA: Harvard Business School Press.

Udwadia, F. E. (1990). Creativity and innovation in organizations: Two models and managerial implications. *Technological Forecasting and Social Change: An International Journal, 38*(1), 65–80.

West, M. A., & Farr, J. L. (1990). Innovation at work. In: M. A. West & J. L. Farr (Eds), *Innovation and Creativity at Work: Psychological and Organizational Strategies* (pp. 3–13). Chichester: Wiley.

MANAGEMENT IN THE GLOBAL "RISK SOCIETY": RE-CONSIDERING RATIONALITY, TECHNOLOGY AND CONTROL

Per-Arne Persson

EDITOR'S NOTE

In the nineteenth century, the comparative method was seen as essential, if not fundamental, to growth and production of knowledge in the human sciences. However, over time the categories that formed the basis of nineteenth century comparative research (civilized: savage for example) were discredited. And so, in time, was the comparative method itself.

The decline continued as we moved into the twentieth century, and kinder, more genteel terms were used. For example, in the anthropology of the early twentieth century we find the discussions that were once framed in terms of "primitive" and "advanced" replaced by discussions of "same" and "different."

But in the end, the comparative method itself was discredited and abandoned. Often this is explained by historians of the social sciences as the result of the development of more rigorous, more empirical methods and units of analysis. Having said this, the comparative method still offers us ways to think (by contrast) about things we generally either take for granted or just assume, often on little factual basis, to be "true."

Advances in Library Administration and Organization
Advances in Library Administration and Organization, Volume 21, 131–162
Copyright © 2004 by Elsevier Ltd.
All rights of reproduction in any form reserved
ISSN: 0732-0671/doi:10.1016/S0732-0671(04)21004-5

Persson's paper on the military is comparative in that it provides a model against which library organizations can be compared. As such, it provides the ALAO readers who may know little about the military and may even find comparisons drawn between what goes on the military and in the library to be at best suspect or at worst ideologically repugnant. Nevertheless, Persson's paper provides a way to ask when it comes to the library and its operations the most central of social science questions "What is [really] going on here?"

It does this by giving readers an opportunity to think past biases and to reconsider those elements we tend to associate with the military and to ask what role these elements play in the library in relationship to how work is organized and carried out there. Among the elements and categories Persson would like to have us think about are rank, hierarchy, power and control-all key issues in any modern organization.

But these issues that often for reasons of culture (in America, we are all equal; hierarchy is an anachronism) and ideology (individual competence and worth can not be equated with rank) have not been well explored in the recent literature on library organizations. To put it another way, we think today that we can understand libraries as organizations and make adequate plans for how work and structure there will be organized in the future without reference to any of these terms, and particularly without reference to terms like power and control.

However, by not looking at the role these concepts play out in how libraries operate, we are not making them or the effect they have in libraries "go away." Rather, when we attempt to finesse (or make disappear) these terms as we do with rhetorics of "empowerment" and "flattening the hierarchy," we just leave ourselves with a weaker vocabulary and a more limited set of understandings. This vocabulary and these understandings emerge out of "common sense" and have perhaps more to do with the imagination (how we would like things to be) than science.

In the end, rhetoric and understandings grounded in common sense are not analytically strong enough or precise enough to allow us to make sense out of what is happening to libraries and to those who work in them today. What Persson reminds us is that, if we toss out central categories of social thought (hierarchy, rank, power, control), ones that have a rich analytic and empirical history, they will only come in the back door and confound our best efforts to understand what a library is for both those who work in it and for its clients, and how it does business.

The military represents (as Persson argues) the archetypical bureaucratic operation. But libraries as organizations do have structure and hierarchy, reflect logical and rational models, exercise power, make policy and legitimatize certain actions on the basis of "science" and "rationality." As such, they fit almost perfectly Weber's definition of what a bureaucracy is whether we like it or not.

The question for ALAO readers is what happens when ideology (here false) or at least a partial belief about the nature of our own institutions and practices, obscures the way things are. Persson has presented us with a *Gedankenexperiment* (a thought experiment) – one that allows us to wrestle with the question of how well we really understand the institutions we both manage and work within.

James M. Nyce, *Co-editor*

INTRODUCTION

The development of management and what is called *the scientific method* follow a rationality originally derived from calculability and measurement. Through the 19th century a systematic management approach (Yates, 1989), pragmatically applied in managerial practices, eventually led to what became called scientific management. A parallel process was the refinement of an encyclopedic classification system for the development of modern libraries. One of the pioneers, Paul Otlet from Belgium, in the late 19th century conceptualized the modern library and its supporting IT infrastructure, calling it the *Universal Book*. His concept was a new kind of encyclopaedia derived from all existing books, veritable machines for intellectual work, "reading machines." Otlet also envisaged a "Universal Network for Information and Documentation" linking centres of production, distribution and use, regardless of subject matter and place. The term "Documentation" expressed a broader approach to the organization of sources of knowledge than "bibliography"; occasionally the word "information" was used, related to facts and data. "Information science" did not get its name until the mid-1950s (Rayward, 1997). This early modern development reflected needs growing from current social organization practices, itself being dependent on organizing. Later, around 1950, when computer technology was applied, the envisaged machines finally seemed possible to produce, and the modern information science and corresponding technologies evolved. Managerial ideals from the early 19th century already had established the need for still more detailed classification and structuring techniques. Half a century ago technical control methods were refined with the help of electronic data processing and eventually information systems as we recognize them today. The technologies successively have formed the practice, been equated with the organization itself, and are not just, as they were, "tools."

Knowledge has traditionally been defined from the perspective of a certain rationality, structured according to library and bibliographic classification systems to satisfy certain interests, not the least those of libraries. However, "knowledge" interests and definitions sometimes grow from the work where other criteria for rationality and relevance are designed and applied, occasionally leading to frictions. The encyclopaedic way of looking at knowledge may have to be integrated with other perspectives. Moreover, modern sociology has developed new views on technology, as for instance Anthony Giddens' "structuration theory," according to which humans create technologies which become structures, in turn affecting the creators' doings (Walsham, 1993), information technology being the prime example. Being one of the leaders in this tradition, Giddens means that the reflexivity of modernity actually undermines the certainty of knowledge, even in the core domains of natural science. Such shortcomings as regards "scientific knowledge and methods" justify attempts to develop alternatives to the Technical Rationality that has been called a "positivist epistemology of practice" (Miser, 1985, p. 287): professional activity consists in instrumental problem solving made rigorous by the application of scientific theory and technique. The first step of a reorientation is to investigate why conflicts appear. If "best practice" is not enough, what to do then?

The LIS community can learn much from looking at a case history of how rationality gets expressed in a "pure" form of bureaucracy. This community can also learn much about how rationality, power and organization intertwine and construct modern institutions by following the argument set out here. The military from the time of Weber on has been seen as the prototypical bureaucracy, the "purest" expression of what a bureaucracy and a hierarchy is. It is true that libraries and other not for profit organizations are not committed ideologically or practically as much as the military is to both. Military requirements promoted the development of information artefacts, demonstrating a rationality seldom being questioned. One could believe that the military practice was consistent with this ideal, but a closer look has revealed that rationality is a construct – one that needs to be defined and analysed so as to understand how rationality "plays out" in a particular organization under certain conditions.

We can say that rationality is pragmatically created ad hoc or post hoc. However, the common sense view of rationality uncritically is left unaffected, guiding the construction and governance of organizations. The research behind this paper sheds light on details in the military command work and information systems design. It demonstrates how different activities within the military organization are linked and that the different perspectives on rationality and the design of business activities and output might lead to problems. Designers of computer-based information systems might have found alternative design rules which had been more relevant for practitioners, had designers recognized the need and roles for non-formal interaction. Consequently other technologies than information technology might have been crucial, or conversely, that information technology had been conceived differently.

This paper summarizes an ethnography that has been ongoing since the late 1990s, aimed at the definition of principles for information systems design (ISD) for military command work and organizing within the military national defense. This kind of research was deliberately chosen in order to discover new aspects in military command work. The study is presented here as a comparative, contrastive example to LIS institutions, representing the kind of rationality which has been consciously created and a normative framework for science and management alike. Three case-stories are presented and discussed briefly. Through contrast and comparison LIS readers will be able to reflect on their own practice, stepping from what they take for granted as logical and natural, in the organizations and institutions they know best. They may use this example to think about how rationality, power and technology together build, justify and make these institutions "manageable." Another "twist" when doing this introspection is to make visible what is commonly labeled "invisible work," making it controllable. This transformation is not magic. It does not make physically hidden actions appear, but instead, it shows what may happen when new perspectives are applied, when concepts become available, and when people train their contextual sensitivity, broadening their view. Both researchers and managers can benefit from an ethnographic view of an organization, and may want a knowledge system that supports their work.

Re-reading the foundations of Western management science, technology, and rationality thus promotes a deeper understanding of modern society, its organizations, and what might be "best control practices" of complex social systems and thereby the design of technology. New structures and relationships evolve. The relations between technology, control, and decision-making have to be understood, re-evaluated, and put into the context of the modern "Risk Society." One conclusion is that scientific and/or rationality is neither self-explanatory nor "natural." On the contrary, several rationalities may be interwoven in both IT design decisions and business operations. Nevertheless, the LIS community has to fulfil its mission.

DEVELOPMENT OF MANAGEMENT PRACTICES AND MILITARY ORGANIZATION

Management within global business and modern networked organizations consists of highly controlled activities relying on sophisticated control technology, read "IT." However, since ideals change, management becomes an aggregation of sometimes contradictory control mechanisms. IT artefacts can be consciously designed or applied ad hoc, in either case aiming at a trade-off between stability and a flexible strategy for managing power, meaning and norms. Socially acceptable IT solutions for some may be overshadowed by contextual conditions and competing views on rationality, design and organizing. Hidden or overt design contradictions may lead to implementation failures and augmented risks instead of efficient risk management.

Unless discovered and analyzed, cause-effect relationships underlying organizational breakdowns remain in place as common sense constructs that lack empirical support. Wishful thinking leads to irrelevant organizational design solutions; more and thorough "repair work" is then required in order to establish satisfactory operations.

The immediate background to this paper is the growing difficulties in designing military command structures that have developed over the last few decades. Several contradictions appear. While the ideal is a very flexible, agile organisation and, while development techniques and tools become more powerful, solutions tend to become very expensive without showing a positive relationship between design effort and outcome. High-level analysis and problem solving remains problematic, probably best demonstrated in the September 2001 events in the U.S.A. and their aftermath. "Information overload" is commonly considered the culprit. Of special interest (but probably not well understood) is the relationship between context, bureaucracy, and operations. We need to study both the design of systems and operations, mainly in peace time, and their implementation and use in training or actual operations. Historically, pre- or post-battlefield "soldiering" and organizing have always put conflicting demands on people, different from the demands of battle where other priorities reign. This situation makes problem definition and the design of remedies confusing, "IT" being a common but seldom fully satisfactory answer. Unfortunately, mistakes are expensive and may result in military management and command work that reflects faulty design.

In a broad sense, military organizing follows a *rationalistic engineering and management strategy* but an adequate balance during ISD between technology and human action has been hard to define. Ultimately, ISD *should* lead to IT artefacts that enable rationalization and control efficiency without raising costs, but the opposite seems to be more the rule than the exception. During several military operations since the early 1990s, especially UN missions, the meeting between complex operational environments and traditional organizations has seemingly challenged established truths about organizing and command practices. Several cases, for example, illustrate Weber's notion of the struggle between charisma and routinisation (Schroeder, 1992), between human ideas and management structures (technologies), indicating the difficulties with balancing these factors properly. As was the case in the last century's development within (American) management (Barley & Kunda, 1992), practices evolve like waves, rising from an ideological foundation of integrated normative and rational rhetoric of control. If one does not work, the other is applied.

There are, within the military, several contradictions which lead to increased uncertainty regarding the design of control mechanisms: between peacetime bureaucracy and its "offspring," command in war, between design for stability *and* flexibility. New technology is a common remedy but usually means shortcomings in competence, economic resources, and uncertainty as regards security and reliability. A common response to this growing uncertainty involves intensified efforts at control, accompanied by a search for new (control) technologies as supposed "silver bullets." For about the last 15 years there has been, in Sweden and abroad, a search for a "Science of Command" (Davis & Blumenthal, 1991; Sorenson, 1989). However, command and development practices in general, including ISD, are still based mainly on the scientific tradition within the natural sciences. Progress has been slow, and when new organizational forms seem possible (Groth, 1999), new approaches for research and systems analysis are required, presupposing new perspectives and theories. The historical record makes Operations Research (OR-) techniques (close to Systems Analysis) part of this effort because, in the same way as within management (Barley & Kunda, 1992), research practices form "waves" where previous and new ideals and practices are integrated, but not without conflicts.

Military OR has traditionally been focused at high-level decision-making or tactics, and the analysis, development and implementation of technology and organizations. Even if these activities have been based on empirical data, the modern military organization (like current society) is very complex, often "opaque" and difficult to study. Unless searched for, much activity and many important actors in the modern organization remain invisible. Research has to recognize this complexity in order to make these factors more visible, and make sense of seemingly confusing actions and events in the modern organization. This sense-making requires support from LIS and other domains.

RESEARCH OVERVIEW AND THE ARTICLE

In summary, the research rationale for this study was the current lack of proper theory for the combination of pragmatic command work and ISD, related to the often very costly and uncertain attempts to develop efficient supporting IT-systems. This paper describes an attempt to achieve this through a combination of high-level theory and empirical data. Kahan et al. (1989), working from the cognitive and information processing perspectives, discussed previous research, forming the opinion that it was flawed, lacking conceptual and situational frameworks, and divergent as regards results. Consequently, the ethnography, aiming at the discovery of possible underlying cause-effect relationships, first produced a grounded theory for command (Persson, 1997). It continued as ethnographic fieldwork within army command organizations during domestic exercises. The qualitative analysis of empirical data led to a model (see Fig. 3) where the relationships between social

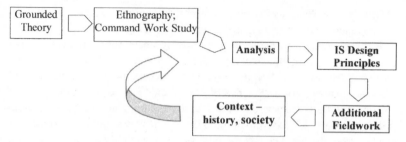

Fig. 1. Overview of the Study. *Note:* Bold marks later phase.

action, technology, power and rationality were elaborated, subsequently stimulating the formulation of ISD principles (Persson, 2000). Complementary fieldwork has provided more work design examples, supporting and elaborating previous results. A review of history, especially the development of theory, accounting and organizing practices has given other insights. Figure 1 illustrates the process.

In the introduction, the paper recalls how Western managerial practices and corresponding theories about social and technological development have been implemented in military command practices, which I call *command work*. It gives an overview of current military control thinking and practices, a cultural portrait: What people do in their work, the artefacts they use, and the environment in which they operate.

After this brief look at the first research results, in order to outline further work, the paper discusses "modernity" from Anthony Giddens' (1991) theoretical position, specifically the relationship between *rationality, technology*, and *action*. The paper then presents some results from later fieldwork, specifically from work design and IT use within military management and command work that demonstrate life in a modern military organization where new control technologies are implemented and contradictions are abundant. These glimpses of research methods, a final discussion and a look at the technical skills involved and the scientific standards underpinning them, suggest what may be viable lines of the military practice and of research when designing the modern organization.

RATIONALITY, MILITARY MANAGEMENT AND COMMAND WORK

Control of the military institution is a primary concern for the nation state, setting many standards that also are applied inside the organization. *Bureaucracy* has long been the common denominator (Brown, 1995). The introduction of systems analysis and modern management practice in the form of the Program Planning

Budgetary System (PPBS) during the 1960s (Ways, 1969), set the standard. It was a logical continuation of a long period of development of scientific management which rapidly spread to the U.S. military, being one of the waves described by Barley and Kunda (1992). PPBS reached the Swedish defence organisation in the 1970s, piloting the current trend of Business Process Re-engineering (BPR) and Total Quality Management (TQM)-inspired best practice.

e-Business has its counterpart in military command work, sometimes being transformed into a globally distributed system of precise and co-ordinated operations. As in civilian business, a central concern is how to pragmatically apply control technologies, allowing large-scale organizing, stable, long-term operations, *and* a rapid, flexible and tailored response to any situation. The latest approach is "networking," creating specific organizational structures and procedures for large-scale and flexible operations, often titled "Network-Centric Warfare" (NCW). It rests to decide whether this networking gives us a new kind of organization (see for example Groth, 1999) or just a (technically) networked bureaucracy.

For centuries now, but with a marked acceleration over the last few decades, the military institution itself has been searching for a Science of Command and Control, a system of superior control and command methods and technologies (Gat, 1989; Howard, 1983). There are a number of paradoxes. One is that the "science of command and control" is primarily investigated within the context of the battlefield or a war situation. Another is that criticism is voiced in the increasing belief in technology and the power of modelling as a decision-enhancing technology. Davis and Blumenthal (1991) claim the lack of a vigorous approach to military science and too much dependence on quantitative modelling replaces thinking and erodes the role of experience, a concern shared by others:

> This rather touching faith in the efficacy of electronic gadgetry was further expressed by the same group of officers, who indicated that the newly devised electronic means would give the commander more time to practice the art of command. Disillusionment was not long in coming, however, as the new technical means continued to inundate decision-makers with floods of information (Holly, Jr., 1988, p. 275).

What then about modern management control theory? Bourgignon (2001) discusses modern management control, which, she argues, basically uses a Taylorist approach of scientific management, corresponding to a reinforcement of control. This reinforcement ("what counts is what is counted," ibid., p. 7) occurs in firms where there is simultaneously an increased and officially acknowledged demand for autonomy, creativity and initiative. This dichotomy causes frictions. New methods enlarge the scope of management control, including control of non-financial dimensions of performance (often called *qualitative*) with the help of balanced scorecard-techniques.

Bourgignon comments on formal (or control) regulation and informal (or autonomous) regulation. The former is written into an organization's system of rules or in function descriptions, these being recognized management principles, while autonomous regulation is founded on effective relations hidden behind "official fiction" (ibid., p. 6). Control and autonomous regulations are juxtaposed. Negotiation tends to reduce the friction between the two, which, however, is never totally eliminated.

Management control formalises an organisation's budgetary expectations, and plans are "areas of negotiation in which control regulation and autonomous regulation are competing through the opposition of local and central interests" (ibid., p. 7). Labouret (2001), analyzing accounting and budget practices supports this view, concluding that budgets may be *tools for rational choice*, its processes selecting and retaining information, or *political tools*. In addition they are standardized but highly rational representations of reality according to economy-control principles. Concluding from the discussion by Schäffer et al. (2001), they even represent a *superior rationality*.

Computer science and industry have provided generations of control technologies for all kinds of management. Since the computer was introduced, its use within organizing, for social control purposes, has reflected both the long tradition of strategic management (Hoskin et al., 1997), computer history and changing conceptualisations of what an "information system" is (Cecez-Kecmanovic, 2000). New computer applications, aims and areas in the field of command work have evolved, from Management Information Systems (MIS), Artificial Intelligence (AI), to Group Decision Support Systems (GDSS) for distributed "networked" teams. The following overview shows how the ethnography led to a view of the modern military practice and its evolution, including the processes of thinking, work-based experience and the design of technology.

COMMAND WORK TODAY,
THE CULTURAL PORTRAIT

Ethnography and its Outcome

The purpose of the ethnography has been to produce a cultural portrait (Fig. 2) of the domain of command work; what people *say*, *do* and *use*. Field data consists of notes, documents, photographs, and audio recordings (from action and follow up interviews). The fieldwork produced a rich picture illustrating the kind of practices described by Davis and Blumenthal (1991). Ingredients are the conflicts between "scientific" models and the practice where knowledge is embodied in procedures

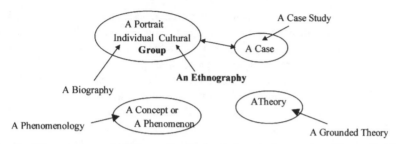

Fig. 2. Ethnography and Different Qualitative Research Approaches (Creswell, 1998, p. 37).

rather than being formalized, leading to difficulties in using technology while maintaining autonomy and command authority (Holly, Jr., 1988).

Military actors are experts in the modern command organization, transforming the operational environment and controlling it through a series of pragmatic and opportunistic control actions. They rely on many kinds of technology, some being effective, some causing friction (cp. charisma/routinisation). Command work, on a generic level, is not a system of ordinary managerial routines but rather a kind of engineering or dynamic *design work* that is hard to define and control.

The military uses a great variety of control mechanisms and attributes in order to achieve reliability under war conditions and to be perceived as a potent, rational and trustworthy institution both by their own national government and by potential enemies. Discipline, leadership, bureaucracy, ethos, and training constitute traditional control mechanisms. Rational control mechanisms operate in parallel with others dealing with emotions and interpersonal trust. Thus, "decision-making" and "leadership" are integrated with military management.

Furthermore, the work is knowledge-intensive, designing and producing signs and symbols used as representations on maps, in the HQs and in the field. These signs must be visible and credible, made from recognized components. They represent the world for operators who use them as controls and as a means of communication. The whole process is very flexible, involving interpretation and negotiation of both its content and the signs that are its products. Accordingly, actors define, design, apply or reject technologies according to their needs. Ongoing evaluation guided the continuation of the process. Formal bureaucracy is either meticulously used or circumvented in order to achieve desired results. Let us have a closer look at this portrait.

The theoretical understanding of modern IT is limited. The military, as well as other institutions and businesses, is confronted by this technology, growing business complexity, and demands for cost-efficient and reliable control mechanisms in peace and in war. Several contradictions arise within military control practice, illustrating the dichotomy between mechanical and organic solidarity and between communalism and individualism (Barley & Kunda, 1992). As in other environments, division of labour and specialization is necessary both within the military practice and within ISD. The dilemma experienced by the military can be expressed as the tension between the rigidity of the bureaucratic modern Communication and Information Technology (CIT) – dense environment, the charismatic leaders' desire to lead in their own styles, and their dependence on internal and external experts. The organization's main line of approach involves a certain rational perspective on the design and use of control technology and a reliance on routinisation for stability and reliability.

A COMMAND WORK MODEL AND SOME CONCLUSIONS

When composing and analysing the cultural portrait of the military group, observed phenomena had to be considered in the light of theory during the whole research process. Figure 3 expresses a theoretical command work view, developed during the study.

Clearly, theoretical constructs like *power, autonomy,* and *rationality* could explain the social interaction during work. *Autonomy,* a prerequisite to dealing with evolving events and frictions, and *power,* became core issues, varying between being goals and prerequisites for flexibility in social interaction and control. In theoretical terms, what is happening in heterogeneous organizations and work groups (and most groups *are* heterogeneous), is that different competing rationalities are being applied, motivated by a change of strategy and reinterpretation of previous actions, events and technology. The social character of work makes *rationality* a central concept when designing action and interaction, as for instance in decision support technologies. By definition, decision-making means

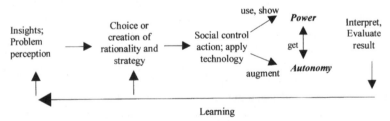

Fig. 3.   Theory, the Pragmatic Command Work Principles.

the application of a system of beliefs and its associated methods and techniques, often known as "rational." The paradox is that a purely *rationalistic* organising and design process seems to fall short of requirements in the work. If we compare this with design theory, we see (in theoretical terms) the same kind of integration of rationalities (Holmström, 1995) where people do what is practicable (creating a kind of *rationality of practice*). This rationality means that *social value* and not just rational control efficiency, defines what will be the appropriate and preferred design, both in the IS development process and in practice. The interpretation of "social value" varies and cannot be given a definitive meaning.

When facing new situations, staff organized control actions individually or with others are required to either achieve *more autonomy to build power* or to *exploit existing power* and, ultimately, to gain better control of the environment using the resources at hand. People sometimes have different goals, each with their own rationality, in what looks like a harmonious joint effort. Alternatively, transformations occur between different aspects of rationality, for example between formal decisions and informal contingent action that are later formalized.

Control systems design, method development, and research are strongly influenced by the combined OR and engineering traditions, and later by cognitive engineering (Whitaker & Kuperman, 1996). "Best practice" implies a preference for studying and supporting high-level decision-making, and for modelling ideal (often automated) control systems for rapid processes (Davis & Blumenthal, 1991). Designing control technologies using empirical data from concrete studies of work is less common. This bias towards a future-oriented and technical design approach reflects corporate interests, including problems in actually carrying out studies of work and action under both war (access) and peacetime conditions (prioritizing resource allocation). However, failures to adapt "perfect technical systems" are abundant, costly, and deserve closer analysis in order to provide insight, supposedly from new perspectives. This concern is shared within the information systems domain (Denning, 2002).

CONCLUSIONS CONCERNING SCIENCE AND RESEARCH DRAWN FROM THE MODEL

Humans apply technology in order to overcome their weaknesses rather than to achieve autonomy and/or power. Traditionally, technology has been specified through the practices of systems engineering, implying a mixture of experience, common-sense practice and systems analysis, and then purchased from industry. The difficulties in establishing a cause-effect relationship between technology and capability prevail, justifying continued investigation of issues such as autonomy and power, how rationalities interact, and how social actors function as "rationality brokers." The current debate and development of the military for future operations require close and critical investigation.

Let us recall Weber's theories before outlining some research considerations. In his view, there is a dichotomy between control and co-ordination ideals for war and peacetime respectively, visible in generals' decisions in battle, often seen as inspired by intuition, and rational action (administration) within accounting and office procedures. This dichotomy exemplifies Weber's notion of the struggle between charisma and routinisation (Schroeder, 1992), between ideas and operations, or simply stated, between *mind and matter*. This dialectic appears in the design of coordination tools, e.g. MIS, and in other systems of this type, but is often invisible within the modern organization. Fieldwork was directed at illuminating this conflict and finding approaches to solutions involving the transition between these positions, primarily the design and the use of control technology.

New kinds of technology often result in new "divisions of action" between man and technology and technologies' effects that recurrently surprise people. In computer and information science, experimental computing in order to build and test experimental systems and hypotheses is an important research element. However, research cannot shed light on how newly implemented technologies will be received, on the actual operator workload or on the optimal competence required.

The ideals from the natural sciences ("the Scientific Method") have had a strong influence when organizers search for models and theories. Military practice, however, often emphasizes the role of art and intuition. Davis and Blumenthal (1991) believe that this tradition, emphasizing the intuitive military "art" over science leads to conflicting opinions as to whether a science could be developed, but recommended that "... the science at issue is a social science. As a result, there are many "squishy" aspects, and the need for forthright use of subjective judgments as well as quantitative data" (pp. 24–25).

Questions were raised as early as the 1950s (Lowental, 1957) about the suitability of (the then modern) social science and its employment for cultural studies:

Empirical science has become a kind of applied asceticism. It stands free of any entanglements with foreign powers and thrives in an atmosphere of rigidly enforced neutrality. It refuses to enter the sphere of meaning [. . .] Social research takes the phenomena of modern life, including the mass media, at face value. It rejects the task of placing them in a historical and moral context. In the beginning of the modern era, sociology had theology as its model, but today the natural sciences have replaced theology . . . Theology aims at salvation, the natural sciences at manipulation; the one leads to heaven and hell, the other to technology and machinery. Social science is today defined as an analysis of painstakingly circumscribed, more or less artificially isolated social sectors (p. 52).

Still, social science has a tendency to neglect context or to position action within less relevant, "artificial" theoretical frameworks, especially when it comes to studies on or development of IS.

If additional progress is to be made, a qualitative research approach can provide complementary and different data than a quantitative approach. In this work, key concepts, related to social value, are *functionality* and *visibility*: only visible actors and actions can be controlled. By using signs that can be communicated across an organization and added on to maps, informating social action, command work and its effects become visible. The "muddling factors, squishy aspects and subjective judgements" (Davis & Blumenthal, 1991), belong to the empirical domain and have to be considered in context if research is to justify its existence. It has to contribute to the visibility of social actions and then provide a basis for ISD. There are then two aspects of progress, one being the level of knowledge within and support for command work, the other being the research itself as regards methods and output. The research has to be self-reflective and adaptive to changing research conditions. Moreover, a qualitative research approach presupposes consideration of *contextual factors* (Strauss & Corbin, 1990). A relevant *theoretical frame of reference* is a prerequisite to define and then analyse the context (modern society and its institutions) and its evolution. Anthony Giddens' theories about modern society, framing the military institution, provide a suitable foundation against which action can be seen and interpreted. His modern social theory encourages a look at the relations between power, technology and individuals' actions which is central if one is to understand what goes on in a modern organization. As already mentioned, Weber's work will also be used.

MODERNITY, RATIONALITY AND TECHNOLOGY IN "RISK SOCIETY"

"Risk Society" and Rationality

Giddens' view of modern society, characterized by the globalized economy where state boundaries become less important, is based *on capitalism, industrialism, surveillance* and *the industrialization of warfare* (Bryant & Jary, 2001). Continuous rationalization transforms the familiar contours of industrial society: In this society reliable foundations for knowledge no longer exist, not even in the natural sciences. Giddens introduced the concept of a "risk society" where increased control is exploited in order to avoid "existential anxiety," preserving "ontological security."

High modernity involves the disembedding, or lifting out, of social relations, practices, mechanisms, and competencies from their specific, usually local, circumstances of time and space ('locales'), and their extension, thanks to the developments in communications, over much wide spans of time and space (Bryant & Jary, 2001, p. 22).

Local social relations are replaced by *abstract systems*, labelled *expert systems* and *symbolic tokens*, both dependent on trust. Money is the prime example of such tokens. Disembedded social relations allow global extension, enabling immediate action worldwide. Because of the necessary specialization caused by the complexity of organizations, everybody is simultaneously expert and novice (Giddens, 1991). Widespread operations require new control mechanisms, both technically and socially, ideally balancing control and sufficient autonomy for those who are controlled (cp. Fig. 3). An unconditional trust in technology and abstract systems is a prerequisite of society and has to be upheld by its institutions. From their birth, nation states are information societies because they must know who their members are. Surveillance in modern society is not only a military concern. It is the foundation of society and business in general. The surveillance machinery of the nation state is not directed only at external enemies. Large enterprises contribute to the surveillance trend. Actually, modern management has advanced the development of surveillance since F.W. Taylor's days. The borders between the military and civilian fields have become blurred.

Webster (1995) recalls Giddens and modernity when critiquing and analysing the "Information Society" to which the military belongs, and with which it shares attributes. Modern societies and thus urban societies are much more socially organised than previous "communal-based modes of life," having to gather extremely detailed knowledge about their publics in order to function. The information gathered by its institutions is more detailed, precise and individual than anything garnered in a pre-industrial community. Market research, credit-checking agencies, and electronic footprints contribute to the "informatisation of society." This surveillance society is also a disciplinary society and a vulnerable one, nurturing anxiety. "Risk society" has no problem justifying the need for security, its conditions clearly motivating the use of new technologies for surveillance.

The new *Network Centric* perspective on warfare (adopted in most Western nations) influences current military thinking and operations. The vision matches modern society, being an equivalent of e-business, depending on a technical capacity for augmented "richness and reach" (Alberts et al., 2001): that more information can be communicated and operations coordinated easier thanks to IT. The concept is closely related to Giddens' outline of the economical, social and technical options in "Risk Society," presupposing the disembedding of social relations, their replacement by abstract systems, and human actors managing to remain in control through the tailored definition of knowledge. As in previous military organizing, theory – except from a technical, rational perspective – is merely absent. It becomes "rational" to continue along the same road. The intensified use of technology and the industrialization of warfare, with regard to its means, methods and processes thus seem "natural." Its rationality and pace leave little room for critical analysis, but tensions evolve around needs, problems and solutions. This applies not only to the military but also to any institution that has a right to understand, influence and then use technology for its legal organisational needs. Rather than taking them for granted, Giddens' framework promotes an understanding of risk society as context. Thus, what we may perceive as rapid neutral technical development is an intense, conscious launch of products searching for a market. More often than not, a technology precedes a need. Therefore, what appears to be justified control technology and its application might be the outcome of several agendas, of combined (and flexible) rationalities.

COMPLEMENTARY VIEWS ON RATIONALITY

In organizations, complementary aspects of rationality are applicable. Most know about "bounded rationality": we cannot learn everything, get all information, or consider every alternative in a choice/decision situation. Brunsson (1989) discusses *action rationality* and *decision rationality* respectively, and rational or *irrational* actions. Groth (1999), and Orlikowski and Gash (1994) use a similar perspective, by discussing *modes of rationality* (or technological) *frames*. Groth (1999) discusses modern organizations where humans act within a set of frames, *modes of rationality*, providing rationales for action. "Acting within frames" means constructing organizations in a way that makes sense, understanding that organizational politics can make it subjectively rational for an individual to behave in ways that are economically irrational for the firm. No single solution will achieve total domination, but similarities will coexist with local adaptations:

> Since frames will be different in different parts of the world, and even within different local regions in the same society, modes of rationality will also differ, and no single organizational solution will achieve total domination – although solutions that are successful in certain settings may inspire actors elsewhere to adopt certain aspects of them that are compatible with the local conditions (Groth, 1999, p. 29).

Rosenhead (1998) points to the relativism inherent in dominating theories, and how opportunistic adaptation and fashion flow to science and practice. It is often a political process of reaching agreement on what to do, a

> heaving mass of power plays, rhetoric, self-interest, deals and ego-involvement all carried out in smoke-filled rooms – and of which he thoroughly approves as a mechanism far superior to

central control for generating the decisions from which strategy emerges. In effect [Stacey] treats politics as essentially a no-go area for rational thought. Yet all the participants do have their own separate rationalities.

We see the similarities between command work, where political and not only rationalistic actions were frequent, decisions being commonly acknowledged as "rational" ingredients but at the same time as possible "rationality junctions." Barley and Kunda (1992) support the relativistic development of at least American organization theory and practice. Their overview demonstrates how two types of rhetoric have succeeded each other in waves since the late 19th century, *normative* and *rational*, supporting theory development. OR belongs to the period of systems rationalism between 1955 and 1980. The latest normative phase (beginning in the early 1990s), after the late 1980s "hyperrational ideology of financial ruthlessness," they say, will probably be replaced by a new wave of rationalism during a period of economical expansion where automation will become a strong element. According to them:

the presence of this hyperrational ideology could be variously interpreted as the culmination, the continuation, or even the institutionalization of the previously surging rhetoric of systems rationalism (ibid., p. 394).

I conclude that there *has* been a new wave of rationalism, visible in the evolving e-business environment, driving or being a consequence of new organizational ideals, where social action (following Giddens' theories) becomes a matter of abstractions and remotely controlled business operations, in the military and elsewhere.

In summary, there are actions (including decisions) of several rationalities at hand. Without understanding the politics and the "rationality game" within organizations and how technology can be exploited, politically and economically, research has little chance of widening the perspective on organizing. Before returning to the field, because of the central role of technology, let us share some perspectives and theories about technology.

THE ROLE OF TECHNOLOGY IN ORGANIZATIONS

In a general sense, technology has several social purposes and roles, some being linked to control actions. Fieldwork revealed tensions between imposed technologies and traditional ones and between informal and formal, technically structured mechanisms. By and large, efforts to implement IT often end in an unexpected result where users/customers become dissatisfied with what they are given. Clearly, humans depend on technology, the field of military organizing being a prime example, but the common perspective on technology leads to a view where humans have a central position, use technology, but have to struggle in order to overcome the gap between themselves and technology as object. Instead of this human-centred position where humans passively get technology, one which defines social action as integrating human and machine capacity, and sees humans as actively making sense of technology, should be applied.

Orlikowski's (2001) phrase, the *"interpretive flexibility of technology,"* means that actions constituting technology are often separated in time and space from the actions that are constituted by technology. Moreover, Orlikowski makes an important distinction between the *design mode* and the *use mode*, where technology is constructed technically and socially respectively. While many technologies are perceived as fixed structures, practice shows that technology has to be comprehended and activated by human agency if it is to be effective. In such interaction users interpret technology and evaluate its effects. IT is deceptive, sometimes showing human-like qualities: the superior brain, Artificial Intelligence (AI), setting the standards for humans, simultaneously establishing a hierarchy. While the critical human role of interpretation of symbols is recognized (Whitaker & Kuperman, 1996), many feel confused. Gray and Tagarev (1995) state

> Critical researchers . . . note the cultural disparity within our information society. We live in a world in which not everyone has equal access to the tools of the Information Age – a global culture of the inforich and the infopoor, a culture feeding into and upon imbalanced information relationships. Technology, while socially inevitable, is not politically neutral and the oppressive characteristics of technology are being seen and experienced in the global community, adding a new dimension to the intricate complex of reasons for conflict (pp. 4–5).

Giddens' structurational model of technology has four components (Bryant & Jary, p. 49):

(1) Technology as a product of human action.
(2) Technology as a medium of human action.
(3) The institutional conditions of interaction with technology.
(4) The institutional consequences of interaction with technology.

When we create structures (technology, organizations), we become "stuck" within what is possible to express, measure or see. Everything outside the structure merely becomes invisible. Without an analysis, we might take technology for granted. Conditions and consequences are hard to imagine or discover in advance.

Now let us have another look at the inner life of a modern command organization, home of the struggle between charisma and routinization, between humans and bureaucracy. It has been made visible through the ethnography meant to provide new insight, and after a brief description of context, three in-depth cases provide material for further analysis. The first two originate from a Command Post Exercise under winter conditions, while the third was a ISD modelling session when new technology was discussed in a design team.

RETURNING TO THE FIELD – THREE CASES

Command Work Under Field Conditions

Military (army) tactical low- and medium-level command organizations are designed to be protected, mobile and capable of operating in battle environments independently of societal infrastructures for communication. Headquarters (HQs) are normally divided into separate subunits where the command work is distributed according to functional requirements, to include combat support (engineering, transport, logistics), integrated operational battle planning and control (combat functions), an intelligence cell, and facilities to form a forward command post (FCP). There, commanders can position themselves together with an integrated team of staff officers for close-up surveillance and control of combat operations and active presence close to subordinate units.

An HQ relies on a dedicated communication system for radio and data communication, connecting it to higher echelon networks. Its FCP usually consists of a few armoured vehicles and tents where work is done, linked by a LAN, and powered by a generator. In all, about 20 staff officers and support personnel work in shifts. The Commander is often there (the FCP being "active"), and the FCP is supplied with information and resources by other (rear) HQ units. A tactical FCP must be able to move regularly, day and night. When not active, HQ units try to monitor the tactical situation as close as possible. Some functions (combat support, logistics) may still be active even if the site is "passive," maintaining control organization-wide.

We shall first have a brief look at two situations during a winter Command Post Exercise (CPX), where HQs and supporting units (signal and communication, logistics) formed a full scale division command and control structure, within a traditional war scenario. New communication, information and computer systems were brought together for the first time, and several analyst teams and researchers participated. The first situation evolved during a few morning hours in an FCP illustrating "invisible work" and how researchers perceived what did, or rather, did not happen. The second situation is one that exemplifies what low level command work really can be like. We will see the effects of a rational perspective on ISD and operational activities.

The third situation is a modelling session within an ISD team where consultants and practitioners together worked out new command methods and tool-sets. It demonstrates another aspect of rationality, one where methods structure ideas and experiences into work processes, procedures and formal routines. Methods rely on assumptions about work and what are suitable products – in other words they grow from a certain rationality. Together the situations illustrate contradictions, the dialectics between ISD and work, and effects of different perspectives and organizing frameworks.

The relation between the cases is that modelling and ISD (the third case) define what is (later) used in actual situations (case one and two), the design defining constraints for people trying to interpret and make sense of their technologies. Case one could have informed ISD, helped identify requirements, but what actually happened did not make sense for researchers and analysts who worked from a mindset that did not help them identify and make sense of what they experienced. In such circumstances, little feedback is possible from the field to designers. In other words: Case one describes one source of knowledge production about military command work and how this production is positioned in a given mindset, ontology, and knowledge structure. Case two reflects how practitioners struggle to overcome the limitations in their tools ("survival-kit") resulting from the superordinated management and ISD rationality. The third case illustrates how experience is formalized into ISD knowledge with the help of ISD experts and knowledge engineers.

DATA: OPERATIONS RESEARCH AND INVISIBLE WORK IN A FORWARD COMMAND POST

The drive from the exercise control HQ to reach the divisional FCP took almost two hours. There, the arctic winter morning hours saw communication breakdowns, partly caused by the severe cold, partly by technical malfunctions in the computer systems where new applications were tested. My resources were a notebook, camera, audio recorder, and my formal pass to the CP.

One of the ISD ideas is to produce force situation data (positions, activities, resource status) automatically or on command (as reports) from each site to all nodes, mostly bottom-up, within the command organization via the LAN/WAN network connecting the command structure. The desired capability also was continuous distribution and presentation of force data as symbols (fine-tuned by operators depending on their roles) on PC-hosted electronic maps in each HQ section. Communication delays, however, degraded the supposedly common, continuously updated, accurate situation overlays. Staff officers tried to substitute traditional paper maps with plastic film overlays for the computer-based electronic maps. Enemy symbols were separately updated on the screens, but, as a result, the information system only gave operators partial support for situation assessment.

Operators continually discussed problems and tried to find remedies. At 10.56 AM the Chief Operations Officer (COO) asked a colleague:

Have you got any incoming mail? I haven't got any messages at all.

His comrade had gotten a message at 09.46 AM. At the same time the COO asked a sergeant assistant to announce (via the LAN) a local FCP staff briefing by 11.10 AM. The latter logged into the LAN by 10.57 at one of the workstations in order to send an e-mail via the local LAN. In the meantime some officers tried to get in touch with a subordinate unit but in vain.

Op off 1: *We should have had a divisional telephone list.*

A check proved that there was only one, the internal HQ list.

At 11.00 AM: No outgoing line available.

The COO: *We cannot communicate with anybody.*

By 11.05 he summarized the units he was unable to reach.

At 11.09 a telephone message from a subordinate unit announced the landing of airborne enemy troops within its area of responsibility (AOR). Operators at the FCP tried frenetically to find out more.

At 11.45 AM an officer-analyst and a senior OR-analyst entered the tent. They worked for the exercise analysis unit. After some minutes they concluded:

This does not provide us with anything, let's get out of here.

Whereupon they moved on to another HQ/subunit.

At 11.52 borders between units were plotted manually on the traditional large paper map. The COO talked to a colleague over his GSM cell-phone: They agreed on the poor quality of the official communications network and discussed what to do.

Comments on the Situation

The case demonstrates what a normal morning can be like in a "passive" FCP where the overall tactical situation was monitored, the character and visible parts of this work, and how people tried to remain informed. An observer can monitor only a limited part of what happened, not what people thought. It also shows, given that the CPX was a test occasion for technical support systems, how work easily becomes invisible (in effect non-existent), and the importance of personal communication between individuals/operators.

Some obvious reasons for invisibility in this case are the access problem (HQs are remote places) and weather conditions (arctic winter). Also important are the attitudes and pre-conceptions regarding the criteria for qualified command and staff work displayed by the researchers/analysts. These two, who left disappointed after only a short while, had probably appeared at the FCP because they thought that the CO would be there, the FCP itself being active, and that they would be able to get a glimpse of critical decision-making, *charisma in action*. They behaved in common with many systems analysts and OR researchers, confirming biased views of what command work is like, and how technology should function (alternatively: that there is a gap between man and technology).

Technology does not normally function very well when new and untested. Any evaluation of technology that does not consider cause and effect under operational conditions cannot properly assess the technology in question and important side effects may be missed. We see the relation between *design mode* and *use mode*, and how the routinization of work, a prerequisite for the use of information technology, takes its toll. Because of technical and design-related data distribution problems actors instead turned to their GSM cell phones (few routines being applied), thereby contravening Standard Operating Procedures (SOP), and further reducing the chance of seeing whether the SOP and the information systems were relevant.

It takes time, and requires people on location to observe and understand social action and interaction. Instead of regarding breakdowns (the whole morning) as relatively uninteresting anomalies, researchers should try to analyse them. The technical breakdowns caused OR analysts to abandon the site because they interpreted the absence of visible actions as the lack of researchable issues. A deeper understanding of technology and the interaction between man and machine can be developed given an analytical attitude, sufficient time and an observation position allowing the accumulation of sufficient data. In summary, we can trace different rationalities behind the ISD, the exercise, evaluation, and how operators tried to overcome frictions and survive, with and without technology. In addition, we see how researchers/analysts (including the author if this article) work according to their pre-conceptions of the empirical domain, according to what seems rational to them.

CONTROLLING TECHNICAL COMMUNICATION SYSTEMS – AND PEOPLE

The next case illustrates control of the mobile radio network and the kinds of efforts needed to accomplish that. Network operations are controlled from vehicles belonging to the mobile command structure (Fig. 4, adapted from Rice & Sammes,

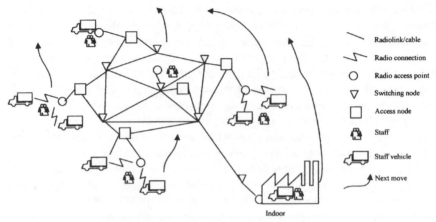

Indoor

Fig. 4.   The Networked Mobile Command Structure and its Operating Principles, Using Outdoor or Indoor Positions for HQ sub units.

1989). Usually, this system is looked upon merely as technology without considering human operators as controlling, mediating and executing agents (Fig. 4).

During the same exercise, I spent some hours with a few operators who described their job, the technical management of mobile radio networks. Continuous control operations sometimes mean urgent handling of technical breakdowns or personnel matters. The operators used a variety of artefacts and tools, from communication media, computers, notebooks, Post-it notes, spreadsheet and text documents. In their work, they relied on technical capability graphics presenting details about routers, nodes and links, while constantly interacting with other remote and co-located operators. A common visualization technique is to present the links and connecting nodes, geographically oriented on computer screens, and their transmission capacity with its variations in real-time mode.

Operations were difficult to plan in advance because the movement of nodes, consisting of a few vehicles and operators, was often made with short notice. Because of the winter conditions, the snow situation was monitored and recorded in tables. Moreover, HQs wanted to remain in position because of a shortage of suitable new HQ positions while the tactical force movements were to follow operations plans. In order to get an overview of the situation and control capability, operators themselves designed additional tools based on MS Office-products.

One invention was a spreadsheet summarizing reports from distributed node operators about technical operations and technical resources, a kind of dynamic situation overview designed according to local needs: "*Only we can use it*." They had not had time to produce a more systematic solution but realized that, via a common web interface, each operator could have typed his report. A MS Excel spreadsheet could then have been designed to automatically compile messages. A further step in speeding up the reporting would have been to integrate and then get data from a few autonomous data systems and computers monitoring and controlling different aspects of the technical system. Some of the compiled lists contained data that was a few hours old, while overviews of some artefacts, by necessity, had to be real-time, continuously receiving data from technical systems and machinery. Operators tried frenetically to augment the visibility of technical and human operations using computer-based tools, voice communication and standard reports. Trying to influence remote fellow operators, a manager shouted in his telephone microphone:

I want to know within milliseconds when a link has been moved or interrupted!

In spite of such efforts, node movement could not be predicted and controlled totally. The crew in some node was reduced because of illness. One brigade HQ wanted to pull out its resources (parts of the total network) prematurely when the exercise was about to end. In general, operators had to fight all these frictions in the real field *and* in "cyberspace," trying to make clear what happened, be it inside computers or involving people.

The network operators form the backbone for any tactical move, relaying decisions and reports, and fixing faults. Their needs are seldom analysed together with "higher-order requirements" and the design of tools for staff officers and decision-making COs. Invisible, often remote, network control operations are somewhat taken for granted or completely neglected, not the least because these operations are very complex and few have sufficient experience to really understand them.

Comments on the Situation

Because of the limited understanding of the human aspects of "networking," social relationships can disintegrate. Much energy then must be devoted to repairing them, to re-establishing the necessary social environment and conditions. Without a deep understanding of technical network operations and their control, few social relations can be first disembedded (Giddens) and then replaced, allowing the control of widely distributed operations.

The social aspects that caused frictions were not and could hardly have been considered or anticipated by system designers, neither do we look at operators' skills nor the evolving frictions caused by our own forces and the (fictitious) enemy. Certainly, a technical redesign of control technology can help people in their work, but a considerable portion of it will depend on human-to-human communication, clear understanding, and action. When Technical Rationality dominates, the mechanistic portions of the work occupy designers' mind-sets, supporting the view that control is about the transmission of facts and, consequently, easily formalized for computer support and processing. As we can see, however, not only facts were involved in the drama. The operator had to struggle to influence people, not by providing facts, but by trying to get commitments. Without these ingredients, nothing can be done. The expert operator (an officer) left the army for a civilian job in a telecom company a short time after the exercise, but to the author's knowledge, there is no connection between the case-three-situation and this decision. Rather, he realized that his expertise could be valued differently somewhere else.

Clearly, ideas and command efforts were launched (illustrate *charisma*), when the technical and organizational infrastructure (*routinization*) gave rise to frictions. Operators tried to design technologies that could satisfy particular needs, and because of their technical skills, they were successful. In summary, we can decide on what constitutes good and bad design and the kind of tools needed as resources to realise those designs. The next case illustrates design and the kind of systematic work that underpins the two first cases.

COLONIZATION OF MIND

Mignolo (1995) describes and analyzes the colonization of America and the simultaneous introduction by the Spanish conquerors of a new language, literacy and an encyclopaedic knowledge system. He uses the concepts *Colonization of Mind* and *Colonization of Memory*. This historic process has its counterpart today in organizations. Another, but no less revolutionary "colonization," takes place and a new world order appears (the global economy), defined in its own special kind of language, implying intense use of IT "colonizing" practice and work with its implications for current and future practice. This new language, part of the systems engineering and methodologies applied for ISD is English or strongly influenced by English, but it means a kind of colonization which easily alienates practitioners from each other and their practices.

I will use Mignolo's examples and conclusions in order to illustrate the processes in another corner of the military workplace. The actors are all various experts in a modern workplace, finding themselves influenced (mild expression) by two forces, both illustrating *routinization*: One is the internal military bureaucratic power aiming at social control, underpinning the ISD. The other is the technological push. The latter streamlines their perception of their work and of themselves according to what can be expressed in the official "method-language." The case describes how, during a design workshop aimed at clarifying ISD issues and requirements, work groups were discussing other artefacts and methods for the future system design. Consultants, contracted by higher authorities, thereby represented a certain rationality and perspective for "good" control practice and technology, acted as facilitators in order to elicit ISD ideas. One of the topics was "unit cards," traditionally meaning a kind of "register card" containing key data about subordinate units that were designed to provide an overview of critical issues. Suddenly, one senior consultant objected to the use of a "traditional" military concept, "unit card":

Consultant: *I frown when you use the term 'unit card'.*
Operator: *We know what we mean when we say 'unit card'.*
C: *I thought you meant punched cards.*
O: *We won't use the word 'unit card' again. But we use the word to mean the form, the template, the artefact, in the same way as we think in terms of paper when we say 'map'* (There is another debate over the kind of maps to use, traditional ones or electronically displayed maps, produced from terrain data bases).
C: *I use it to mean the data, the information content.*

Comments on the Situation

The method-driven ISD may easily result in premature formalization and technical solutions that confuse operators, leaving certain ideas behind even if these make sense to practitioners. When human operators cannot make sense of their tools, they may abandon them altogether (cp. Fig. 3), disrupting the organization, even if they themselves can operate them effectively.

This fragment from the conversation illustrates the perceptual differences between the consultant and an officer-practitioner. The latter, reasoning from his pragmatic work perspective, sees the social value of the artefact in the work, ideally serving him according to his ideas. For him, "unit cards" are meant to print out or be used in other ways. The former is interested only in data and information, the formalizable aspects of events and facts in the world, soon to be programmed and stored in computer memories and databases, which will then *support work routines.* When everything becomes categorized in terms of "information," then social actions and value become irrelevant and only the semantic and syntactic expressions count because of their role in supporting administrative routines.

Consultants do not normally have to demonstrate *charisma,* because they represent and are empowered by the rationality of science, IT and engineering, using its core resources and concepts. Conclusions: in order to reach a satisfactory solution, it is necessary to identify and to consider what stakeholders there are and whose interests should have the highest priority.

INTERPRETATIONS, RATIONALITY, CONTROL AND CULTURE

Objectivism and technical rationality (although operators do not use these terms) guide most research, ISD and management in the military because this approach normally promises to produce the desired control efficiency and stability. It is also trustworthy. Throughout the cases studied, the struggle between charisma and routinization within the modern organization was evident, resulting in different types of trade-offs. The underlying intention was to support organized action, but frictions evolved, promoting workarounds and problem-solving actions.

The belief in our ability to understand, map, and objectively represent a world in symbols, and process them through a cognitive effort leading to knowledge (Whitaker, 1996), is widespread. It is based on a belief in technical rationality. The ISD, in general terms, was designed to serve a supposedly charismatic leader, the Commanding Officer. The command work model (Fig. 3) shows that there should be a fit between technology and action, but the social world is not static. Consequently, because others' evolving needs were not satisfied, complementary initiatives were needed, exemplified by the network operators' frenetic design efforts and actions. For them, urgent and pragmatic action was needed. Even before objectivism and rationalism are introduced, there is no straight line between design and the desired result, except that participation and local use facilitate sense-making.

The first case demonstrates how technical design causes frictions in use mode because of the aggregated effects of technical rationality in the ISD, one being the rationale (distribute symbols as knowledge), another the technical solution which implied a detailed but fragile routinization. The case also shows how researchers followed common sense thinking, finding a site, the FCP, that they supposed, was the centre of the action, one designed to be a union between power and technology. Unfortunately, they did not understand what was happening. Invisibility prevailed. In accordance with Batteau's (2000) observation, the FCP did not live up to a 'facade of order'. The normative-rational command and research thinking involved was hardly challenged, even when they became disappointed.

The second case illustrates the consequences of having a dominant-normative (and rational) thinking person decide on priorities and the top-down design of technology that results to some extent impractical or insufficient in use mode. The third case is about the imposition of certain rational norms related to and dependent on the dominant culture. However, these norms ultimately make the organization dependent on external competence rather than being independent. Various power centres find common interests, leaving others out of the game.

Both "leadership" (supporting charisma) and more technology (routinization) are rational solutions to these situations but from different viewpoints. The conclusion is that "good" control artefacts should be able to be used across rationalities, like work when ideas evolve. Traditional artefacts (less routinized) have social value even if they require work and are objectively less efficient, like those developed by the network operators.

Weick (1993), after having re-analysed the flow of events during a forest fire where several people were burned to death, concluded that, when communication in an organization is interrupted, the organization disintegrates. As long as our environments allow or even promote the creation of more relations, culture is "updated" and recovery from breakdowns is possible. I will be more precise in this conclusion: When people can no longer develop a relationship and interact, or when "culture" means ready-made representations or administrative routines, the latter are no longer meaningful by themselves but may instead give rise to a breakdown in understanding. Additional challenges face those who design new types of organizations based only on technical rationality, so pervasively powerful. Unfortunately, reconciliation between them might be difficult.

DISCUSSION, FUTURE WORK AND ASPIRATIONS

Modern organizations' social and cultural environments tend to be less intelligible for those concerned only with technical efficiency, or for those using systems analysis techniques in pursuing technical rationality (Miser, 1985). This, in turn, leads to a perspective on social and human resources and action as abstract systems components and processes respectively. Much remains invisible and confusion grows. Each alternative interpretation and problem analysis has its roots in a different rationality. For example, even if technical rationality is powerful and tends to be predominant, management means more.

This situation probably has parallels within organizations, from which basic understandings and problem solutions evolve, based on the dominant view on knowledge and work practices. Action/decision sensibility and awareness, however, must accompany and balance strength, especially in military operations. Therefore, complementary systems analysis methods and OR techniques should be developed and applied by managers and researchers respectively. By proclaiming or enforcing concepts (the third case) the world is given names, actually created, and power relationships change. The first two cases demonstrate the consequences of such production. Basic research and OR as craft have to define what methods are to be used, trying to anticipate their consequences.

Research must avoid a position within dominant thinking and organizing practices that fails to consider the impact of a number of attributes:

- operations are often remote and fast, even automated and hard to investigate;
- the application of an abstract systems view during research and organization development, making the social aspects all the more invisible;
- developers, weak on theory, suffer from "conceptual depletion," especially when it comes to analysing the role and impact of technology and bureaucracy;
- there are few humans around in the organization;
- the implicit and often explicit dominant top-down organizing perspective.

Research should try to get a close view of human actions, augmenting their visibility in the modern organization. Because it may not be evident where the core business takes place (politics and rationalities may intervene), a research team must understand cultural issues, managerial politics, and practices. As the military cases show, when expanding the research perspectives of the technical rationality, ethnography certainly can contribute to both understanding and design, advancing thinking beyond objectivism and rationalism (Whitaker, 1996). Thereby new knowledge perspectives and requirements evolve.

Any means to illustrate, even solve the struggle between humans and technology (in Weber's words: between charisma and routinization) will surely be welcomed. The prerequisite is that researchers also, in the same way as people in the work, acknowledge that rationality can be "manufactured," maybe even being an unintentional consequence of how knowledge usually is defined and stored. It is not sufficient just to support humans' work, as long as its ontology is not critically investigated, and possibly adapted to new conditions. The ethnography illustrates the notion that the world is socially constructed, "knowledge" underpinning sense-making, but abandoned when considered necessary. The construction relies on the available tools, which, consequently, must allow relevant constructs. Whether LIS can support reinterpretations or instead contributes to the struggle between charisma and routinization is a question for further studies, which this paper cannot answer.

ACKNOWLEDGMENTS

This study was supported by the Swedish Army, providing access to a series of exercises between 1998 and 2001.

REFERENCES

Alberts, D. S., & Garstka, J. J. et al. (2001). *Understanding information age warfare*. Washington, DC: Department of Defense.

Barley, S. R., & Kunda, G. (1992). Design and devotion: Surges of rational and normative ideologies of control in managerial discourse. *Administrative Science Quarterly, 37*, 363–399.

Batteau, A. W. (2000). Negotiations and ambiguities in the cultures of organization. *American Anthropology, 102*(4), 726–748.

Bourgignon, A. (2001). New management control: Is it really new? Is it really safe? *5th International Management Control Systems Research Conference.* Royal Holloway, 4–6 July, University of London.

Brown, H. G. (1995). *War, revolution and the bureaucratic state.* Oxford: Clarendon Press.

Brunsson, N. (1989). *The organization of hypocrisy, talk, decisions and actions in organizations.* Wiley.

Bryant, C. G. A., & Jary, D. (2001). Introduction. In: C. G. A. Bryant & D. Jary (Eds), *The Contemporary Giddens, Social Theory in a Globalizing Age* (pp. 3–39) Palgrave.

Cecez-Kecmanovic, D. (2000). The discipline of information systems: Boundaries crossed, boundaries pushed. In: *Transcending Boundaries: Integrating People, Processes and Systems Conference.* Brisbane: Griffith University.

Creswell, J. W. (1998). *Qualitative inquiry and research design: Choosing among five traditions.* Sage.

Davis, P. K., & Blumenthal, D. (1991). *The base of sand problem: A white paper on the state of military combat modelling.* N-3148-OSD-DARPA Santa Monica, CA: Rand's National Defense Institute.

Denning, P. J. (2002). The profession of IT. *Communications of the ACM, 45*(6), 15–20.

Gat, A. (1989). *The origins of military thought from the enlightenment to Clausewitz.* Oxford: Clarendon Press.

Giddens, A. (1991). *Modernity and self-identity: Self and society in the late modern age.* Stanford, CA: Stanford University Press.

Gray, A., & Tagarev, T. (1995). Modern information technology and shifts in the military culture. *Communication: Organizing for the Future Conference.* Rome (http://www.natcom.org/conferences/Rome/Rome%20papers/Gray.htm 14 April 2002).

Groth, L. (1999). *Future organizational design: The scope for the IT-based enterprise.* Wiley.

Holly, I. B., Jr. (1988). Command, control and technology. *Defense Analysis, 4*(3), 267–286.

Holmström, J. (1995). The power of knowledge and the knowledge of power: On the systems designer as a translator of rationalities. In: Gothenburg Studies in Informatics. Report 7 Part 1, pp. 257–268, June 1995. F. Kämmerer, F. Ljungberg, J. Stage & C. Sørensen (Eds). *Design in Context – IRIS 18 (Proceedings of the 18th Information Systems Research Seminar in Scandinavia),* 11–13 August, Gjern, Denmark.

Hoskin, K., Macve, R., & Stone, J. (1997). The historical genesis of modern business and military strategy. *Fifth Interdisciplinary Perspectives on Accounting Conference (IPA97)* 7–9 July, 1997, Manchester. http://www.les.man.ac.uk/IPA/papers/papers/73.html 19 February 2000.

Howard, M. (1983). *Clausewitz.* Oxford: Oxford University Press.

Kahan, J. P., Worley, R. D., & Stasz, C. (1989). *Understanding commanders' information needs.* Santa Monica, CA: RAND Corporation, R-3761-A.

Labouret, V. (2001). Premise for a simultaneous measure of paradigmatically different budget behaviours. *5th International Management Control Systems Research Conference,* Royal Holloway, 4–6 July, University of London.

Lowental, L. (1957). Historical perspectives on popular culture. In: *Mass Culture, the Popular Arts in America* (pp. 46–58). New York and London: Free Press.

Mignolo, W. D. (1995). *The darker side of the renaissance: Literacy, territoriality and colonization.* Ann Arbor: University of Michigan Press.

Miser, H. J. (1985). The practice of systems analysis. In: H. J. Miser & E. S. Quade (Eds), *Handbook of Systems Analysis, Overview of Uses, Procedures, Applications, and Practice* (pp. 281–326). Wiley.

Orlikowski, W. (2001). The duality of technology. In: C. G. A. Bryant & D. Jary: (Eds), *The Contemporary Giddens, Social Theory in a Globalizing Age* (pp. 62–96) Palgrave.

Orlikowski, W. J., & Gash, D. C. (1994). Technological frames: Making sense of information technology in organizations. *ACM Transactions on Information Systems, 12*(2), 174–207.

Persson, P.-A. (1997). Toward a grounded theory for support of command and control in military coalitions. Department of Computer and Information Science. Thesis No. 607. Linköping University, Sweden.

Persson, P.-A. (2000). Bringing power and knowledge together: Information systems design for autonomy and control in command work. Department of Computer and Information Science, Dissertation No. 639. Linköping University, Sweden.

Rayward, W. B. (1997). The origins of information science and the International Institute of Bibliography/International Federation for Information and Documentation. *Journal of the American Society for Information Science, 48*(4), 289–300.

Rice, M. A., & Sammes, A. J. (1989). *Communications and information systems for battlefield command and control*. Brassey's U.K.

Rosenhead, J. (1998). Complexity theory and management practice. (http://www.human-nature.com/science-as-culture/rosenhead.html 4 July 2002.)

Schroeder, R. (1992). *Max Weber and the sociology of culture*. Sage.

Schäffer, U., Weber, J., & Prenzler, C. (2001). Characterising and developing controller tasks: A German perspective. *5th International Management Control Systems Research Conference*. Royal Holloway, 4–6th July, University of London.

Sorenson, H. W. (1989). A discipline for command control. In: S. E. Johnson & A. H. Levis (Eds), *Science of Command and Control: Part II, Coping with Complexity* (pp. 7–15). Fairfax, VA: AFCEA International Press.

Strauss, A., & Corbin, J. (1990). *Basics of qualitative research: Grounded theory procedures and techniques*. Sage.

Ways, M. (1969). The road to 1977. In: F. E. Emery (Ed.), *Systems Thinking* (Vol. 1, pp. 372–388). Harmondsworth, Middlesex, England: Penguin Books.

Webster, F. (1995). *Theories of the information society*. Routledge.

Weick, K. E. (1993). The collapse of sensemaking in organizations: The Mann Gulch disaster. *Administrative Science Quarterly, 38*, 628–652.

Walsham, G. (1993). *Interpreting information systems in organizations*. Chichester, England: Wiley.

Whitaker R. (1996). *Objectivism, reductionism and cognitivism*. Manuscript. (http://www.informatik. umu.se/~rwhit/ObjRedCog.html 6 July, 2002.)

Whitaker, R. W., & Kuperman, G. G. (1996). *Cognitive engineering for information dominance: A human factors perspective*. AL/CF-TR-1996-0159. Dayton, OH: Crew Systems Directorate, Human Engineering Division, Wright-Patterson AFB, OH 45433–7258.

Yates, J. (1989). *Control through communication*. London: Johns Hopkins Press.

HIERARCHICAL TO VERTICAL: PUBLIC LIBRARY ORGANIZATIONAL DEVELOPMENT

Cynthia A. Klinck

HIERARCHICAL AND BUREAUCRATIC ORGANIZATIONAL STRUCTURES – NO LONGER RELEVANT?

As libraries endeavor to respond quickly to changing business conditions, even those libraries with well-organized hierarchies find themselves in difficulty. Jessica Lipnack and Jeffrey Stamps in their book "Virtual Teams," state that hierarchies "use force to defend resources, maintain social ability and control technology" (Lipnack & Stamps, 2000, p. 145), and this characteristic causes the further slowing down of new developments. As a result, public libraries are placed at a disadvantage as they struggle to meet today's challenges and prepare for the future. Libraries are coming to realize, as many businesses already have, that hierarchies may no longer be the best model for successful operation in a rapidly changing environment.

In the past, the monopoly of power in a hierarchical organization structure may have offered stability to libraries and their administrators; however, it does not support innovation. So notes theorist Mintzberg (Mintzberg & Quinn, 1988), who affirms that innovation requires lobbying, maneuvering, and negotiating past blockages of opinion among colleagues in a hierarchical organization.

Advances in Library Administration and Organization
Advances in Library Administration and Organization, Volume 21, 163–179
Copyright © 2004 by Elsevier Ltd.
All rights of reproduction in any form reserved
ISSN: 0732-0671/doi:10.1016/S0732-0671(04)21005-7

Those libraries that cling to the hierarchical model are likely to find that

> ... simple hierarchies are notoriously unstable in the face of the unexpected. Ancient empires rose and fell as populations expanded and capacity became overextended. Boom-bust cycles and on to bureaucracies.... (Lipnack & Stamps, 1994, p. 40).

Bureaucracies have long been recognized as moribund, nonresponsive structures, not known for their ability to deal with change or to embrace the creativity required by the knowledge era. Bureaucracies grow larger until finally, "Today's complexity outruns bureaucracy's ability to organize it" (Lipnack & Stamps, 1994, p. 40).

How are the organizational structures in public libraries falling short of meeting the needs of the future and what must be altered to improve the abilities of these organizations to perform?

WANTED: ORGANIZATIONAL STRUCTURES THAT WILL EMBRACE CHANGE AND SUPPORT LIBRARIES IN DOING KNOWLEDGE WORK IN COMPETITIVE ENVIRONMENTS

Step One: Understanding the Competitive Environment

Competition faced by libraries is vast and relentless. Public libraries must take a cue from the marketing books on their non-fiction shelves and improve "speed to market," bringing materials and services to patrons more quickly in order to stay even modestly competitive with bookstores and other commercial and entertainment enterprises and to maintain competitiveness with that technological information provider, the Internet. Advances in technology coupled with expanding competition demand that our libraries become better positioned for responsiveness to customers in both service design and in promotion of offerings, as well as in development of organizational relevance to support that responsiveness.

Our reference departments face massive competition. The Internet now provides a bewitching trove of ubiquitous information offered through a medium that is both instantly available and much more engaging than many of the products offered by the local public library. The Web falls short of being a library in a number of ways. First, in the quality of the information itself: Although there is an illusion of depth and comprehensiveness, the information is not all there, with shortfalls in depth, breadth, accuracy and quality. Standards and validation are often missing, and while search engines appear easy to use, searching is simply not sufficient to discriminate among collections, let alone among individual items or further disaggregations of content (Griffiths, 1998). And yet, the Web offers riches that library collections can and do not.

Libraries offer other information services that the Web does not: At the public library, a trained researcher can develop a search strategy that pinpoints the best information, regardless of format or source. A library researcher can offer background or supplemental sources that evaluate, support or repudiate the information secured. A librarian can easily provide relativity regarding how the information relates to the overall knowledge base through identification of seminal authors and key works. Librarians can locate primary information that has not been altered in nuance or accuracy through rewriting.

Librarians provide value-added services such as referral to other collections and acquisition of needed materials through interlibrary loan from research collections. Librarians can often assist in finding information with scope, organization or format tailored to the patron's intended uses. Libraries provide databases, at no charge to customers, which are not available for free on the Web, and library staff assist patrons in both finding and formatting on-line information to expressly meet their needs.

In spite of these dynamic, highly refined, personalized offerings, libraries have found it difficult to convince a preponderance of citizens that library services provide a competitive advantage over casual, untrained research on the Web. Libraries have also found it difficult to successfully promote value-added services or demonstrate their worth to a public often satisfied with superficiality. Continued efforts are needed to promote the importance of quality information, to sell the services and added values that libraries provide, and to maintain a competitive position in the information side of the library business. To do that, in the months and years ahead, librarians must find ways to provide new and expanded services to both new and existing publics. Reference librarians may be challenged to do research instead of reference; to assist individuals and companies in knowledge management; to reformat, evaluate, summarize, manipulate or otherwise manage information; and to become involved in the theoretical side of information work, expanding their role as practitioners. These practitioners must engage in significant promotion. These changing roles require different skill clusters, additional staff with different personality types, and new organizational structures to support staff and enable their productivity.

Public libraries also have a strong mandate to discover the needs and interests of users and potential users for library programs, services and materials in areas other than research, and to effectively promote those to the populace. Without the availability of tempting materials found in quantity as they are at the local bookstore, without programs as alluring as those in the community's sports venues or on cable television, libraries will be unable to compete successfully for the time and attention of their users.

To stay competitive, then, libraries and their personnel must task themselves to maintain a dedication to patron-centered values and to use marketing research to quickly discover viable niches in both information and recreation markets. Upon learning what services and materials will excite patrons, libraries must conduct gap analyses to see how their own services and collections fall short and set about to quickly implement those services that fall within their purviews. Libraries may well need to expand beyond traditional purviews. Then, to fully assume a competitive position, the library must find new and glitzy ways to fully promote the materials and services desired by patrons. Libraries must, in effect, learn to create a demand through marketing and promotion, and then must insightfully and speedily change the market mix of offerings to both anticipate and respond to the evolving interests of the community and the culture.

Libraries must prioritize in ways that allow them to meet the demands of their various publics in spite of the resource limitations imposed by the vagaries of public funding.

Competition, technology, and funding are not the only pressures. Shortages of qualified personnel are problematic, as staff struggle to handle work in libraries that has changed from routine to knowledge work. Retraining of current personnel to develop skills in technology, marketing, service design, knowledge management and virtual teaming puts massive pressure on libraries, whose managers are also finding that they must recruit new types of individuals with different skill sets and even different personality types to design, build and promote, rather than just respond to demand.

Step Two: Finding Organizational Models That Embrace Change for Doing Knowledge Work

As diversity in the work force increases and types of work and requisite skills are amplified, libraries will increasingly find that "organizational designs that were suitable for routine work in stable environments no longer fit most organizational settings. Increasingly, organizational success depends on making complex trade-offs, learning and implementing new approaches, and applying advanced knowledge"(Mohrman et al., 1995, p. 11).

For long term survival, organizations require structures that are capable of flexibility and change. Those individuals working in organizations still dominated by hierarchical, two dimensional thinking are focused upward, toward the management layer above and ultimately to the Director or CEO. This is fundamentally at odds with emerging concepts of virtual teamwork and knowledge management and is also at odds with a patron-centered decision-making ethos that must be the central tenet of a marketing-based organization.

For the public library willing to move beyond hierarchy and look for an organizational structure that supports a more responsive, patron-centered approach, what comes next? What might the flexible, evolving library organization of the future look like? Inspiration may come from theoreticians who, in the late 1990s, identified the tenets of the nimble organization.

> Organizations need to be incredibly smart, fast, agile, and responsive. They need to respond and make smart decisions at ever-increasing speed, even as the unintended consequences of speedy decisions flare up in a nanosecond and keep leaders focused only on fire-fighting. The old days of 'continuous improvement' seem as leisurely as a picnic from the past. In this chaotic and complex twenty-first century, the pace of evolution has entered warp speed, and those who can't learn, adapt and change moment to moment simply won't survive (Wheatley, 2001, p. 29).

Margaret Wheatley continues, describing her hopes for the effective usage of fundamentals of Knowledge Management, through which

> The organization that knows how to convert information into knowledge, that knows what it knows, that can act with greater intelligence and discernment – these are the organizations that will make it into the future (Wheatley, 2001, p. 29).

Nimbleness can be defined as

> no more than the means by which an organization is able to accomplish its true objective, which is to make the adjustments necessary to stay aligned with its market (Conner, 1998, p. 31).

Daryl Conner, organizational change consultant, defines nimbleness as

> the ability of an organization to consistently succeed in unpredictable, contested environments by implementing changes more efficiently and effectively than its competitors (Conner, 1998, p. 31).

Conner predicts that

> Soon the competitive advantage will be not in delivering what is needed today but in being able to have a nimble response to the next generation of needs that are not yet known by the customer (Conner, 1998, p. 32).

A CASE STUDY IN ORGANIZATIONAL DEVELOPMENT: THE WASHINGTON-CENTERVILLE PUBLIC LIBRARY EXPERIENCE

This case study presents an organizational model that allows for a rapid response to changing needs. Washington-Centerville Public Library possesses value systems and an organizational structure that allow for quick response to the needs of external and internal customers and to both organizational and situational requirements. This model may serve as a bridge from supplanted hierarchical models to structures more suited for the virtual future. Washington-Centerville Public Library is a successful nimble organization, although this evolution took place before the defining literature on that topic was published during the late 1990s.

Rapid growth has been a constant during the past 25 years in this suburban Ohio public library. This growth has provided a fertile climate for re-engineering and development of a new type of library organizational structure. The staff has grown from seven to 150 while circulation has increased six-fold, literally doubling three times over, to two million per year.

During these growth years, Washington-Centerville Library was almost a textbook model – one in which the management employed all eight of John Kotter's well-researched process steps for leading change: (1) Establish urgency (growth of the community and the responding development of the library, along with six building additions, remodelings or new buildings supplied ample urgency); (2) Create a guiding coalition; (3) Develop vision and strategy; (4) Communicate the change vision; (5) Empower broad-based action; (6) Generate short-term wins; (7) Consolidate gains; and (8) Anchor new approaches in the culture (Kotter, 1996).

TECHNIQUES AND VALUES INCLUDE VISION-DIRECTED LEADERSHIP, CONTINUOUS IMPROVEMENT, SELECTIVE HIRING AND MANAGED CHANGE

While all of Kotter's steps were employed, perhaps the most evident to employees and customers through the years has been the strong emphasis on vision, values, and standards. This, along with strategic planning, is taught to every new employee. A cornerstone of the long range and annual planning activity, the vision is articulated and strongly embedded in the organizational culture and the institutional identity.

In addition to vision-directed leadership, the application of continuous improvement, selective hiring and managed change were instrumental in bringing a new and constantly evolving organizational design into reality. Continuous improvement was a necessity at Washington-Centerville, as both community and library growth resulted in a rapidly expanding and ever more complex library organization. Constant evaluation and responsiveness were employed to direct the operation, develop new facilities, expand the size of the staff, teach new skills, implement new systems, and develop the organizational structure itself.

Selective hiring and strong training initiatives created skilled, capable staff. The availability of a well-educated labor pool and the library management's consistently high selection standards resulted in an outstanding group of paraprofessionals and support staff. These individuals were hired during a period when it was difficult for this small, growing library to compete with surrounding university and large public libraries for MLS candidates. The Director and Board were committed to promoting from within, and the library invested substantial resources in training and staff development. These alternate hiring practices supported excellence, resulting in a trained group of staffers with extremely high standards of performance and the skills to effectively support those standards. The emphasis on internal employee development also helped strengthen employee commitment and reduced turnover.

Change was planned and managed for best organizational effect, as new values were intentionally fostered. As the library progressed through the steps of Kotter's change process, high levels of internal communication allowed change to proceed more comfortably for staff and assured that changes were both more quickly inculcated into the culture and more lasting.

A final influential value, employed rigorously in the culture, was an ethos of patron-centered decision making. Marketing theory, supported by needs assessment, drove resource allocation, and determined core services. Patron wishes, expressed and anticipated, brought focus to collection development decisions as well as to prioritization of and initiation of services.

ORGANIZATIONAL DESIGN COMMITMENTS RESULT IN SUCCESSFUL STRUCTURE

Through the past 25-year period of growth, the following commitments were applied with intentionality to develop a unique and successful organizational design:

(1) Dedication to a *horizontal, team-based structure.*
(2) Commitment to *upward mobility and training* of staff to support that mobility.
(3) *Emphasis on level of responsibility and job content* rather than primarily on education in job design and classification.
(4) *Use of self-directed teams.*
(5) Design of a management structure *with team leaders guiding the programs and planning*, with support and human resources management provided by managers.
(6) Recruitment of *managers from non-library settings.*

ORGANIZATIONAL DEVELOPMENT (OD) BRING SUCCESS AND OUTSTANDING RESULTS

The Library's organizational development and design commitments brought about outstanding results, among them:

- Organizational change occurred fluidly, with an effective structure designed for each period of organizational growth, evolving readily to the next stage.
- Utilization of marketing principles developed patron-centered services and collections with speed, creating an upward spiral of continuous growth.
- Quality emphases resulted in extremely high patron satisfaction ratings, possibly the highest in Ohio, according to a professional survey consultant and the results of numerous community surveys.
- Repeated national recognition occurred for Washington-Centerville Public Library – three times ranked first among libraries of similar size in Hennen's American Public Library Rating Index, and twice ranked second among all the nation's libraries. This objective statistical ranking rates efficiency, effectiveness, support and usage.

Following is further information about the intentional commitments to organizational design that brought about these successes. Aspects of this case study may offer illumination to libraries seeking reengineering strategies.

Organizational Design Commitment 1: Structure
Retains Horizontal, Team-Based Character

As the Washington-Centerville Public Library grew, deliberate efforts were made to retain a horizontal organization structure, which was essential for several reasons. For effective training and establishment of evolving organizational vision and values within the culture, a flatter organization was more effective. The Library Director constantly did informal needs assessments and then provided immediate coaching as well as small group and individual training to reinforce growth and change.

A strong team basis for the organizational structure became more and more prevalent as the collegial working style of the Director and the many new hires, most of whom were baby boomers, became dominant in the culture. In a fast-growing organization like this, there was less inclination for employees to cling to outdated but comfortable models. A small number of employees accustomed to working in hierarchical settings found some discomfort with the flexibility and fluidness of the new culture, but additional support and an explicit focus on tasks overcame most of their concerns.

Organizational Design Commitment 2: Job Design Emphasizes Levels of Responsibility Rather than Education

Few employees had library school educations since competition from larger university and public libraries in the area gave the smaller Washington-Centerville Public Library little edge for hiring MLS/MLIS librarians during the early years of this period. Therefore, a staff of motivated para-professionals was built, and a classification system was put into place that emphasized responsibility levels rather than relying solely on educational credentials; MLS librarians and para-professionals resided in the same classification group according to responsibility assignments and job content. Para-professionals with degrees in early childhood education, recreation programming, and other related disciplines brought their own expertise to the library. With in-house training in library work, these talented para-professionals made significant contributions, and in so doing, confirmed the Library Director's belief that the skills required to be an outstanding librarian do not come only from an MLS/MLIS education.

Organizational Design Commitment 3: Training Supports Upward Mobility and Reinforces Culture

Training and upward mobility were required to support the growing organization. Very few new employees had library experience, and all needed substantial amounts of training. Para-professionals were hired in great numbers and trained for library work, and, since there were few staff members available to offer on-the-job training, the Director performed a great deal of that training herself. Self-taught in employee development and in training subjects such as adult learning theory, instructional design and effective transfer of training, the Director used that theoretical grounding to prepare peer trainers within the library and developed in-house certifications for certain types and levels of trainers and training.

Training provided support to staff and offered consistent values clarification that proved to be another effective way of managing change. In addition, training in small groups or one-on-one resulted in the building of stronger and deeper communications channels, enhanced collegiality, and provided personal support for change and growth. Training conducted by the Director enhanced not only the knowledge of the staff, but also their confidence in themselves, their reliance on the ease of interaction with the Director in current and future situations, the confidence that they could speak honestly, and the knowledge that their ideas matter.

This organizational attribute also points to several limitations and concerns for a rapidly growing library – the reliance on close relationships that is both comfortable and effective in the small-sized organization is disrupted as growth continues and new levels of middle management are inserted. Like many other aspects of change, this must be managed carefully and with intentionality to assure ongoing continuity of organizational values and effectiveness. Seemingly paradoxical, mutually exclusive skills are required as new middle managers must learn the ability to guide, control and limit within the focused operational sphere while simultaneously developing vision and an organization-wide purview. Changes in the number of levels as the organization grows require new expectations for the front-line staff, new skills for the Director to work through middle managers, and a great deal of emphasis on building trust and expanding the overall team through controlled, articulated means. Substantial resources must be continuously devoted to maintaining the cultural transfer of this array of unique values, which is not always easy during times of rapid growth.

Organizational Design Commitment 4: Self-Directed
Teams Characterize the Culture

At various times during the growth of the organization, self-directed teams were employed. When the manager of one of the library system's two full-service libraries retired, the strong team at that facility recommended to the Director that no replacement manager be hired. The Director concurred, and for the next two years, the group directed that library until the staff and collection moved into a new building six times larger. The team, composed entirely of para-professionals, effectively designed and improved work processes, orchestrated projects, planned and implemented new services and programs, departmentalized the library, and integrated new personnel into newly created positions. The Director provided weekly communications and a link to the sister library, reinforced values, provided support, validated successes, and affirmed the integration of many of the concepts and values taught in training and employee development activities.

This emphasis on self-directed teams provided within the culture a strong feeling of success, both self- and team-satisfaction, and an underlying knowledge that teams work. This early effort in self-directed teams was pioneered before there was much information in the business or library literature describing this concept.

The model for multi-departmental teams and task groups is now an integral part of the culture of the organization, although it too must be intentionally tended and reinforced as the organization grows.

Organizational Design Commitment 5: Management
Team Supports Team Leaders and Front Line Staff

As outstanding patron-centered library services resulted in ever higher usage, the library continued to hire new staff in order to be able to respond to public demand. To provide guidance for the rapidly growing staff, team leaders were promoted from within the ranks and given responsibility for overseeing planning and provision of library services. Simultaneously, a management-by-objective philosophy was introduced in the strategic planning process at the library to assure that the work of the departments was aligned with the goals of the organization. Team Leaders focused on serving customers, and served as program managers, rather than assuming full supervisory, human resources or administrative duties.

Initially, all Team Leaders reported to the Library Director, but as the organization grew, it became apparent there was a need to begin to develop a middle management level. Consideration was given to assigning additional supervisory, administrative and HR responsibilities to the Team Leaders, thus making them full-fledged department heads, the typical middle managers found in most public libraries. A second option was considered and eventually employed: Hiring trained managers with supervisory experience to support the Team Leaders.

Positions were created on a Management Team and filled through the years as the organization grew and new positions were funded. The individuals sought for these management positions were experienced, trained supervisors and managers, who were assigned as liaisons to one or more teams – Technical Services, Youth Services, Information Services, and Public Services (often known in public libraries as Circulation). This method had some unique characteristics and a number of benefits:

(a) Administrative work like scheduling was handled centrally for the library by one of the managers and support staff, thus maintaining organization-wide standards, facilitating planning for personnel resources, and freeing each Team Leader to spend more time in public service, planning, and implementing projects.

(b) Team Leaders, the senior practitioners in each department, were still able to do the work they loved – provide top-notch service directly to the public, thus serving as models and maintaining involvement in the important work of direct service because they were not burdened with heavy administrative duties.

(c) Managers were often more suited by both personality and desire to the sometimes tough decision making and limit-setting work required in management and supervision, whereas practitioners promoted from service jobs often had difficulty breaking out of the service-oriented modality that appeared contradictory to effective human resource practice. (These new managers were trained internally in library practices, which was often much easier than training librarians to become managers or supervisors.)

(d) Following the lead of business, the Washington-Centerville Library Management Team served as an Executive Committee, operating in lieu of an Assistant Director by providing administration and top management under the leadership of the Library Director. This practice continues to provide more continuity, specialization, and redundancy than employing a single assistant director, a common practice in other public libraries.

Organizational Design Commitment 6: Effective Managers
Are Hired from Outside the Library Profession

To support the Team Leaders and front line staff, some of the managers who were hired possessed experience in supervision and management in bookstores, business, retail, administration of professional service firms, as well as non-profit management. These managers did not have library experience or MLS degrees. They possessed skills that were not often found in the MLS population – strong skills in supervision, managing performance, and human resources work. They successfully learned the library business as they had learned other businesses, and they brought into the culture such useful skills as process improvement, project management, and employee development. These managers coached the Team Leaders and the library professionals in effective methods of supervision, motivation and performance management as their front line supervision roles expanded.

The enthusiasm for learning that came with these non-library managers was exploited by the Library Director, who actively engineered opportunities for employee development within the entire culture with a happy result: A positive upward spiral of internal promotions occurred as people learned new skills and employed them. New positions were constantly being created due to growth, and these were often filled by internal candidates. (To honor the commitment to high standards in staffing, the best candidate was selected, whether internal or external.) Then, to provide a pool of candidates for entry level positions, a program to employ substitute customer service workers was implemented to provide backup; substitutes were hired, trained and were soon available for promotions into regular, non-substitute positions.

The resulting organization structure as designed was not unlike that of a hospital, where the administrative staff supports the clinical personnel.

RESULTS CHARACTERIZE A NIMBLE ORGANIZATION

The results of these organizational design commitments were substantive and epitomized the flexibility of a nimble organization, including, among others:

- a high performing management group, adept at facing problems and solving them;
- a highly effective supervisory structure, able to deal with problems rather than engaging in avoidance;
- a well-trained, effective staff, highly dedicated and directed toward public service;
- a learning organization that predated the published description of the same; and
- a structure that grew effectively to support each new stage of organizational development.

THE ORGANIZATIONAL CHART SHOWS THE PRESENT AND FUTURE

The Washington-Centerville Public Library's non-hierarchical, team-based organizational chart is shown in Fig. 1. The entire organization reports to the patrons of the library. In the organization, communication occurs horizontally as well as vertically, among teams and individuals, and as a good practice, is conveyed both to individuals who are stakeholders by virtue of their supervisory role (hierarchy) and to those with subject interest (team investment).

The Director and other managers are shown orbiting a central circle that represents the Management Group. Other groups providing service to various internal and external customers are located adjacent to the Managers who support them. In addition to these departments, other ad hoc teams and committees are also formed as required.

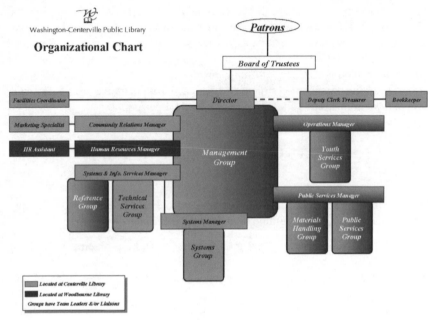

Fig. 1.

BEYOND THE PICTURE: THE EBB AND FLOW OF AD HOC TEAMS AND COMMITTEES

Rather than relying solely on a few individuals in hierarchical positions of leadership such as the team leaders and managers shown, this organizational chart also positions the library for distributed leadership to ad hoc committees by vesting authority in these groups as well. An example of how a multi-departmental team might be added to the organizational chart is shown in Fig. 2, although groups may be convened by and report to any group shown on the organizational chart. Some hierarchy is still essential, as approvals must exist for the sake of resource procurement and budgeting.

Membership in committees is based upon interest, initiative, time availability, willingness to serve, existing project load, departmental work loads, and requisite balance in representation from various departments within the organization. The decision making needs, reporting requirements, composition, and scope of work for these committees are variable, and are determined as the group is convened. Time frames and available resources are defined in advance. Committees at

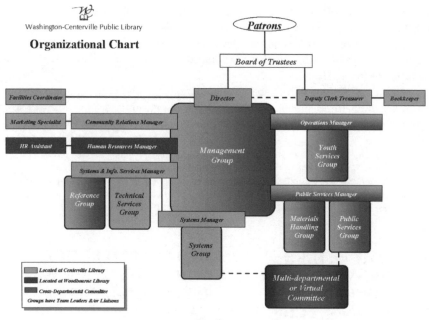

Fig. 2.

Washington-Centerville Library have handled projects, managed the roll out of new services, and developed and implemented new processes.

Integration of personnel from various groups and levels into these committees provides both dynamism and high levels of investment. Directing these committees by "leading from behind," as one staffer described it, requires skills in motivation and leadership. Not all staff are skilled or empowered in this leadership function, but training to that end is planned to further broaden the base of individuals able to guide teams.

SUCCESSFUL FUTURE ORGANIZATIONS WILL CONTAIN A BLEND OF HIERARCHY, TEAMS AND VIRTUAL WORK

As the Washington-Centerville Public Library organizational chart already combines a blend of structural influences, so will those of other libraries as they evolve and reengineer to meet the needs of the future. Hierarchy does and may continue to have a place, but it is not the be-all, end-all structure that it has been for libraries in the past. Nor is the new organization formless. While adaptability and flexibility are key in the new corporation, formless or free-form organizations are not necessarily the most direct route to that flexibility, according to organizational planning consultant Robert Tomasko (1993).

Virtual capabilities will enable teams, individuals, and organizations to work together in real time, online, whether in physical proximity or not, and with new paradigms for timing, structure, protocols and other working modalities.

> Decisions no longer have to go up a hierarchy to get someone with aggregated information and a broad understanding of the parts of the organization. Organizations that can capitalize on this technological capability by establishing the appropriate fit between their information technology architecture and their organizational design will achieve a competitive advantage in terms of time, cost, and responsiveness (Mohrman et al., 1995, p. 11).

THE FUTURE OF OD: FROM FLAT TO LUMPY, FROM UPWARD ORIENTATION TO EMERGING CONCEPTS OF CLUSTERED, MULTI-LEVELED, CIRCULAR TEAMWORK

As organizations progress from hierarchical, upward-oriented organizational structures to newer models that will allow them to operate successfully in the future, they will be moving to organizational charts that look more like solar systems, or so report a number of thinkers in the field of organizational development. Organizational charts may also resemble pizzas, sideways trees, and even geodesic domes. Software for developing complex organizational charts incorporates concepts from such fields of study as social-network analysis, network mapping processes, and relationship mapping. From that description, one can quickly deduce that these charts are intent on recognizing what actually happens in organizations, not just what appears on their organization charts.

To respond to the quickly evolving work of the knowledge industry in a networked society, organizational charts are developing in three dimensions, to incorporate hierarchy, bureaucracy, networks and teams, both physical and virtual. A fourth dimension is added to convey the element of motion associated with rapid organizational change and team work. Corporations are using three-dimensional models that can be altered and changed in moments to reflect a dynamic world of work. These models attempt to describe the complex and ever changing ways that people actually work together in organizations. Clearly, the phrase "change in moments" is an indication of the fact that both groups and organizations will need to reinvent themselves with greater frequency and in quicker time frames than ever before. The nimble organization will own the future.

MOVING TO THE FUTURE: PAVING THE WAY FOR EVOLUTION IN ORGANIZATIONAL STRUCTURES FOR LIBRARIES

In their 1995 book, *Going Virtual*, the authors present this paradigm for organizations in the future:

> Virtual teaming is an optimal way to work in the current environment of time compression, distributed resources, increasing dependency on knowledge-based input, the premium on flexibility and adaptability, and availability of electronic information and communication through networks (Grenier & Metes, 1995, p. 8).

The organization chart presented here may be worth consideration as a potential bridge to that paradigm, offering, as it does, an organizational model combining business and library values, a team-based structure, and a framework for the evolution to the use of fully vested, knowledge-based, virtual teams in a nimble organization.

REFERENCES

Conner, D. R. (1998). How to create a nimble organization. *National Productivity Review*, Autumn, 31–36.

Grenier, R., & Metes, G. (1995). *Going virtual: Moving your organization into the 21st century*. Upper Saddle River, NJ: Prentice-Hall.

Griffiths, J.-M. (1998). Why the web is not a library. In: B. L. Hawkins & P. Battin (Eds), *The Mirage of Continuity; Reconfiguring Academic Information Resources for the 21st Century*. Washington, DC: Council on Library and Information Resources and Association of American Universities.

Kotter, J. (1996). *Leading change*. Boston, MA: Harvard Business School Press.

Lipnack, J., & Stamps, J. (1994). *Age of the network: Organizing principles for the 21st century*. New York, NY: Wiley.

Lipnack, J., & Stamps, J. (2000). *Virtual teams: People working across boundaries with technology*. New York, NY: Wiley.

Mintzberg, H., & Quinn, J. (1988). *The strategy process: Concepts, contexts and cases* (3rd ed.). Prentice-Hall.

Mohrman, S. A., Cohen, S. G., & Mohrman, A. M., Jr. (1995). *Designing team-based organizations: New forms for knowledge work*. San Francisco, CA: Jossey-Bass.

Tomasko, R. (1993). *Rethinking the corporation: The architecture of change*. New York, NY: AMACOM.

Wheatley, M. J. (2001). The real work of knowledge management. *IHRIM Journal*, 5, 29–33.

PART II:
SYMPOSIUM PAPERS THE CHANGING FACE OF SERVICE: PAPERS FROM THE FIFTH ANNUAL JOHANNAH SHERRER MEMORIAL LECTURE, LEWIS & CLARK COLLEGE, OCTOBER 2003

INTRODUCTION

The Johannah Sherrer Memorial Lecture in Library Service was established in 1999 at Lewis & Clark College in Portland, Oregon, to commemorate the contributions and legacies of a respected friend, colleague, and champion of service. Johannah Sherrer (1947–1998) served as Director of the Aubrey R. Watzek Library at Lewis & Clark College from July 1993 to September 1998 when she passed away following a gallant battle with melanoma. Previous Sherrer Lecture presenters have been: 1999 – Walt Crawford, "Service in a Complex Future"; 2000 – Jerry D. Campbell, "The Fate of Service in an Increasingly Digital and Commercial World"; 2001 – Elizabeth A. Dupuis, "The Importance of Being Learned"; 2002 – Joan K. Lippincott, "Service in a Collaborative Way."

For the fifth event in recognition of Johannah Sherrer's contributions to library service, a symposium was held on "The Changing Face of Service," examining how library service has changed in the five years since Johannah's passing and where it might be headed in the future. Panelists included friends and colleagues of Johannah. The papers that follow include some presented at the symposium or serving as background information for comments made at this event.

James J. Kopp
Director

Aubrey R. Watzek Library
Lewis & Clark College

JOHANNAH SHERRER: COLLEAGUE, MENTOR, FRIEND

Richard W. Hines

In my mind, there are two Johannah Sherrers: one is the paper Johannah that you would know from reading her vita; the other is the personal Johannah that you would know if she were your colleague, your mentor, or your friend. I'd like to examine briefly both of these Johannahs.

From her vita you would learn that Johannah Sherrer was a graduate of the University of Portland (BA), the University of Kentucky (MSLS), and the University of Dayton (MA, History). You also would learn that her career began at the University of Dayton in 1970 where she was a Reference Librarian and then Head of Reference. In 1979 she moved to the University of Northern Colorado where she first served as Coordinator of Reference Services/Collection Development and then as Director of Public Services. She assumed the role of Head of Reference at Duke University in 1986, a position she held until 1993 when she became Director of the Watzek Library at Lewis & Clark College in Portland, Oregon. Johannah authored and co-authored numerous articles and book chapters and was a frequent speaker and panelist at library conferences. She received the American Library Association's H.W. Wilson Library Periodical Award for Excellence in 1984 and the Media Award for Journalistic Contributions to Libraries in Colorado from the Colorado Library Association. She chaired the ALA's Professional Ethics Committee and several other committees at the national, regional, and state levels.

While all this gives us some insight into Johannah and her contributions, my personal memories of this wonderful person offer a deeper glance into who she

Advances in Library Administration and Organization
Advances in Library Administration and Organization, Volume 21, 185–187
© 2004 Published by Elsevier Ltd.
ISSN: 0732-0671/doi:10.1016/S0732-0671(04)21008-2

was. I first knew Johannah as a colleague. We met in April 1988, and were friends until her death in September 1998. I had come down to North Carolina from MIT to interview at Duke for the position of Visiting Librarian. Although I had been a librarian for four years, it was the next nine months of working for Johannah that shaped my career to this very day. I remember being picked up at the hotel the night before the interview by Johannah and being led off into the woods for a potluck supper at the cabin home of one the librarians. What a warm feeling; what a great way to start an interview. One of Johannah's great qualities was that she could put you at ease in an instant. At the end of the interview process Johannah had a dinner reception for me (as she had done for all the candidates) at her house that night. Sometime during the evening she scalded herself badly while making coffee or tea. She never mentioned it. She just buckled down and went on with the evening. It was only much later that I learned about the incident. Johannah just went ahead and did it, despite the obstacles. I think that this incident is very indicative of the way Johannah operated her life and even the way she approached death.

Working for Johannah at the Duke Reference Desk perhaps was the most exciting year of my professional life. This was 1988, and if you will remember back, we (meaning librarians) were still pretty much in control of the access to information. There was no Web eating into our reference statistics. Individual help with all questions was still very much the norm. The Reference Desk was frantic, often triple staffed until 10 at night. This was the atmosphere that Johannah thrived in. It was her thing. I can remember her taking questions from the most difficult, cranky faculty at Duke, then charming him, then spending a couple of hours in the stacks making sure he got just what he needed. And she loved every second of it.

I can also remember her talking about bibliographic instruction and her distrust of it as a vehicle of learning. She would say that you always seemed to see the same people from the BI class a couple of days later at the Reference Desk. They couldn't remember how to access that database and needed help. Over and over she would talk about how libraries failed their service mandate by forcing users to access our resources on our terms, rather than theirs. Personal service was the bottom-line ethic Johannah lived. We all lived it at that reference desk. In all of this, Johannah was a mentor.

I also knew Johannah as a friend. Whether it is the memory of sitting around an old fashioned metal kitchen table on a warm Saturday afternoon in Durham, North Carolina or it was taking the grand tour of Oregon on my first visit here, with Johannah seemingly tireless in her devotion to her guests. Johannah was a charmer and an entertainer. She was much more comfortable at home having a dinner party than she was going out. Personal, one-on-one, intimacy was her thing.

I often think of those last days, and her courage fighting melanoma. Never complaining to me about an unfair life. Always interested in what others were up to. Brave, personable, and charming to the very end.

THE CHANGING FACE OF SERVICE – A PERSPECTIVE FROM PRIVATE HIGHER EDUCATION

Elaine Heras

There is a plaque on the wall near the reference desk in the Aubrey R. Watzek Library at Lewis & Clark College where Johannah Sherrer served as library director from 1993 to 1998. It reads, "In Memory of Johannah Sherrer." I always imagine that Johannah is watching over us as we staff the desk, answer questions, and provide service. For in addition to being a library director, Johannah was a reference librarian par excellence. She not only knew her stuff, but she also had a way with people, a way of engaging them and showing that she really cared about them and their needs. She would go the extra mile to find the answer to a tough question, and she instilled her service values in her staff.

As we examine the "changing face of service" in the past five years, I would like to reflect on the changes in service at a moderate-sized, private, liberal arts college. The Aubrey R. Watzek Library provides service to the College of Arts and Sciences and the Graduate School of Education of Lewis & Clark College in Portland, Oregon. Enrollment is approximately 1800 undergraduate and 600 graduate students. A separate library, The Paul L. Boley Law Library, supports the Law School. The Watzek Library houses some 280,000 volumes and over 450,000 microform units, and subscribes to 1300 print periodicals, many more in electronic format, and over 120 electronic databases. The libraries at Lewis & Clark participate in the Orbis Cascade Alliance, a consortium of 27 academic libraries in Oregon and Washington that share a union catalog and participate in

Advances in Library Administration and Organization
Advances in Library Administration and Organization, Volume 21, 189–192
Copyright © 2004 by Elsevier Ltd.
ISSN: 0732-0671/doi:10.1016/S0732-0671(04)21009-4

Table 1. Watzek Library Reference Desk Inquiries, 1997–2003.

Fiscal Year	Reference Questions	% of Total Inquiries	Total Inquiries
1997–1998	14,145	84.3	16,785
1998–1999	11,390	77.5	14,696
1999–2000	9,502	72.9	13,031
2000–2001	8,085	69.0	11,721
2001–2002	6,905	70.5	9,797
2002–2003	5,718	58.1	9,836

direct borrowing and other services. Twenty-three staff members provide service in the Watzek Library, including 24-hour access to the building during the weekdays during the academic semesters. Seven librarians provide service at the reference desk, in addition to collection development and other duties.

Reflecting on the changes in service at Watzek Library over the past five years or so, the first thing that comes to mind is that in 1998, and for several years before that, we double-staffed the reference desk. There were enough questions to keep two librarians busy, and the extra staffing afforded us the opportunity to spend an adequate amount of time with each patron. Two or three years ago we abandoned that practice when it became very clear that it was no longer necessary, nor prudent, to continue having two librarians at the desk. The number of actual reference questions fell from 14,145 in 1998 to 9,502 two years later. Last year, the number was only 5,700. See Table 1.

A primary reason for this, of course, is the widespread use of the Internet that has impacted so many aspects of our lives. The availability of information has grown by leaps and bounds and people find that the answers to many of their questions are at or near their fingertips on the computer keyboard. It is a challenge at times for those of us who have been in the profession more than ten years (and even those newer to the profession) to imagine what goes on in the minds of today's students in regard to locating information. Today's students have grown up with computer technology and have had access to the Internet since grade school. They have been doing their own Web searches for years and have been taught research skills in high school. Many of them either think they already know, or should know, how to find information and do college research, and so they rarely, if ever, ask for help.

Another factor in the downturn of reference statistics, a trend that is happening across the country in academic libraries, is that research databases and other online tools are becoming much easier for people to use. Librarians used to have to show each new user how a particular database or interface worked. Today the majority of database interfaces are pretty much self explanatory. Even help pages, once an oxymoron, are more understandable now. Until recently one of the most frequent questions that we librarians were asked was which research databases should be used to find information on a particular topic. We still field some of these questions; but for the most part, we have built our library Web sites into such fountains of information that students can go to the online research guides we have compiled to find for themselves the most useful sources. In some cases the large vendors that offer multiple databases are also pointing students to the best databases for a given topic as they logon to the system. We used to expend a lot of energy explaining the procedures for finding periodicals in print or in microform in the library. Now, so many journals are available electronically that sometimes students can do their research without ever getting up from their chairs. Students can see with one click, and without exiting their database search or re-keying the journal title, whether or not we have the journal they need, regardless of its format.

If Johannah were with us today she would certainly be pleased with the changes in interlibrary loan service that have taken place in the past few years. The speed with which we can get materials from other libraries is truly remarkable. The majority of our journal requests arrive in less than two days. Patrons are able to submit requests themselves from some of the databases, directly to a library that has the item. Most libraries now scan the articles and transmit them electronically. At our library, we then email the requestor to let them know how to pick up their copy online. These improvements in speed and ease of service help facilitate the research process.

Believing that we should provide service at the point of need, Johannah was not a great proponent of library instruction classes. Her emphasis was on giving help at the reference desk or giving one-on-one help to individuals. As the liaison for the International Affairs department, she used to meet with each student in that program to discuss resources for their thesis topics. Although we have always accommodated anyone seeking in-depth individual help, we did not promote this. Last spring we decided to formally offer a research consultation service, as many other libraries have, as a means to provide service at a different level to our students and faculty.

Since students do not come to the desk much these days (except to use our stapler for their electronic reserve printouts), it is difficult to reach many of them on a one-to-one basis. Even going out and roving among the reference area computers does not elicit the questions it did in years past – we're more likely to get looks that say, "Why are you looking over my shoulder?" So, we have been attempting in recent years to work with faculty who teach research-related courses to see that the students acquire the information skills they need in some way. Sometimes we do this by meeting with a class to talk about important resources in that discipline. Other times we might collaborate with a professor on a particular assignment, for instance to compare and evaluate scholarly and popular literature on a topic.

We might help a faculty member keep up a course Web page by updating links to resources. Like many libraries, we are exploring chat or virtual reference as a means of addressing the evolving service needs.

In 1998 we were only just beginning to develop a library Web site. It consisted of the catalog and little else. Today we spend a great deal of time providing as much helpful information as we can on our Web site, from Circulation policies to electronic reserves and lists of our videos and CDs, and much more. We also try to ensure that we are using terminology that is understandable to our users and that our Web page design facilitates navigating our site. In each of the last two years we conducted usability testing of our Web pages. We have done significant redesigns of the site and consider it a work in progress. The initial "point of service" for many of our users is our Web site, and, as a result, we have shifted our energies to make this as helpful as possible.

What does the future hold for library service here and at other academic libraries? What will it be like five years from now or even next year? There are numerous unknown influences from outside the library and from off campus with which we will have to deal. Changes in the past five years have made it more apparent that planning, both strategic and tactical, is a critical part of our activities. Through planning we are attempting to become better prepared for the challenges and opportunities that present themselves. It is important to involve our various constituencies in this activity. For us, that includes the Faculty Committee on the Library and a Student Advisory Committee. We also incorporate such activities as usability studies, user satisfaction surveys, and even our suggestion book into the analysis of the service we provide.

We have made numerous and quite dramatic changes in service within a relatively short time span. The constant in the service we provide – the element that has not changed in five years – is our service attitude. It is an attitude of friendliness and helpfulness, one of respect and caring for those we serve. I believe this was Johannah's legacy to Lewis & Clark. We remember her enthusiasm for helping people, especially the students, whom she always put first. We remember her ready smile, her friendly demeanor, and her unquenchable thirst for the right answer. She used to tell us that if we were to make an error in judgment, we should make it on the side of generosity. This is the face of service that will never become outdated or obsolete. Sometimes we may need a little reminder, like that plaque on the wall near the reference desk, but Johannah's spirit touched everyone who knew her.

INFORMATION PRIORITIES: REVISING OUR "WORLD-VIEW" OF SERVICE

James J. Kopp and Dan Terrio

THE EVOLVING INFOSPHERE

In an intriguing and provocative paper in *Social Epistemology*, Luciano Floridi (2002) seeks to define library and information science as applied philosophy of information. In his examination of what the philosophy of information is, Floridi notes:

> The subsequent growth of the information society and the appearance of the infosphere (the semantic environment in which millions of people spend their time nowadays) have further influenced the development of contemporary philosophy. This has moved from focusing on the domain represented by the memory and languages or organized knowledge – the instruments whereby the infosphere is managed – to focusing on the nature of its very fabric and essence, information itself. Information has thus arisen as a concept as fundamental and philosophically important as 'being', 'knowledge', 'life', 'intelligence', 'meaning' or 'moral good and evil' – all pivotal concepts with which it is interdependent – and so equally worthy of autonomous investigation (p. 42).

Floridi goes on to state that "The philosophy of information revitalizes old philosophical questions and poses, or rather identifies, new crucial problems. It also helps us to revise our world-view" (p. 42).

The intent of citing Floridi's study is not to delve into a discussion of the philosophy of information, although that would be an interesting discussion. Nor is it to delve [too] deeply into Floridi's examination of one of the leading librarians of the twentieth century, Jesse Shera, who in 1965 wrote, "Librarianship

Advances in Library Administration and Organization
Advances in Library Administration and Organization, Volume 21, 193–199
Copyright © 2004 by Elsevier Ltd.
All rights of reproduction in any form reserved
ISSN: 0732-0671/doi:10.1016/S0732-0671(04)21010-0

is the management of human knowledge, the most interdisciplinary of all the disciplines – and because it is concerned with the philosophy of knowledge it is potentially the most deeply philosophical of all the professions" (p. 176). Rather the intent here is to suggest how *information* itself is increasingly becoming not just part of the environment in which we live (the "infosphere") but increasingly an element of the disciplines that make up the scholarly environment. Of course, information has always been intertwined with scholarship and the academy, but when even our philosopher colleagues have, as Floridi points out, "begun to address the new intellectual challenges arising from the world of information and the information society" (p. 41), it suggests that it is perhaps time to examine more closely how information, and information services, are being addressed in our institutions of higher education.

Ten years ago Arthur Harkins (1993) noted, "The speed of change is accelerating more rapidly with each passing year. By the year 2010 human information, now doubling every 18–24 months, is likely to double every one to three weeks" (p. 46). Harkins argued that, with this rapid change, we entered the knowledge age where, to be effective workers and citizens, we must employ the values, outcomes and competencies that are often associated with the liberal arts. In this way, we can shape and increase the impact of information, transform information into knowledge, and communicate that knowledge as new information which in turn continues the growth of knowledge. The observations and predictions Harkins and others made have generally proved to be true, if not even underestimated. But has our own information environment, our infosphere, evolved to keep pace with the rapidly expanding external infosphere? More significantly, are we preparing our graduates to enter the broader infosphere of the world of the 21st century with the knowledge and understanding to be able to be productive and effective participants in whatever field they enter and to continue to be learners beyond their undergraduate experience? Is our immediate infosphere one that meets the needs of our students, faculty, and staff?

The "interdependent" aspect of information, as Floridi suggests, and the "interdisciplinary" nature of librarianship, as Shera stated, are important elements in assessing an infosphere that meets those needs. This paper seeks to outline the argument that our immediate infosphere, although meeting many of the perceived needs of our students, faculty, and staff, is not operating in the most effective ways to address the rapidly evolving needs of these constituencies. Interdependency is a critical element of how any institution of higher education functions (or functions well) and that same concept and role should be found in the key elements that make up the infosphere of the institution. Similarly, the values of the interdisciplinary elements of "librarianship" (as Shera described it and here expanded to cover "information services") are vital for a healthy infosphere.

Two of the principal components of the infosphere at many institutions, the library and information technology organizations, are too often viewed solely as support mechanisms that are expected to react to information needs on campus when they should be more involved in the information processing activity in all stages of the academic endeavor. J. Gary Augustson, Vice President for Information Technology at the Pennsylvania State University (and recipient of the 2001 EDUCAUSE Award for Excellence in Leadership) states that senior management (trustees, presidents, chancellors) "must come to understand that the effective support of, planning for, investment in, and operation of the IT enterprise are critical to the success of your institution" (Augustson, 2002, p. 14). This is easily expanded to include the library or all information resources and services. However, the interdependency and interdisciplinary components of the infosphere as they relate to these key functions are restricted by organization, culture, and attitude. The result often is a model that is functional but incomplete and inefficient because of this disconnection with the broader aspects of the information components of the institution. This leads to an infosphere that only partially meets the total information needs of students, faculty, and staff. This disconnect affects how the information resources and services are aligned with an institution's mission, strategies, goals and objectives.

In the past decade many, if not most, institutions of higher education have undertaken reviews of their academic priorities in some general fashion or as part of a more direct evaluation of such areas as general education, writing across the curriculum, teaching and learning, etc. In fact, such activities have periodically gone on for decades, but the shift in the past five years in the assessment "culture" of higher education has placed a higher priority and more visibility on these endeavors. Much of this is prompted by accreditation organizations, which, in turn, have been driven by a call for greater accountability from several quarters, including Congress. In most of these endeavors, the information priorities are not specifically identified as a key aspect of these assessments. The library (more likely) and the information technology entity (less likely) may be addressed, but the nature of the criteria for assessment are based on traditional and outdated standards, failing to reflect the changing infosphere within the institution and beyond.

Information Literacy and Information Technology Fluency

One area in which there has been some degree of effort of addressing the evolving infosphere in many academic institutions is in information literacy and the related information technology fluency. But the means by which these steps have been taken often proves to be insufficient and incomplete. The report issued by the National Research Council (1999), "Being Fluent with Information Technology," notes that information technology fluency seeks to provide individuals who understand "information technology broadly enough to be able to apply it productively at work and in their everyday lives, to recognize when information technology would assist or impede the achievement of a goal, and to continually adapt to the changes in and advancement of information technology" (p. 15). This is a goal of information literacy as well as information technology fluency and many institutions have sought to develop programs to address this lofty goal.

However, the assumption is increasingly made that students arriving at institutions of higher education are more computer and technology literate, but there is an important distinction between *using* information technology and *understanding* information technology. Most students enter college with "low-level" skills such as word processing knowledge, Web browsing expertise, and e-mail skills. Students also come with certain proficiencies with respect to technology for entertainment purposes, such as games, music, and videos. Such skills made them experienced users of certain applications but it does not mean that they are fluent with information technology. Relatively few students (and one can add faculty and staff here also) understand foundational concepts such as the basic principles and ideas of computers and networks and the how and why of information technology and technology issues. Some (but not all) have application skills in databases, spreadsheets, and creating and editing Web pages. A smaller number have the capabilities to apply information technology to complex situations and solve problems. Are such skills necessary for our students? If we seek to provide an education that will make our students productive in both their academic endeavors while attending our institutions and productive graduates and life-long learners, addressing information technology fluency is critical. Information technology fluency may only be realized by integrating these programs into the learning process, which would be aided by collaborations and partnerships with IT, the library, and faculty.

There are many types of evolving information landscapes among higher education institutions to address this and other issues. The Coalition for Networked Information (CNI) sponsors a project on "Collaborative Facilities" (available at http://www.dartmouth.edu/~collab/index.html), which are spaces that "integrate the services of information technologists, librarians, instructional technologists, multi-media producers, and many others to serve a wide range of faculty and student needs." CNI also sponsored a study of "New Learning Communities" in which 20 institutions participated in the mid-1990s. This examined the collaborative efforts at institutions in dealing with their evolving infospheres. The "collaborative development" of these new learning communities was mirrored by "collaborative learning" among the faculty, librarians, information technologists, instructional technologists, and students who participated in these activities. Joan Lippincott, Associated Executive Director of CNI, reports on these activities in several publications and offers lessons that are very applicable today (Lippincott, 2002, pp. 190–192).

External Factors – Accreditation and Granting Agencies

Along with the changing infosphere of higher education are changing expectations of the agencies that serve as accreditation bodies and those that offer much needed financial support through grants. Ronald L. Baker, Deputy Executive Director of the Commission on College and Universities, has noted, "Shifts in societal values, attitudes, and expectations are forcing colleges to move toward meaningful assessment and documentation of the quality of outcomes as well as the quality of intentions, infrastructures, and processes" (Baker, 2002). The shift to "quality" measures indicates, as the title of Baker's presentation suggests, that we have moved "Beyond Space, Stacks, and Sources" and that "Institutional constituencies are questioning the relevance, significance, and efficacy of traditional measures of quality and effectiveness" (Baker, 2002). The impact is that more emphasis will be placed on how library and information resources and services assist in achieving the mission of an institution in a way that goes beyond the number of volumes, databases provided, and network connections.

Similar to the shift in accreditation agencies, granting organizations also are moving toward more qualitative and "holistic" views of how organizations meet their academic missions. Funds for the physical aspects of supporting the information needs of the institution are almost a thing of the past and programmatic activities that provide evidence of an integrated approach to teaching and learning are getting the attention of the agencies that are distributing fewer and fewer funds.

Where Do We Go From Here?

So where should institutions of higher education go from here in assessing their own infosphere and perhaps revising their "world view" of information services? One of the first steps is to ascertain what role the institution feels that information plays in the academic mission of the institution. Most mission statements of institutions of higher education do not include the word "information" but other elements of their missions like "liberal learning," "seeking knowledge" and "preparing students for leadership," imply that the student who attends and graduates from these institutions should understand and appreciate the role of information in the world view, not just while at the institution but beyond.

If these indeed are part of the expectations of our students, and the faculty and staff who assist them on their educational expedition, then the institution should examine its information priorities and its information services in the same way that they have addressed academic priorities, the role of teaching, and writing across the curriculum. The challenge is for administrators of these institutions (CEOs, CAOs, Deans, and others) to come to terms with the evolving infosphere and the changes in service needs that are taking place.

CONCLUSION

In another article in the issue of *Social Epistemology* noted at the outset of this paper, Ashley McDowell (2002) examines "Trust and information: the role of trust in the social epistemology of information." In this study, McDowell offers these observations:

> We are told that we are living in an information age; however, the business of information is extremely complex. Those who attempt to handle the world's recorded information cannot touch a billionth part of it. Their goals could be merely to control, categorize, and subdue that information; but, of course, those are not their goals. Their most crucial goal is to *disseminate* that information, and in a way that gets it to those who want or need it. Thus information science, along with social epistemology, must be centrally concerned with how we can get the right information to the right people in such a way that those people end up with the knowledge they need (p. 51).

McDowell presents several important points in this paragraph, including the obvious one that dealing with information is complex and there is just too much of it to handle. She also dispels the notion that those whose profession centers on the business of information (one might consider information services in that respect) are seeking to place barriers and obstacles in the way of information seekers. In fact, it is the dissemination of information that is key along with the important added element of presenting it "in a way that gets it to those who want or need it." What particularly stands out in McDowell's statement is the concluding sentence regarding getting "the right information to the right people in such a way that those people end up with the knowledge they need." This has long been the intent and focus of library and information service, but the landscape has changed, in as little as the last five years. As a result, we must be vigilant and proactive in assuring that we are looking toward the horizon and are not behind it. The challenge is to ensure that we are centrally concerned in an interdependent and interdisciplinary way in getting the right information to the right people in an effective and efficient manner. To do this, a new "world view" of information services (and our infosphere) is required.

REFERENCES

Augustson, J. G. (2002). Leading the IT team: The ultimate oxymoron or the ultimate challenge. *EDUCAUSE Review, 37*(2), 12–18.

Baker, R. L. (2002). Library and information resources: Beyond space, stacks, and sources. Presentation to the Northwest Association of Private Colleges and Universities Libraries, October 17.

Floridi, L. (2002). On defining library and information science as applied philosophy of information. *Social Epistemology, 16*(1), 37–49.

Harkins, A. (1993). Knowledge base learning. *Futurics: A Quarterly Journal of Futures Research, 17*(3–4), 46–60.

Lippincott, J. K. (2002). Developing collaborative relationships: Librarians, students, and faculty creating communities. *College & Research Libraries News, 63*(3), 190–192.

McDowell, A. (2002). Trust and information: the role of trust in the social epistemology of information. *Social Epistemology, 16*(1), 51–63.

National Research Council. Committee on Information Technology Literacy (1999). *Being fluent with information technology.* Washington, DC: National Academy Press.

Shera, J. H. (1965). *Libraries and the organization of knowledge.* Hamden, CT: Archon Books.

REFLECTIONS ON SERVICE

Scott Alan Smith

In reflecting on the theme of "The Changing Face of Service," I considered service in a broad context – not just in libraries, not confined to the academy, not focusing on scholarly publishing. Instead, I gave some thought as to how our views and expectations of service are shaped throughout our daily experiences, and how we might compare and contrast service as framed in different contexts. When should we expect it? How do we measure service (indeed, do we?)? When should we demand it?

One major shift in the presentation and delivery of service for consumers has occurred over the last few years and is a direct consequence of globalization. We inhabit a world closely scrutinized by corporate marketing organizations, who seek to build brand identity and differentiate their products from those of their competitors. The companies who package and franchise these products routinely display their mission statements in their sales literature and on their websites, invoke references to their outstanding, excellent service, and endeavor to paint a gauzy picture of luxury, efficiency, and total customer satisfaction. We are seldom invited, however, to peer behind the curtain. When we do, we see what we already know to be the case – phone banks staffed with poorly paid employees parroting responses from the corporate script; web sites designed to reduce staffing and payroll; and all too often sheer, fundamental indifference.

Sadly, because the speed of change has accelerated so rapidly in recent years, we will soon have (if we do not have already) a generation who knows no alternative, and assumes that this is the way it should be, or at least the way it is. The late Robert Neil, professor of history at Oberlin College, was fond of referring to the "inevitability of the actual." What is, is what must be.

Advances in Library Administration and Organization
Advances in Library Administration and Organization, Volume 21, 201–202
© 2004 Published by Elsevier Ltd.
ISSN: 0732-0671/doi:10.1016/S0732-0671(04)21011-2

If our knowledge of service is informed exclusively by those who profit by not providing it, how will we know what is truly possible? If "service" is offered as an assumed tenet of the overall package, but never actually tested or delivered, how can we know whether we have been the recipients of service in the first place, and whether that service was in fact good or bad? If all we know of service comes from the general definition rendered daily by thousands of e-tailers around the planet, how can we reject this transparent hypocrisy and demand genuine attention, resolution, and satisfaction? Can we hold out any hope that in generations to come we will have achieved anything more than consistent, predictable mediocrity?

I think the answer is: yes, we can. We can because there are those who refuse to accept these definitions, who do not permit such limitations to be imposed on themselves or the organizations they represent, and who sustain a clear sense of purpose; a succinct and undiluted understanding of mission.

This is not to suggest that academia is in general immune from crass commercialization – witness the ways so many admissions offices now market their institutions to prospective students, promoting upgraded residences, trendy food courts, and hip on-campus clubs. But libraries are different, and in libraries we still find people dedicated to preserving and sustaining an honest allegiance to service. It is not that changes are not happening in library buildings, as they are being upgraded with trendy information commons and even coffee shops. But behind it all is service and the type of service for which Johannah Sherrer was an advocate. Johannah was a librarian who would not compromise her beliefs, her obligations, or her professional responsibilities. And she most definitely would not accept consistent, predictable mediocrity in service, nor should any library.

Libraries still invest substantial resources in attracting and retaining capable staff, and in guaranteeing that staff are well trained and motivated. Instruction, in a variety of formats, ensures that students are provided ample opportunity to become familiar with library collections, real and virtual, and their use. On a daily basis, librarians continue to provide dedicated, substantive support, and deliver genuine service.

This does not happen by accident. Quality service is a direct reflection of capable management. It is because of people like Johannah that libraries retain a real and ongoing commitment to service. Even in an era of declining budgets, increasing costs, and a myriad of administrative pressures, good librarians bring a spirit of innovation and true vision to library operations, development and administration. The environment around us and within libraries has changed in the five years since Johannah left us, but the face of service is still very much the same as that provided by Johannah Sherrer.

THE CHANGING FACE OF SERVICE – A PERSPECTIVE FROM PUBLIC HIGHER EDUCATION

Patricia J. Cutright

Public institutions of higher education have experienced a myriad of changes in the past five years. These changes have demanded a re-evaluation of not only how higher education conducts its business but the even more fundamental question as to what is the mission or purpose of our colleges and universities today. With enrollment increases and state funding decreases, public universities are faced with a more diverse student population and the challenge of providing a quality education to all who seek it – in residence or off campus. Also, entangled in the primary role of higher education is the responsibility of the institution to serve the community at large. The question at hand is how the library approaches the service issues associated with the many different constituencies that we serve.

Eastern Oregon University, though small and situated in the rural eastern side of Oregon, has been impacted much the same as its sister institutions on the west side of the state. Experiencing a continuous average growth of 9% annually, with much of that increase in distance learning enrollment, the library has been particularly challenged to provide adequate service for this student population (Eastern Oregon University [EOU], 2002).

Advances in Library Administration and Organization
Advances in Library Administration and Organization, Volume 21, 203–207
Copyright © 2004 by Elsevier Ltd.
All rights of reproduction in any form reserved
ISSN: 0732-0671/doi:10.1016/S0732-0671(04)21012-4

THE GROWTH IN DISTANCE LEARNING
DEMANDS CHANGE

They call in from near and far, they drop by, e-mails fill your box, and, as the term approaches an end, there is a flurry of paper that flies from the fax machines. The activity that surrounds this student population is all part of the "customer service" that constitutes meeting the academic support needs of the distance learning student. Designing a program that provides the most appropriate and expeditious method of delivering information to these students is a challenge that libraries have had to face as e-learning has gained popularity on our campuses. Since its entrance into distance learning in the late 1970s, Eastern Oregon University has been recognized nationally as a leader in the field. As demand for expanded curriculum grows, so does enrollment, Eastern's Division of Distant Education (DDE) program is experiencing the same growth trends reflected nationally, demonstrating an average 61.3% increase over the past 5 years (EOU, 2002).

As the concept of e-learning becomes a burgeoning business for both public and private educational institutions there is much speculation as to what constitutes a successful service-oriented operation. Is it the availability of a wide variety of courses and programs; the modality of delivery of courses; the faculty quality and involvement in teaching? With distance learning on the upsurge, it has become an increasingly popular subject for study by those attempting to understand and explain the phenomenon.

In a project being conducted by the Western Co-operative for Educational Telecommunications (WCET) and the Western Interstate Commission for Higher Education (WICHE) entitled, "Beyond the Administrative Core: Creating Web-based Student Service for Online Learners," the basis of the work is an investigation of support services. The premise is that, like traditional campus-based students, online learners need access to other support services such as library services, tutoring, and academic advising. It is unrealistic to expect that those students who do not come to campus for their education will, in fact, be able to come to campus to access student services (Western Co-operative for Educational Telecommunications, 2002).

Many colleges and universities providing distance education have stepped back, taken a breath, and are now looking beyond the rush to get the student on the class roster. Addressing student support concerns has lead to the creation of "one-stop shops" for a more holistic approach to student services support. With program completion rates at 73% for Eastern's DDE programs compared to national statistics of 10%–35% (Ryan, 2001), the EOU distance learning experience is one that substantiates the assertion that the difference is attributable to the institution providing a much stronger support network for the student (EOU, 2002). Eastern's Pierce Library's efforts in partnering with the Division of Distance Education to establish a system which empowers the student to achieve corroborates the work in progress by the WCET partner institutions.

The Goal: Full Library Service for All

Pierce Library has for many years lead in providing library services to, not only the students, faculty and staff at Eastern Oregon University, but to the easternmost 10-county region of the state, as well. In developing library services for the distance learner the staff at Pierce Library has focused on delivering a full service package that gives the student 24/7 access and levels the playing field for our off-campus population. Examples of some of the services provided are:

- Electronic Research Center: 24/7 access to 74 indexes and full-text databases that are searchable on-site or remotely via the World Wide Web. All distance students are entered into the university's student information system and given a barcode which provides access authentication for off-campus use of bibliographic databases.
- Interlibrary loan and Ariel Internet document delivery service: Students may electronically place interlibrary loan requests for materials using the library's web site. Materials will be shipped via ground delivery with a 24–48 hour receipt time or journal articles and short documents can be scanned and sent via the Internet directly to the student's e-mail box.
- Electronic Reserves: The electronic collection of course support materials put on reserve by the teaching faculty traditionally was photocopied and sold in the campus bookstore as course packets or put in the Reserves section in the library. With the advent of scanning and Web access to materials the Electronic Reserves service generally alleviates the need for the hard-copy service, while providing 24/7 access to this information.
- Pioneer and Orbis-Cascade Alliance Consortiums: These integrated library systems provide access to nearly 23 million books, journals, government documents, and more from the holdings of 90 different libraries. The Pioneer Library System comprises the collections from 70 academic, public and school libraries in eastern Oregon. The Orbis-Cascade Alliance represents 26 academic libraries in Oregon and Washington. All students, faculty, and staff may initiate a direct patron borrow through the systems, eliminating the need to place the request through the interlibrary loan department, thus providing 24/7 access to resources.

- Information literacy: Workshops are provided on-site at the 11 DDE Centers throughout the state. The workshops and other reference assistance is provided by two librarians on staff with 30% of their time dedicated to distance education students and faculty. The library staff also teaches two library courses which are taught on-site as well as online and recommended to all DDE students, with both listed as General Education course electives.

While focusing on services for our students through various collaborative efforts, Pierce Library often finds itself to truly be eastern Oregon's library. The mission of the University states that "We have a special commitment to the educational, social, cultural, and economic needs of eastern Oregon." This service philosophy carries over to the library by providing outreach to the ten county region through many co-operative projects that improve the quality of life in the region.

One area of involvement entails providing information and expertise for economic development in the region. An emerging plan to introduce new strategies for economic revitalization in the region is called "Economic Gardening." Economic Gardening is the process by which resources are provided to help grow local entrepreneurs. This is in contrast to economic hunting whereby the community's limited resources are used to attract outside companies to relocate (Gibbons, 2003). There are three main elements to this program:

- Information.
- Infrastructure.
- Connections.

The library staff plays an integral role in two of the three elements: first, working with the business or economic development coordinator in providing valuable information ranging from market trend analysis to GIS and, secondly, collaborating with the economic development team to ensure the connections and networking are established to promote the success of the project.

In the Carnegie Foundation report, *Reconsidering Scholarship*, Ernest Boyer (1997) illustrates the necessity for the academy to rethink the role of "service" to the larger community. He states that "Beyond the campus, colleges and universities are being asked to account for what they do and to rethink their relevance in today's world" (p. 76). In rural America, as in the beginnings of the land grant institutions, higher education is being drawn upon to provide the insight and expertise, creating an interdependence that blurs the line between "town and gown."

The Politics of Entanglement

While working at Pierce Library, the impact that the unification of ideas and collaboration can have on the students, faculty and citizens of a community is evident. In my tenure at Eastern Oregon University I have been exposed to the benefits of "consortium attitude" that comes from co-operation and partnerships. Time and again the library demonstrates the positives of what is referred to as the "politics of entanglement." As Shepard (1997) describes this philosophy he states, "the politics are really quite simple. We maintain an intricate pattern of relationships, any one of which might seem inconsequential. Yet there is strength in the whole that is largely unaffected if a single relationship wanes" (p. 4). Eastern Oregon University and specifically Pierce Library, have learned that entanglement and co-operation can lead to a strengthening in services that no institution could afford alone.

REFERENCES

Boyer, E. L. (1997). *Scholarship reconsidered: Priorities of the professoriate.* San Francisco: Josey-Bass Publishers.

Eastern Oregon University (2002). *Did you know?* Retrieved November 22, from http://www2.eou.edu/dde/.

Gibbons, C. (2003). *Economic gardening: An entrepreneurial approach to economic development.* City of Littleton, Colorado. Business/Industry Affairs. Retrieved September 15, from http://www.littletongov.org/bia/NewEcon/default.asp.

Shepard, B. W. (1997). Spinning interinstitutional webs: The politics of entanglement. *AAHE Bulletin,* 49(6), 3–6.

Western Co-operative for Educational Telecommunications/WICHE (2002). Beyond the administrative core: Creating web-based student services for online learners. Retrieved November 11, from http://www.wcet.info/projects/laap/about/about.htm.

CONTRIBUTORS

Patricia J. Cutright is Director of Libraries at Eastern Oregon University in La Grande, Oregon. She is the 2003 recipient of the LITA/Gaylord Award for Achievement in Library and Information Technology and the 2002 recipient of the Oregon Librarian of the Year award from the Oregon Library Association.

Elaine Heras is Associate Director of the Aubrey R. Watzek Library at Lewis & Clark College in Portland, Oregon where she has been employed since 1985. She has also worked at Portland State University and the Boston Public Library.

Richard W. Hines is Dean of Information Resources and University Librarian at the University of Portland in Portland, Oregon. Prior to his current appointment, he held positions at Colorado State University, Duke University, and the Massachusetts Institute of Technology.

James J. Kopp is Director of the Aubrey R. Watzek Library at Lewis & Clark College in Portland, Oregon. His previous appointments include positions at the University of Portland, Washington State University, Columbia University, and the National Library of Medicine.

Scott Alan Smith is Regional Sales Manager, Pacific Northwest/Northern Tier, Blackwell's. He has been a key player in several library activities in the Northwest, including the Timberline Acquisitions Institute.

Dan Terrio is Chief Technology Officer at Lewis & Clark College in Portland, Oregon. He previously held positions as CTO at Lewis-Clark State College in Idaho, Director of Information Technology for the Richard T. Farmer School of Business at Miami University in Ohio, and Manager of Academic Computing at Augsburg College in Minnesota.

PART III

INFORMATION LITERACY: INTEGRATING INTO THE INSTITUTION'S ACADEMIC CULTURE – ONE COURSE AT A TIME

Jean Donham

INTRODUCTION

Liberal arts education has traditionally emphasized critical thinking and other components of information literacy. Because knowledge is accumulating and changing even more rapidly than in earlier eras, it is more crucial than ever that students develop the motivation and ability to become lifelong learners if they are to flourish personally and professionally in this information age. Cornell College has established a campus-wide emphasis on information literacy since 2000. While the skills and knowledge that constitute information literacy have been a part of the curriculum long before, an intentional effort to integrate information literacy into coursework in all disciplines has revitalized the dialog about teaching these critical thinking skills and has re-invigorated effort toward information literacy goals. That dialog causes us to ask one another and ourselves "What is information literacy? How is it to be taught, nurtured, learned, and utilized?" These questions and others were highlighted as the College undertook its re-accreditation self-study where information literacy was a particular point of emphasis.

Advances in Library Administration and Organization
Advances in Library Administration and Organization, Volume 21, 213–235
© 2004 Published by Elsevier Ltd.
ISSN: 0732-0671/doi:10.1016/S0732-0671(04)21014-8

Cornell College defines information literacy as the attainment of the skills, knowledge, and dispositions that enable one to locate, evaluate, use, and communicate information effectively for the purposes of gaining knowledge, solving a problem, or making a decision. This definition is fully congruent with specific Association of College and Research Libraries (ACRL) and American Association of Higher Education (AAHE) competency standards associated with information literacy. Cornell has adopted these standards as a part of its information literacy model, and librarians, faculty, and writing center staff regularly collaborate to integrate the standards into courses in point-of-need instruction. According to these standards, the information literate student:

(1) determines the extent of the information needed;
(2) accesses needed information effectively and efficiently;
(3) evaluates information and its sources critically and incorporates selected information into his or her knowledge base and value system;
(4) uses information effectively to accomplish a specific purpose; and
(5) understands many of the economic, legal, and social issues surrounding the use of information, and accesses and uses information ethically and legally.

Information literacy is a pre-eminent concern for college and university libraries. The *ACRL/AAHE Standards for Information Literacy* provide a conceptual framework for the skills, knowledge and attitudes that students need to develop over their college years. A challenge is determining how best for librarians to teach to these standards in the higher education environment. Various solutions to this problem are documented in the literature (Kasowitz-Scheer & Pasqualoni, 2002), including required courses in information literacy, online tutorials, orientation programs at the beginning of the first year, as well as integrated instruction in either the first year or throughout the academic program. The choice of strategy is dependent upon the pedagogical philosophy as well as the academic culture and structure of the institution. At Cornell College, for both theoretical considerations and institutional reasons, the library has chosen to implement a program that integrates information literacy instruction into courses in all four years of the undergraduate program.

THEORETICAL CONSIDERATIONS FOR AN INTEGRATED INFORMATION LITERACY MODEL

The overall intention of instruction in the library is to develop concepts that will transfer to new environments as students graduate and encounter new research needs, tools, and information. Such transfer of learning requires consideration of tenets of learning from the literature of educational psychology. Several theoretical constructs are particularly relevant in the effort to teach for post-collegiate application or far transfer as well as for the immediate needs. Among these are concept formation, constructivism, transfer of learning, and a conceptual model of the information search process. To relate these theoretical constructs to information literacy, it may be helpful to describe each briefly.

Concept Formation

A concept is "the accumulated knowledge about a type of thing in the world. Learners accumulate this knowledge through multiple opportunities to explore, examine, and integrate perceptions and inferences" (Wisniewski, 2000). Concept formation requires multiple experiences in multiple contexts. As a learner experiences and re-experiences a concept, he/she develops an understanding of its features, properties or critical attributes, its exemplars, a framework, and its contexts. In information literacy, after various experiences, students develop a concept of a database or a search engine, for example. Teaching information literacy across disciplines and over years in college increases the likelihood that such concept formation occurs.

Learning for concept formation differs from procedural learning. Procedural knowledge "is knowing how, or the knowledge of the steps required to attain various goals" (Byrnes & Wasik, 1991). Information literacy involves, in part, procedural learning. Students must learn how to use features of electronic databases, for example, how to save selected records or how to use the search screen. However, in order to increase their ability to learn new databases independently, for example, they benefit from learning the concepts of controlled vocabulary, Boolean logic, and the distinction between keyword and subject or descriptor searching. Procedural learning and conceptual learning interact to develop a deep understanding of information searching.

Integrated instruction can be focused in such a way that students have the opportunity to consider information literacy in the context of a specific discipline. The approaches to information in the natural sciences are substantively different from the approaches in the humanities, for example. By teaching information literacy in context, these disciplinary idiosyncrasies become an aspect of the instruction; the intentional opportunity exists for students to experience these differences, as they participate in information literacy instruction in different contexts throughout their college experiences. These repeated experiences in different contexts lead to conceptual learning.

Constructivism

According to this theory of learning, people actively build or construct their knowledge of the world (Cobb, 2000). Three prominent theorists in constructivism are John Dewey (Dewey, 1933), George Kelley (Kelley, 1963) and Jerome Bruner (Bruner, 1986). Of these, perhaps most relevant here is Kelley. Kelley posits that learners form constructs in a highly individualized way to organize their perceptions of their world. As new information is available, the constructs are restructured in a continual process of rediscovery and integration. Each new learning experience offers the opportunity to reconstruct the meaning of previous experiences. By integrating information literacy into courses for all four years, students accumulate knowledge and experience so that each time they confront information literacy instruction, they bring more prior knowledge to the setting, and hence take away new insights and skills.

Transfer of Learning

Transfer of learning depends on students acquiring a deep understanding of the initial instruction (Barnett & Ceci, 2002). Deep understanding "occurs as one looks for, tests, and creates relationships among pieces of knowledge around a reasonably focused topic" (Newmann, Secada & Wehlage, 1995, p. 10). Such deep understanding is unlikely to develop after one-shot instruction sessions. It requires students to have multiple experiences in different contexts in order to look for patterns and relationships.

Deep understanding is enhanced by a positive motivation to learn. Need strengthens the motivation to learn. Consider the plight of a person who needs a driver's license for employment. The need to learn the factual information covered on the driving test increases the intensity of learning effort. Since that need also results in immediate application of the knowledge, there is further support for deeper understanding. Likewise, college students in the library are highly motivated to learn information literacy concepts and skills when they see the immediate need for it and have an opportunity for immediate application. Instruction in the context of a specific assignment creates this sense of need, and in some cases even urgency.

In addition, transfer of learning is enhanced by the identification of essential elements in the concept to be learned and transferred (Hunter, 1971). In information literacy, learning the essential elements of a citation (e.g. publisher, place of publication) or a database (e.g. field, record) will help students understand these concepts in future contexts.

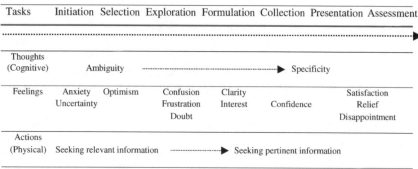

Adapted from Carol C. Kuhlthau, *Seeking Meaning*, Ablex, 1993.

Fig. 1. Kuhlthau's *Information Search Process Model. Source:* Adapted from Carol C. Kuhlthau, *Seeking Meaning*, Ablex (1993).

Conceptual Model

The research of Carol Kuhlthau resulted in a conceptual model of the information search process. This model serves to guide development of the information literacy curriculum at Cornell. Kuhlthau's *Information Search Process Model* includes not only this cognitive aspect of the search process but also the affective aspect of information searching. Her research-based model can be summarized in Fig. 1.

Using this model, librarians identify points in the process where students are likely to encounter negative feelings (e.g. anxiety, uncertainty, frustration) and engage students in consultations to help them over the hurdles that are creating these feelings. Also, librarians use the model to help students appreciate the normalcy of their experience and map where they are in the process. This is particularly important at the exploration stage when students are likely to become anxious before they have really developed a focus for their research. Using a theoretical model of the process helps encourage students to be patient as they gain enough familiarity with a new topic to begin to develop a clear research question and then a thesis.

Integrated or point-of-need instruction provides good circumstances for learning. By integrating instruction into courses, students experience information literacy instruction over their four years in a variety of contexts, with varying degrees of complexity in their tasks. They learn concepts through direct instruction, followed closely by guided and independent experiences in applying what they learn. They experience the continuity of support from a faculty member and a single librarian throughout a project. Cornell has intentionally chosen an integrated approach to information literacy instruction because it situates us well to apply these tenets of learning theory for the best instructional outcome.

INSTITUTIONAL CONSIDERATIONS FOR AN INTEGRATED INFORMATION LITERACY PROGRAM

Foremost among institutional considerations for an integrated information literacy program is the relationship between librarians and faculty. As a step toward developing a collegial relationship between librarians and faculty, Cornell reorganized the professional librarian positions in 2000. Positions as reference librarian, serials librarian and public services (instruction) librarian were transformed into three consulting librarians, one for the Arts & Humanities, one for Social Sciences, and one for Natural Sciences. The College Librarian assumed responsibility as the consulting librarian for Education. The primary responsibility in each consulting position was to work collegially with the departments in the respective academic divisions to design and deliver instruction; to evaluate, build and maintain collection; and to serve as the "personal librarian" for those departments. Other responsibilities (e.g. interlibrary loan, serials, college archives) were divided among the librarians, but their professional identity on campus would be with the academic division. Faculty members showed immediate enthusiasm for this new model, and likewise, students quickly saw the librarians as consultants to the courses in which they were enrolled.

Each institution has its unique character and organizational schemes; these must be part of the formula for design of an information literacy program that works institutionally. In Cornell's one-course-at-a-time (OCAAT) calendar, the academic year is divided into nine terms. Students enroll in one course each term and faculty members teach one course at a time. To complete a full year's requirements, students take courses at least eight of the nine terms. Faculty members teach six of the nine terms. Because Cornell's students take only one course at a time, students seek out and consult with the librarian for the division of their current course. Faculty members encourage this consultation strategy.

Cornell librarians provide formal instruction to classes within their respective divisions, focusing this instruction on the specific assignments required for the course so that information literacy instruction is contextual. In addition, librarians provide individual consultation to students either in formal, scheduled sessions, or in less formal impromptu meetings. These constitute information literacy tutoring. Such sessions may focus on any of the aspects of the information search process. It is common for students to consult with librarians early in their search process to brainstorm a topic or focus for a research project or to develop a research question.

On the other hand, these sessions can cover citation styles and the intricacies of either in-text citation or the formatting of reference lists. Similarly, the topic might be search strategies or selection of databases. These sessions are driven by student need.

The One-Course-at-a-Time calendar gives the college nine term beginnings per year. In traditional semester settings a flurry of instructional activity characterizes the first weeks of the semester followed by relative calm. These "flurries" occur monthly in the OCAAT calendar. At Cornell, information literacy class instruction typically occurs during the first two weeks of a term. The mathematics tell us that we have many more opportunities for teaching among the four consulting librarians than we would have in a two-term academic year, given the availability of only two electronic classrooms in the library. In each term, formal instruction sessions are scheduled for as many as eleven courses. In short, librarians have tried to take advantage of the OCAAT calendar to intensify the information literacy instruction program.

The "personal librarian" model means that each course has its own librarian, depending on which academic division offers the course and which librarian consults with that division. Since students are taking only one course, for that term they have one librarian who is the point of contact for all their library needs. This helps deepen the relationship between the librarian and the students. Each librarian has a unique style and unique strengths. Over time, students benefit from working closing with a variety of librarians, but in any given term, it is a one-on-one relationship.

The OCAAT calendar affords flexibility in class time and schedule. Classes typically meet from 9:00 to 11:00 AM and/or from 1:00 to 3:00 PM. In this schedule, for example, a class that typically meets mornings only can have additional sessions scheduled in the afternoon. These sessions can be information literacy sessions, written into the course syllabus from the beginning. These time periods can be used for direct instruction, or work sessions in electronic classrooms where the librarian assists students, or for one-on-one consultations between student and librarian. This eases the pressure for faculty who are concerned about using too much class time for information literacy topics.

The OCAAT schedule also allows opportunities for immediate application and feedback. Again, with the option of scheduling morning and/or afternoon sessions, students can learn a strategy in the morning and use afternoon time to apply it to their particular research. Ready availability of the librarian and the faculty member provides an excellent opportunity for prompt feedback and correction if there are misunderstandings.

Sustained absorption in course content is facilitated by the OCAAT calendar because student and faculty concentration is not diluted by concern with assignments in other classes. This immersion facilitates information literacy instruction as students return throughout the term to the librarian associated with their course. These librarian-student interactions range from defining research topics, expanding the search for information, discussing perspective to applying citation style or learning software for presenting findings. As a result of these repeated interactions between individual students and librarians, students develop the skills they need and learn to work with a library professional.

Most classes at Cornell are scheduled to meet in the mornings or both mornings and afternoons. This daily schedule provides a routine for the library as well. Mornings are times for meeting with classes, and afternoons provide time for consulting with students one-to-one, or communicating with faculty. Librarians can count on students to be available to work with them in the afternoons and students have grown to expect their respective librarians to be available for them during those hours as well.

INFORMATION LITERACY PROGRAMMING

Academic departments have identified information literacy competencies of particular importance to disciplines in similar language and with similar intent. For example, students in the Department of Biology are expected to learn where to go to find information that they need; how to evaluate the reliability of that information; how to read, understand, and incorporate that information into their own view; and how to communicate effectively in either written or oral form. In particular, biology students will learn how to search for, read, understand, and report on peer-reviewed research publications.

Information literacy skills are also increasingly desired outcomes in the social sciences. For example, the Department of Psychology strives to produce gains in information literacy in:

(1) gathering and critically evaluating information from the primary literature in psychology as published in professional journals and scholarly books;
(2) understanding the research methodologies used to produce new knowledge in psychology and their appropriate application and limitations; and
(3) knowing how to apply psychological principles to solve human problems and improve functioning in various settings.

In the Department of Economics and Business, the goal is for students to develop the information literacy skills necessary to become effective decision-makers: (a) acquiring economic and business information; (b) organizing, evaluating, and analyzing the information; and (c) using the information to make and implement policies that accomplish sound objectives.

Humanities and fine arts departments articulate parallel goals. In the English department, information literacy goals include cultivating students' ability to locate information; use literary scholarship, information databases, and indexes; and evaluate information sources. In the theatre and communications studies department, information literacy involves analyzing a script; identifying areas for research; and locating, accessing and evaluating necessary research materials.

Cornell's efforts in information literacy competencies occur in the classroom, in the laboratory, and in the library, which includes the writing resource center and the multimedia studio. Both library faculty and teaching faculty take responsibility for developing information literacy in students. Instruction provided by the consulting librarians emphasizes the search process, selection and evaluation of information resources, use of information, and intellectual property considerations, including citation styles. Professors, too, are involved in guiding students through these earlier stages, but they have a central role in the stages of processing and communicating information. The multimedia studio and the writing resource center are also important resources for instructing students in the final stage of the information process.

A graphic representation of a model of the information process depicts its implications for collaboration in teaching and learning, see Fig. 2. This model shows that faculty and librarians collaborate to provide support for the student researcher throughout the stages of the search process. The multimedia studio and writing resource center supplement that support at the beginning of the process to guide the collection of information based on the format of the final product and at the ending stage to produce and publish results. An important aspect of this model is that information literacy instruction is not only in the domain of the librarian. Responsibility for developing these competencies belongs to all faculty, including librarians as well as staff in the writing center and multimedia studio. This shared ownership is a hallmark of the Cornell approach to developing information literacy.

This model illustrates the stages of the information search process. These stages parallel the five ACRL information literacy standards. At each stage there are intellectual tasks occurring; these are represented in the model; examples include "assessing the quality of information" or "synthesizing." As students engage in these intellectual tasks, they may choose to interact with the supporting "cast" that includes the consulting librarian, the professor, and other key resources. The first stage of the process involves discussing and formulating questions, selecting and perhaps narrowing a topic, and determining the extent of the information needed. This is, of course, a traditional step in college work. Often a professor assigns a paper or project topic, or a student and professor work together to develop a

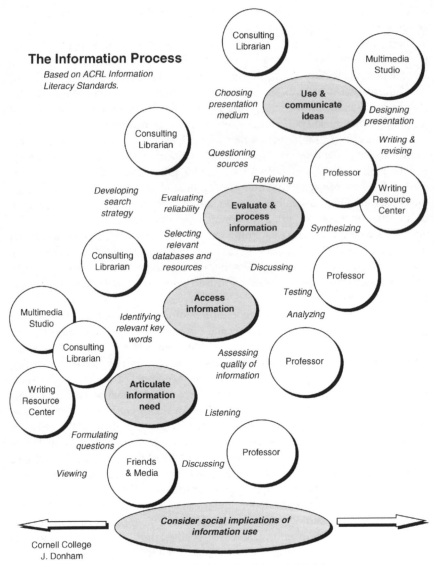

The Information Process
Based on ACRL Information Literacy Standards.

Fig. 2. Cornell's Information Literacy Model.

topic. At Cornell, students discuss topics and information needs primarily with professors, librarians, and classmates, but also with staff in the writing resource center or multimedia studio.

The second stage in the information process involves accessing and gathering needed information. Specific activities are likely to include developing search strategies, selecting relevant databases and resources, identifying relevant key words, and locating printed materials or works. Instruction regarding accessing information occurs frequently. For example, in computer science, a common first exercise in upper-level elective courses asks students to locate reports of research on the Web. Professors in many disciplines commonly ask students to write annotated bibliographies as an early step in the development of a project. In the study of modern languages, students in introductory courses are taught to explore the Web in the target language and to use materials created for native speakers. Such exploration enriches the cultural content and sharpens both information literacy and language skills. Most languages have extensive Web-based activities to accompany texts.

College professors are all too familiar with the result when students merely combine bits of information into an incomprehensible hodge-podge. Once information is obtained, it must be evaluated and processed. The reliability of sources and the validity of arguments must be ascertained, and disparate and sometimes even contradictory information must be reviewed, analyzed, discussed, and synthesized.

It is necessary but not sufficient for students to evaluate the sources of information they have accessed. Students also need background knowledge to evaluate the accuracy of the content, and they need critical thinking skills to evaluate the validity of the arguments presented. In the philosophy department, for example, Logic and Critical Thinking in particular is a course designed to provide training in the rudiments of good reasoning and to sensitize students to fallacious reasoning. Such training and sensitivity require knowing what is and is not relevant to assessing the truth of claims, and it is essential to information literacy.

One result of the information process described thus far – accessing information, evaluating sources and arguments, integrating information – should be the incorporation of selected new information into a student's knowledge base and value system. In fact, this stage of the information process has been traditionally considered one of the most important intended outcomes of engagement in a liberal arts education. To illustrate: The comparative study of religion provides substance for information analysis. This can be seen in the preferred usage by many scholars of religion of the term "worldview" to characterize the primary intellectual object of their study. The two full-time faculty members in Cornell's Department of Religion are both comparativists. The emerging ethos of Cornell's religion department stresses the development of critical perspective on one's own culture as well as on the cultures of others. This critical perspective lends itself to selective altering of a student's knowledge base and value system. In focus group discussions, students reported that the religion courses had improved their thinking skills and increased their appreciation for religious traditions other than their own. For instance, one student commented, "I liked comparing all different religions of the world; I was exposed to beliefs outside of my Christian background. The academic viewpoint helped me understand [religions] beyond social stigmas and stereotypes."

Similarly, in Department of Education classes, students divide their time, observing in classrooms, meeting in class for discussion, and examining the professional and scholarly literature. These students read theory of learning and research on teaching, observe the application of these abstract principles in real classrooms, and then use class time to compare, analyze and evaluate new knowledge as they create their own understanding of their future profession. Similar processing of information characterized by critical analysis, evaluation, and synthesis, occurs in all disciplines as students engage with new information and incorporate it into their prior knowledge.

The final stage in the information process is the communication of information and ideas to others. Specific activities involved in this stage may include choosing a presentation medium, organizing the presentation, creating a web page, creating visual art or graphs, writing and editing, and/or making an oral presentation. The Writing resource center and the multimedia studio have a role in the delivery of the information literacy program. For example, geology students creating web pages participated in information literacy sessions conducted by both the Consulting Librarian for the Sciences and the Educational Technologist (in the multimedia studio).

At every stage of the information process, information literate individuals should consider the social implications of information use. One example: To assess students' understanding of ethical principles in psychological research and professional practice, the psychology department asks them to respond to two hypothetical scenarios in an open-ended fashion and to provide a numerical rating of the degree to which the proposed research or action involves ethical problems. This project provides important direct measures of student understanding. In several courses, including Senior Seminar, the principles of ethical practice and research are discussed. It is expected that students' insights into ethical issues will increase as they advance in their major. Economic, legal, and social issues surrounding the use of information are sometimes addressed in the writing resource. The library has used its web site to address ethical and legal aspects of information use by providing a tutorial on copyright, information on academic honesty, and assistance for citation style.

In addition to instruction from the teaching faculty, information literacy instruction occurs in group and individual, scheduled and unscheduled, consultations between students and consulting librarians. Since the 2000–2001 academic year, the library has been working toward implementation of an instruction program that has the following characteristics:

- Content is aligned with the ACRL Standards for Information Literacy.
- Instruction occurs at the student's point of need.
- Instruction is integrated into courses so that it has meaning and importance for the students.
- Instruction is planned collegially by a consulting librarian and the teaching faculty member.

This program is well begun. In fact, results of an annual faculty survey revealed that 57% of faculty members had arranged for a librarian to meet with one or more of their classes, and those who had done so reported observing improvement in some aspect of those students' library research work. For example, in General Psychology, students attend instructional sessions on how to use the *PsycInfo* database, the primary tool for searching the literature in psychology. Students learn about the basic functions of *PsycInfo* and its use in locating scholarly articles about particular topics. Formal evaluations of specific sessions provided by students and faculty members indicate that they are worthwhile. Faculty who completed the librarians' evaluation forms were highly satisfied with the relevance of instruction to the course assignment, the level of complexity of the content, pacing, interaction with students, students' application of the instruction to their work, and usefulness of the session in meeting the course objectives. Students also offered positive evaluations of the sessions, especially with regard to the relevance to their work, their own application of the instruction session in their work, and the appropriateness of resources for their needs.

In a liberal arts environment, one intention is to develop in students insight into the unique characteristics of the various liberal arts. Strategies, skills, techniques, and even concepts in information literacy vary, sometimes subtly, sometimes dramatically, across disciplines. Students ought to have the opportunity to experience information seeking in a variety of disciplinary contexts as one way of considering the research disposition of scientists as compared to artists as compared to psychologists, etc. At Cornell, instruction in information literacy is distributed across the academic divisions; the distribution for a typical year is shown in Table 1.

The library also classified sessions according to the instructional emphasis for academic year 2001–2002. Not surprisingly, the results indicated that the topics involved were predominantly the earlier stages in the information

Table 1. Information Literacy Classes in Academic Divisions, 2001–2002.

Classes by Division	Classes	Professors
Arts and humanities	28	12
Education	8	4
Natural sciences	9	9
Social sciences	29	13
Total	74	38

process – articulating information needs, accessing information, and evaluating information, see Table 2.

The predominance of the earlier stages of the information process in library instruction reflects the choices of faculty members. These professors may assume, perhaps correctly, that they are especially qualified to provide education related to the later stages of the information process, whereas librarians are especially qualified to provide education related to the earlier stages. While intensive information literacy instruction is an important ingredient in a student's first-year college experience, there is much to be gained by a spiraling curriculum that brings students back in subsequent years for instruction that elaborates on those initial lessons. Such a developmental approach to the topic is an intention of the Cornell program. Introductory lessons in the first year may focus attention on defining a researchable topic or question, selecting appropriate databases, or developing effective search strategies. In subsequent years and sessions, greater attention goes to evaluation of information sources, comparisons between Internet search engines and subscription databases, use of discipline-specific terms in search strings, and

Table 2. Information Literacy Across Academic Levels, 2001–2002.

Topic	%
Topic selection/definition	11
Search strategy	25
Selecting and using a database	24
Evaluating database search results	12
Evaluating websites	5
Discriminating among scholarly, professional and popular sources	4
Locating/using locally help resources	12
Discipline specific research sources/style	5
Citation Styles	2
Total	100

Table 3. Student/Librarian Consultations, Term 7, 2001–2002.

Classes by Level	
100	21
200	29
300	19
400	5
Total	74

other techniques and strategies that vary among disciplines. Table 3 shows the distribution across levels in a typical year.

In addition to group instruction in courses, Cornell students also receive individualized information literacy instruction from consulting librarians. These consultations may occur as scheduled or unscheduled events, the former either at the reference desk or in the librarian's office, the latter usually in the librarian's office. The library monitored the topics of these consultations for three weeks (Term 7, 2001–2002), as an assessment strategy. The results indicate, like the topics of group library instruction sessions, that the predominant topics of student-librarian consultations involved the earlier stages of the information process, see Table 4.

Students seeking consultation time with librarians during that term represented fourteen academic departments. The consultation strategy is especially valuable in senior seminars where each student's research is unique and where students'

Table 4. Student-Librarian Consultations, Term 7, 2001–2002.

Instructional Emphasis	Standard	No. of Sessions
Topic selection/definition	1 (determine)	18
Search strategy (keyword/Boolean/subject/)	1 (determine)	48
Selecting and using database	2 (access)	36
Locating/using locally held resources	2 (access)	54
Identifying discipline-specific research sources/style	2 (access)	12
Evaluating web sites	3 (evaluate)	2
Evaluating database search results (relevance, depth, source, authority)	3 (evaluate)	23
Discriminating between scholarly, professional and popular resources	3 (evaluate)	7
Citation style	5 (ethics)	1
Other	–	7
Total		208

Note: An individual consultation may have involved more than one topic.

needs vary, based on their own skill and confidence in research as well as their respective topics. Further, this strategy is consistent with the library's commitment to a consulting model of librarianship. The librarian-student consultation strategy is especially useful for students in the early stages of research in senior seminars. Although some seminar students self-schedule consultations with librarians, with faculty assistance consultations have been formally scheduled for senior seminars in the social sciences, education and physical education, art, and English.

The College web site holds great potential as an aid to developing awareness and competence in information literacy. Concerted efforts at developing web-based instructional support for the use of information resources, for writing and for electronic publishing are in progress. Comments in focus group sessions indicate that these efforts are yielding results. Participants indicated that they use the web site for links to databases and for off-campus access. Five of the twelve students in this focus group indicated that they use "everything" on the library web site. As of early March 2002, when an annual student satisfaction survey was administered, 87% of students said they had used Cole Library Catalog that academic year. The library has reorganized its web site to provide assistance to students in accessing and searching information resources electronically. Provision of research aids on the Research in Social Sciences page is an example of an enhancement of the web site to provide improved access http://www.cornellcollege.edu/library/social-sciences/topic-politics.shtml.

DEPARTMENTAL STANDARDS

Individual departments, working with their respective librarians have developed expectations for their students and faculty. One example is the psychology department, whose faculty members have articulated a series of experiences of increasing complexity to develop incrementally their students' information literacy, and many of these experiences involve evaluating and processing information. Nearly all psychology classes require students to use published professional resources for at least one assignment. Following instruction in using the *PsycInfo* database, students in General Psychology complete one or more critiques of published articles selected by the instructor or by the students through a *PsycInfo* search. Assignments in 200-level psychology courses generally require integration of material from several sources: In Social Psychology, students review the published literature as background for their group research project; in Child Psychology, students conduct a literature review for class presentations; in Learning and Behavior, students write about the work of an individual scientist based on a published journal article, the scientist's web site, and possible e-mail correspondence; and in Cognitive Psychology and Personality Theories, students write more traditional term papers on topics chosen in consultation with the instructor. These assignments are more complex than the library resource assignments for General Psychology because they require that students integrate and evaluate information from a variety of sources. Also, students may be required to obtain at least some of the material from the primary source literature rather than relying entirely on secondary sources. The psychology department's 300-level courses generally require that students write a comprehensive review of published literature in a particular area, and students are encouraged or required to include primary source material in these reviews. All psychology majors are further required to take Research Methods where students collect and analyze data and write research reports in American Psychological Association format. Finally, students complete a major literature review as part of their Senior Seminar project.

Students in politics are regularly required to undertake projects that exercise their information literacy skills, and they are provided with a multitude of tools and strategies to help them achieve proficiency. Among the tools and strategies, the department has:

(1) required information literacy classes taught by the consulting librarian as a regular part of beginning and advanced courses;
(2) in collaboration with the consulting librarian, developed specialized guides which address accessing and evaluating information resources in political science and law;
(3) required early submission by students of working bibliographies and has provided instructor feedback on those submissions;
(4) required students to schedule individual conferences with the consulting librarian to focus student attention on source selection and evaluation;
(5) developed a substantial Internet research guide for politics, government, and law.

The geology department aims for geology majors to be comfortable with three components of information literacy: (1) to use a computer to access and work effectively with any database pertinent to geologic information; (2) to recognize relevant information in the primary geologic literature and synthesize it in both written and oral format; and (3) to facilitate communication, learning a variety of presentation technologies including web page design, Power Point, computer-generated 35 mm slides, and poster creation using the plotter housed in the geology computer laboratory.

ASSESSMENT OF STUDENT KNOWLEDGE AND COMPETENCE IN INFORMATION LITERACY

Assessing information literacy is challenging when the instruction is integrated in courses. The intentions of assessment efforts at Cornell are to create tools and processes that are the most likely to serve more than one purpose for assessment. These tools can serve as guideposts for students to help them know in advance the expectations and to help them learn the criteria for judging their own work in light of those expectations. This requires that students receive the assessment instrument along with the assignment. Another intention is that the assessment instrument help identify what students know and do not know. To date, most of Cornell's information literacy assessment tasks are performance-based rather than tests. The accumulation of assessments over time will inform faculty and librarians about program. Analysis of aggregates of students work using explicit criteria will reveal patterns where students succeed and fall short.

As an example of a performance-based assessment, the biology and psychology departments have designed a procedure for directly assessing students' abilities to evaluate research designs and interpret results presented in peer-reviewed scientific journal articles. Beginning and advanced students are provided with sections of several articles and then present brief responses to short-answer questions about what they read. Faculty members in religion and philosophy have also designed direct measures of information literacy to be used in departmental assessment. Students in both departments are presented with several brief written pieces and are asked to provide informed responses. In the religion department, students are given brief newspaper articles and a political cartoon, all of which cover current events related to religious issues. In a similar procedure, philosophy majors respond to a letter to the editor and an unfamiliar argument made by a philosopher.

With respect to the earlier stages in the information process, there is clearly a need to define specific strategies for assessing not only students' exposure to instruction and their perceptions of learning, but actual achievement. The physical education department in collaboration with their consulting librarian developed a set of criteria for assessing bibliographies in student papers, see Table 5. Using such checklists at this provides students with guidance as they critique their own work and calls attention to the important considerations in selecting and using information sources.

Similarly, in considering the end product of the information process, Cornell faculty in such departments as English, geology, and physics are experimenting with the use of rubrics for assessing student performance. These faculty members have adapted a rubric designed by Shannon Whalen (2003) and published on her website (www.academics.adelphi.edu/edu/hpe/healthstudies/whalen/HED601_r2.shtml)

Table 5. Bibliography Checklist.

Criteria

Sources are authoritative. Articles come from journals whose standards for publication include conscientious editorial review or peer review. Books cited are authored by individuals with appropriate credentials. Web sites are attributed to organizations or individuals with expertise on the topic at hand.

Sources are current (Older articles are justified).

Sources are varied. Citations represent various media (book, journal, website, etc.) Where appropriate, diverse points of view are represented. Sources represent a range of publication dates to show the spectrum of thought on the topic, as appropriate.

Sources are of an appropriate number. At least [five] different sources are included. No single source provides the primary substance for the final product.

Sources represent appropriate scope for the assignment. Books and journal articles are not too highly specialized for the scope of the paper. General reference citations are used as background material.

Information from sources is meaningfully integrated into the text of the document.

Special-interest web resources are acknowledged as such in the text of the document. Biases are explained.

Popular literature is included only when appropriate and is acknowledged as such in the text.

Citations follow APA citation style both in the text and in the list of references.

to describe their expectations and to give students clear understanding of their expectations. Figure 3 shows one example of an adaptation of this rubric for Cornell.

Using techniques for authentic assessment provides faculty with a clear portrayal of their students' strengths and shortcomings. In addition, it provides students with specific feedback upon which to base their next efforts. Accumulation of these assessments over time will reveal strengths and shortcoming of the information literacy curriculum for Cornell.

SUPPORTING THE EFFORT

Two major multi-year grants to the Associated Colleges of the Midwest from the Andrew W. Mellon Foundation provide opportunities for Cornell College to advance the study of information literacy and its connections with teaching and learning. One is a grant related to instructional technology, shared by institutions of the Great Lakes Colleges Association; the other is an institutional collaboration grant that the ACM has decided to use to study the ways that students are provided

	EXPERT	PROFICIENT	APPRENTICE	NOVICE
INTEGRATION OF KNOWLEDGE	The paper demonstrates that the author fully understands and has applied concepts learned in the course. Concepts are integrated into the writer's own insights. The writer provides concluding remarks that show analysis and synthesis of ideas.	The paper demonstrates that the author, for the most part, understands and has applied concepts learned in the course. Some of the conclusions, however, are not supported in the body of the paper.	The paper demonstrates that the author, to a certain extent, understands and has applied concepts learned in the course.	The paper does not demonstrate that the author has fully understood and applied concepts learned in the course.
TOPIC FOCUS	The topic is focused narrowly enough for the scope of this assignment. A thesis statement provides direction for the paper, either by statement of a position or hypothesis.	The topic is appropriately focused but lacks direction. The paper is about a specific topic but the writer has not established a position.	The topic is too broad for the scope of this assignment.	The topic is not clearly defined.
DEPTH OF DISCUSSION	In-depth discussion & elaboration in all sections of the paper.	In-depth discussion & elaboration in most sections of the paper.	The writer has omitted pertinent content or content runs-on excessively. Quotations from others outweighs the writer's own ideas excessively.	Cursory discussion in all the sections of the paper or brief discussion in only a few sections.
COHESIVENESS	Ties together information from all sources. Paper flows from one issue to the next without the need for headings. Author's writing demonstrates an understanding of the relationship among material obtained from all sources.	For the most part, ties together information from all sources. Paper flows with only some disjointedness. Author's writing demonstrates an understanding of the relationship among material obtained from all sources.	Sometimes ties together information from all sources. Paper does not flow. Author's writing does not demonstrate an understanding of the relationship among material obtained from all sources.	Does not tie together information. Paper does not flow and appears to be created from disparate issues. Headings are necessary to link concepts.
SPELLING & GRAMMAR	No spelling &/or grammar mistakes.	Minimal spelling &/or grammar mistakes.	Noticeable spelling & grammar mistakes.	Unacceptable number of spelling and/or grammar mistakes.

Fig. 3. Research Paper Rubric. *Source:* Adapted from: Whalen, S. "Rubric from Contemporary Health Issues Research Paper." http://academics.adelphi.edu/edu/hpe/healthstudies/whalen/HED601_r2.shtml.

SOURCES	More than 5 current sources, of which at least 3 are peer-review journal articles or scholarly books. Sources include both general background sources and specialized sources. Special-interest sources and popular literature are acknowledged as such. All web sites utilized are authoritative.	5 current sources, of which at least 2 are peer-review journal articles or scholarly books. All web sites utilized are authoritative.	Fewer than 5 current sources, or fewer than 2 of 5 are peer-reviewed journal articles or scholarly books. All web sites utilized are credible.	Fewer than 5 current sources, or fewer than 2 of 5 are peer-reviewed journal articles or scholarly books. Not all web sites utilized are credible, and/or sources are not current.
CITATIONS	Cites all data obtained from other sources. APA citation style is used in both text and bibliography.	Cites most data obtained from other sources. APA citation style is used in both text and bibliography.	Cites some data obtained from other sources. Citation style is either inconsistent or incorrect.	Does not cite sources.

Fig. 3. (*Continued*)

a liberal education in ACM colleges during the first year and beyond. During the summer of 2002, faculty members from across the College undertook a campus workshop to consider matters related to information literacy. This workshop strengthened the collaboration of the teaching faculty with the resources, human and material, of the library and alerted faculty members to ways that colleagues have explicitly connected their courses to skills and issues related to information literacy. The workshops also occasioned substantial conversation about the sequence of instruction and practice in skills in information literacy and other aspects of liberal education at Cornell. A mid-year luncheon brought the summer workshop participants together again to hear examples of lessons, assignments, assessment strategies, and activities carried out in the fall semester. A second such luncheon in May addresses the events of spring semester. Examples of ideas shared include rubrics for research papers, concept mapping using Inspiration^{TM} software, strategies such as requiring working bibliographies, and approaches to teaching academic honesty. These events have continued the conversation among faculty and librarians as the information literacy instruction program evolves across the campus.

CONCLUSION

It is clear that information literacy is fundamental to liberal education. In designing a program to meet the instructional needs of students, it is important to consider first what we know about teaching and learning. This requires study of educational psychology. Next comes assessment of the institutional culture and the implications of that culture for collaboration between the library and the faculty. In assessing institutional culture, one must ask such questions as

- How amenable is the faculty to teamwork?
- What kinds of assignments do faculty give students and how can information literacy instruction help students succeed?
- How do our students prefer to work? Independently? In consultation with others?
- How important is understanding of process in contrast to creation of product?

Our institutional goal is to implement sound theories of teaching and learning in a structure consistent with the college culture. Our One-Course-at-a-Time calendar provides unique challenges and opportunities for the integration of information literacy instruction into coursework. The essential questions are, "What do we know about our institutional culture?" and "How can we design instruction to fit that culture?" In answering those questions, we have designed an integrated, point-of-need instructional program characterized by close collaboration between faculty and librarians, active teaching, and engaged consultation with students.

REFERENCES

Barnett, S. M., & Ceci, S. J. (2002). When and where do we apply what we learn? A taxonomy for far transfer. *Psychological Bulletin, 128,* 612–638.

Bruner, J. (1986). *Actual minds, possible worlds.* Cambridge, MA: Harvard University Press.

Byrnes, J. P., & Wasik, B. A. (1991). Role of conceptual knowledge in mathematical procedural learning. *Developmental Psychology, 27,* 777–786.

Cobb, P. (2000). Constructivism. In: *Encyclopedia of Psychology* (Vol. 2, pp. 277–279). New York: Oxford University Press.

Dewey, J. (1933). *How we think.* Lexington, MA: Heath & Company.

Hunter, M. (1971). *Teach for transfer.* El Segundo, CA: TIP Publications.

Kasowitz-Scheer, A., & Pasqualoni, M. (2002). Information literacy instruction in higher education: Trends and issues. *ERIC Digest, ED465375* (June 1).

Kelley, G. (1963). *A theory of personality: The psychology of personal constructs.* New York: W. W. Norton.

Kuhlthau, C. C. (1993). *Seeking meaning: A process approach to library and information services.* Norwood, NJ: Ablex.

Newmann, F., Secada, W., & Wehlage, G. G. (1995). *A guide to authentic instruction and assessment: Vision, standards and scoring.* Madison, WI: Wisconsin Center for Education Research.

Whalen, S. (2003). HED 601: Contemporary health issues rubric for contemporary health issues research paper. Adelphi University. Retrieved January 8, 2003 from, www. academics.adelphi.edu/edu/hpe/healthstudies/whalen/HED601_r2.shtml.

Wisniewski, E. (2000). Concepts. In: *Encyclopedia of Psychology* (Vol. 62, pp. 242–253). New York: Oxford University Press.

DEVELOPMENT AND IMPLEMENTATION OF A UNIVERSITY INFORMATION LITERACY COMPETENCY: ONE PIECE OF THE WHOLE

Kathleen Tiller

INTRODUCTION

In a Dilbert cartoon the pointy haired boss introduces his son to Dilbert, explaining that the young man has been hired to manage the technology development group because he has gone to college. When Dilbert asks him what college he attended, the youth replies that he actually spent four years hiding in the attic. What does a college education accomplish? Will it get you the job of your dreams? What can a person really learn? How does higher education distinguish one from others in the workforce or next door for that matter?

A "*pure* liberal arts education is a utopian ideal that has been realized only in very limited circumstances," according to Knox et al. (1993, p. 182). In actuality, a college degree seems to confer little more than status and acts as a screening device for companies. The authors' research seemed to confirm that, while it is important to get a college education, it is much less important which institution grants that degree. Educational credentials help maintain status and provide

Advances in Library Administration and Organization
Advances in Library Administration and Organization, Volume 21, 237–256
Copyright © 2004 by Elsevier Ltd.
All rights of reproduction in any form reserved
ISSN: 0732-0671/doi:10.1016/S0732-0671(04)21015-X

inroads into professions of choice. What is the value of a college education, especially an expensive one?

The State University of New York (1992) in its report on college expectations states that "a good education is one which helps the student appreciate the richness of options and opportunities and enables the student to appreciate the satisfactions of knowing, doing, achieving, and accomplishing" (p. 17). Such an approach does not lock the student into memorization and single responses to artificial problems. Rather it prepares an individual to continue learning for a lifetime. According to Snavely (2000, p. 81), this learning for one's lifetime is the lasting value that the university experience can contribute to the lives of students. How to learn as the society shifts from an industrial to a knowledge economy is of paramount importance.

DESCRIPTION OF THE UNIVERSITY OF DAYTON

The University of Dayton was founded in 1850 by the Society of Mary (Marianists), a teaching order of priests and brothers. It is one of the top ten Catholic universities in the United States and the largest private university in Ohio. Approximately 10,000 students are enrolled, with 6,600 undergraduates, in more than 70 academic programs in arts and sciences, business administration, education and allied professions, engineering and law. There are 401 faculty members, and the average number of students per class section is 28. UD boasts an active service learning program, a non-medical research facility that attracts more than $40 million in annual sponsored research yearly, and the world's largest collection of printed works relating to Mary.

In 2001 *Yahoo! Internet Life* ranked UD as the sixteenth most-wired university nationally. Every student is required to own a computer, and all University-owned housing is fully wired for direct high-speed Internet connection. A Virtual Portfolio project allows new first year students to experience a virtual orientation prior to arriving on campus and then serves as an advising tool and space to preserve their best work. The Portfolio is intended to follow students throughout their UD experience and serve as a final record of that experience in the form of a CD or other media. Sections of the Portfolio not requiring a password can be viewed at http://portfolio.udayton.edu. During the summer of 2003 UD began offering a limited number of e-Learning classes primarily at the 100–300 levels. In keeping with its commitment to use technology effectively to enhance student learning, the e-Learning Lab was created to support faculty's development of on-line material for the classroom.

BASIC COMPETENCIES PROGRAM AT
THE UNIVERSITY OF DAYTON

In 1985 the earlier question of what makes a university experience valuable occupied the minds of the faculty committee charged by the University of Dayton Academic Senate to determine what made our graduates distinctive. A General Education program was being formalized, and businesses were being asked for feedback on the kinds of skills graduates needed for the workplace. Soft skills such as reading comprehension, writing, oral communication, and group work, along with hard skills such as technology familiarity were easy to agree upon. The difficulty lay in finding the proper vocabulary to describe this group of skills, something not as limiting as the phrase basic skills. The committee felt that competency had a better connotation because it moved to a higher level wherein students began with a skill and then grew with the experience throughout their four years at the university.

The committee initially surveyed twelve schools and saw that, in addition to requirements such as Communication 101, Algebra II out of high school, and English composition, computer skills were also emphasized. Familiar with the type of instruction students were receiving in the library, some committee members strongly felt that a wider concept, something more than basic computer skills, perhaps offered through a single required course, was necessary. Provided with sample materials based on information from the Association of College and Research Libraries (ACRL), the committee added Information Literacy to Reading and Writing, Quantitative Reasoning, and Oral Communication to complete the proposed basic competency program.

UNIQUE POSITION OF INFORMATION LITERACY
IN THE COMPETENCY PROGRAM

With the four competencies established and the professional schools able to buy into the idea of competency versus skill, the delivery of the competencies was the next hurdle. Reading and writing, oral communication, and quantitative reasoning had obvious "home bases" in the form of the English, communication, and mathematics departments. Professional schools and programs would be able to choose which course fulfilled the general competencies for their majors from established classes in most cases. Departments, schools, and programs were expected to determine what level of accomplishment would then constitute graduation competencies. To offer programs and the professional schools as much autonomy as possible, responsibility for the delivery of the general information literacy competency was given to classes in the General Education, Humanities Base, and First Year Experience programs to be accomplished before the end of the sophomore year. Competencies were to be phased in over a period of several years, and a Competencies Implementation Subcommittee reporting to the General Education Committee was established. Each competency had a primary implementer responsible for acting as a resource and contact for departments and schools. An overview of the Basic Competency Program is available at (http://academic.udayton.edu/crc/overview/BasicSkillsReport1998.htm).

While the basic goal of allowing each department the opportunity to deliver the information literacy competency was worthwhile, overseeing the information literacy competency presented an organizational challenge. Since no department was expected to be directly responsible for its delivery, an obvious choice would have been the library based on its contributions to the original competency plan as well as its long history of cooperation with the English department in providing library instruction for the composition classes. The information technology group on campus was very open to taking on oversight responsibilities as well. However, since only one of the information literacy competencies was directly related to technology as such, a representative from the library was chosen as implementer.

Information literacy at the University of Dayton occupies a unique position in the competency program itself and the educational goals set for the student body. It was recognized early on as an essential attribute for our distinctive graduates who are expected to follow the call to "learn, lead, and serve." The information literacy program at UD, unlike others at many institutions, has a formal mandate from an administration that recognized the value of lifelong learning and the role of information in decision making. It is not merely a grass roots librarian-led movement that has to struggle for recognition and legitimacy. It is based on strong pedagogical theory and incorporates a solid model for faculty-librarian partnerships. The rest of this chapter will attempt to explain the elements of a solid information literacy program, as well as the structure, problems, and future of the program at the University of Dayton.

ELEMENTS OF A SUCCESSFUL INFORMATION LITERACY PROGRAM – A LITERATURE REVIEW

Information Literacy Should be Viewed as Essential
to the Successful College Experience

Boyer (1987) promoted user education when he stated:

> The college library must be viewed as a vital part of the under-graduate experience . . . We further recommend that every undergraduate student be introduced carefully to the full range

of resources for learning on campus. Students should be given bibliographic instruction and be encouraged to spend at least as much time in the library – using its wide range of resources – as they spend in classes (pp. 164–165).

Nugent and Myers (2000) suggest building on a conceptual framework while introducing the library during the first year. The library should be seen early on as a campus resource, laboratory, and scholar's workstation. Smith (2000) points out that a new paradigm in higher education is emerging as focus shifts from teaching to learning. Education is no longer to be seen only as knowledge dispensed by an expert source. How students can best learn and transfer that experience to their working lives after graduation is most important. Well thought out information literacy programs can help provide students with the ability to apply new skills to new situations as they progress through their college experience. According to Owusu-Ansah (2001), another reality of the current library is its capacity, not as custodian, but rather as provider of resources that enable a student to merely pass a course. Students must be prepared to operate in a society or environment that requires information to solve problems. This is a direct educational role for the academic library.

Information Literacy Should be Taught Through Active Learning

Bren et al. (1998) report much literature indicating that active learning, a hands-on approach with multiple workstations for example, is the most effective means for teaching. Active learning leads to better retention than passive listening in a typical lecture situation. According to Fosmire and Macklin (2002) as well as Brock et al. (2002), problem-based learning, an active learning technique, is a natural fit for integrating information skills into course content since the approach is based on real world issues. Solutions to such problems usually involve more than one right answer and require decisions based on facts. This is a perfect arena for information literacy.

Information Literacy Should Target a Progression of Skills and Concepts

Valentine (1993) found it to be no surprise that undergraduates preferred the easiest and quickest way to do research. Worse yet, it was regarded as almost a status symbol to procrastinate and then rely totally on full text sources available electronically. This observation reinforces the belief that information literacy needs to be introduced early on and reinforced throughout the college experience. Students need to understand the value of a systematic strategy for research as well as when to use it. Relying on the familiar that Valentine pointed out does not expose students to the wide range of resources that today's academic libraries offer. Emmons and Martin (2002) suggest that the availability of information resources continues to outpace student ability to sort and evaluate them. There is a need to force students to continually question and evaluate each step of the research process as it unfolds just as they are initially taught to view writing as an inquiry process. Several authors think that information literacy basics should be introduced through the various types of programs that help students transition from high school to college. Boff and Johnson (2002), Harley (2001), and Parks (1996) all call for laying down the foundations of information literacy within some common intellectual experience that many First Year Experience (FYE) courses offer. These foundations commonly include an orientation to the library, its services, and simple searching techniques that can be expanded further in other course related library instruction at a later date.

Information Literacy Should Emphasize Transferable Concepts over Instruction on How to Use Specific Tools or Libraries

Barclay (1994) recommended taking a serious look at the traditional placement of library instruction in English 101 that has long been the vehicle for other service classes. While this may be the most obvious place for such instruction, it might not be the most appropriate, and librarians should look carefully at the content of such classes. Their efforts might be better spent in areas that need and showcase their expertise and talents. Tiefel (1995) says, "The increase in complexity of the information environment requires . . . teaching the structure of information, use of new electronic formats, and applying critical thinking to information" (p. 329). She argues that because of dramatic changes in technology and the increasing importance of information in today's society, it is paramount that instruction programs focus on teaching concepts rather than tools. Library instruction has broadened to encompass information literacy and course related instruction needs to replace instruction in a vacuum. Bracke and Dickstein (2002) raise the issue of a pedagogical revolution that questions how to reach students who are both computer-savvy and comfortable living life online. Information literacy must somehow convince those students that there is more to research than finding information on the Web.

Information Literacy Programs Encourage Librarian/Faculty Collaboration

Blandy and Libutti (1995) discuss the value of "learning experiences" which translate into the larger world of lifelong applications. Faculty and librarians should seek ways to work together to design effective projects that promote important or new library resources. Visible faculty/librarian collaborative efforts encourage students to see the library as a vital part of the educational experience. Hardesty (1995) encourages librarians to involve faculty in the library instruction program by recognizing, being sensitive to, and working within the typical faculty culture which includes feelings of being overworked, obsession with coverage of material, class autonomy, perceived privileged status, and lack of self-criticism. One on one informal encounters work best and stand a good chance of spreading.

Many authors speak of the importance of developing collaborative partnerships with faculty. Rader (1995) suggests involving faculty by insisting that any requested library instruction be framed in terms of competencies and working with professors to ensure that assignments reflect a range of resources and increasingly more complex search skills as students progress to the end of a chosen degree program. Iannuzzi (1998) proposes identifying campus "hot initiatives," such as student retention or distance learning, and engaging faculty to consider ways information literacy can help. Black et al. (2001) claim that a successful information literacy infrastructure relies on collaboration resulting from relationships developed either informally or through faculty development sessions and liaison programs. Cunningham and Lanning (2002) warn that a "top down buy in" by administration will not automatically guarantee program success because faculty must still be won over. Any attempt at collaboration is essential and must be nurtured through whatever means possible.

Information Literacy Programs Should Not Stand Alone

Carlson and Miller (1984) remind us that the goal of having students function independently is best accomplished when the information is directly related to a specific class because students are more likely to retain something when they actually use it. Dabbour (1997) says that much research points to active learning even on the academic level as the approach preferred over the passive lecture. Talking, listening, writing, reading, and reflecting either alone or in groups has a positive influence on academic success. Elmborg (2003) advocates stressing information literacy in the context of Writing Across the Curriculum so that students see the library's importance in the development of ideas and writing process as it unfolds in all the classes they are taking.

Information Literacy Programs Should Educate the Faculty

Carlson and Miller (1984) point out that the faculty needs to be reminded of the progression from elementary to sophisticated skills because they may easily have forgotten how to do research now. A single faculty member convinced that research has changed can, and often does, influence colleagues. It is critical to keep faculty updated through seminars and workshops. Enthusiasm is contagious and faculty who value research and knowledge of a wide range of resources will not view instruction sessions as mere fillers. Valentine (2001) argues that faculty should be made aware of a serious disconnect between their expectations and student perception of legitimate effort. Students deserve clearly communicated expectations and the time to master whatever skills will lead to the appropriate variety of sources professors expect them to consult. Leckie (1996) is also concerned about the assumptions faculty have of their students' level of understanding about the research process. Having learned research on their own and knowing their area of research well, faculty tend to apply their own model to student behavior. Gonzales (2002) mentions studies that show a direct relationship between faculty use of the library and what value they placed on library instruction for their classes. MacDonald and Dunkelberger (2000) make a case for alerting faculty that students need to be weaned from a growing dependency on full-text databases and trained to make intelligent choices based on analysis and value of search results. Macklin (2001) urges librarians to help faculty understand that familiarity and comfort with computers and technology in general do not translate into the ability to find, select, organize, and communicate relevant information.

Information Literacy Programs Should Encourage the Responsible Use of Increasingly Expensive Library Resources, Print and Electronic

Oberman (1991) claims that, when it comes to the library and access to information, more is not necessarily more, but often less. Students need to be educated to make informed choices, not only among discrete pieces of information, but also about the sources leading to that information. The stand alone card catalog, for example, has been replaced by the online catalog offering access to collections beyond the walls of the user's home library. Kuhlthau (1987) describes a library research process that argues for the need to move from uncertainty and apprehension to satisfaction and accomplishment, not more anxiety and frustration as the number of information sources increases. Farber (1999) points out that the aim of library instruction has not changed over the last 25 years. The goal remains the same, to instruct users in the most effective use of available resources. This applied to print, and it continues to be just as important for electronic sources. Nimon (2001) claims that simply by virtue of existing in an "economic rationalist world," libraries are called upon to demonstrate that their resources and services are worth the investment in time and money.

Information Literacy Programs Should Prepare
Students for Lifelong Learning

Sonntag and Ohr (1996) claim that the university has a duty to prepare students for a world of information, one where change is rapid and usually leads to increasing complexity. Learning environments should be created that challenge students and faculty to work together to search for answers that serve as the basis for informed decision making in a healthy democracy. Clay et al. (2000) in their description of the CSU Information Competence Project make a case in point for how understanding the research process, familiarity with information sources particular to a profession or discipline, and communication of results with appropriate presentation software are central to lifelong learning.

Information Literacy Programs Should Undergo Continuous Assessment

Colborn and Cordell (1998) note that there is increasing pressure from accrediting bodies and from the media to be more responsible for funds allocated to public institutions. Administrations and boards of trustees respond to this pressure by calling for assessment measures on all levels. Shumaker (2003) pointed out that a current challenge facing the higher education environment is to become accountable for how dollars are spent and whether those dollars are being used efficiently as tuition rises and states cut spending. He claims that universities should exist to serve the student first and not the professional interests of the faculty. Rockman (2002) calls for assessment as something to be viewed, not with discomfort or fear, but with intellectual curiosity as a means of assuring quality.

INFORMATION LITERACY AT
THE UNIVERSITY OF DAYTON

A key aspect of the information literacy program at UD is the recognition by the administration that information literacy is an essential component of the educational experience for our students and the approval and financial backing that accompanies this recognition. When the basic skills program was initially conceived, the committee did not consider inclusion of information literacy. There was discussion that familiarity with computers was important, but the concept of information literacy was not introduced into the plan until late in the process. Thanks to the recognition by a professor attending an English 101 library session that what the students were learning that day should be required of every student, the concept of information literacy was no longer just a banner being waved by librarians. Materials from a few schools and the early guidelines from ACRL formed the basis for further discussion of crafting an information literacy competency as part of the basic skills program. Although the committee chose to write its own version of the competency instead of adopting the ACRL guidelines and no librarian was part of that committee, the stage was set and the groundwork was being laid.

The Basic Skills Committee insisted from the very beginning that the information literacy competency would not be developed and administered by any single department. The responsibility for information literacy was viewed early on as resting in the hands of departments, professional schools, and hopefully individual professors. It was very important that all levels buy into the concept and apply the principles to their curriculum and specific discipline needs. Autonomy for the professional schools was especially important. A characteristic shared by many faculty is the desire for total authority within the classroom. Any structure imposed from the top down is frequently met with varying degrees of resistance. This is especially true of anything perceived as irrelevant to content. It became apparent early on that selling the faculty on the idea of information literacy was going to be difficult.

Many faculty tend to take familiarity with the library for granted, and that assumption spills over into what they expect from their students in terms of research. It is not at all unusual for an assignment to be given with no instruction for students other than what appears in the assignment itself. Fortunately, this approach is becoming less common as professors begin to approach librarians for help in guiding students toward resources that will improve the end product of the paper or project. For the faculty then to be told that they would now be responsible for integrating information literacy into their class schedule was easier said than done. It was also important that information literacy be seen as more than computer competence.

A part-time position was created in the library in part for the purpose of serving on the subcommittee that would implement the four basic competencies. The goal of that position was to make sure that faculty and departments understood the information literacy portion of the document, to serve as a resource for suggestions on how to implement the competency in the various disciplines, and to act as a liaison between librarians responsible for instruction and the different units on campus.

Documents and discussion about all phases of the competency program had been made available to the university community. As with many issues, opportunities for input in the process were frequently ignored due to the usual problems of too much to do in too little time. "Suddenly," departments and their faculty were expected to have made substantial progress, not only with the general competencies, but with the graduation competencies as well. In the case of the information literacy competency, it became apparent that the first item of business needed to be a clear explanation of the five components of that competency and some concrete examples explaining how departments across campus could integrate the competency into their curricula and classrooms. Since very few people on campus had even saved copies of the competencies, a website (http://roesch.udayton.edu/services/ref/infolit/) was created with an explanation of the concept of information literacy, the senate approved document, a link to the ACRL competencies, a bibliography, and a simple mnemonic (PIECEs of the Information Puzzle – Problem, Investigation, Evaluation, Communication, and Ethics) to help remember the five parts of the competency (Appendix 1).

It was essential to assure faculty that they were in many instances already incorporating parts of the competency in their current instruction as well as to offer suggestions about how to include other aspects. A small subcommittee with representatives from the programs (Humanities Base, First Year Experience, and General Education) identified in the document as primarily responsible for delivery of the general competencies was formed to identify ways that faculty could implement the competencies. The results of this discussion created an "Expanded Competencies" list which was then added to the website. The idea of this list was to provide suggestions and useful websites that would serve as examples for classroom use. The list was meant to be illustrative and not prescriptive.

Based on the belief that many aspects of information literacy were already in place and only needed some organized formal structure to ensure concept and skill progression while avoiding random delivery, the next step was to examine the existing library component of the English composition and FYE programs, both of which were targeted as vehicles for delivery in the competency document. English 102 at the University of Dayton is part of the general education requirement, and First Year Experience is a required non-credit semester long course. English 102 teaches students the process of a research paper, and FYE includes a study skills section along with other elements meant to assist in the successful transition to a college environment. Over the years a solid relationship had been built between the library and the English department, resulting in required visits during English 101 and 102. The popularity of an introduction to the library during FYE was also growing. While each of the three contacts with librarians was meant to present varied content and build on previous information offered, there had never been a systematic review of that content. The new information literacy competency provided just the framework needed to examine content as well as delivery for consistency and value.

During a series of meetings with librarians responsible for instruction, class content was examined to determine which competencies were being covered or ignored, as well as which ones had a better fit outside of the library. Since the document specified that the general information literacy competency was to be delivered for the most part by the end of the freshman year, librarians broke down the material offered during those classes and aligned it with the competencies. It became apparent that, with the exception of ethical uses of information and technology and familiarity with computer applications for lifelong learning, the other three parts of the competency could easily be displayed in a matrix showing which class introduced which element of the competency. Librarians felt that they could easily cover ethics under the concept of plagiarism and proper documentation of sources. Ethical use of technology was handed over to the Office of Computing Ethics that later developed a module covering existing university policy. Competency with various computer applications and software was left to the communications department that required knowledge of PowerPoint as part of the oral communications competency. Remaining computer competence was to be covered under classroom use with email to professors, participation in threaded discussions, and papers prepared using Word for various class assignments.

Once the matrix was filled in for FYE and English 101 and 102, the remaining Humanities Base Program departments of history, religious studies, and philosophy were contacted and requested to indicate which competencies they already were or would feel comfortable addressing. The communications department was asked to see which competencies were echoed in its own competency requirement. At the end of this process, there emerged a clear picture of where the information literacy competency was being delivered (Appendix 2). All five parts of the competency were covered and everyone, Competencies Implementation Subcommittee and librarians, felt comfortable with the arrangement. With the submission of the grid to, and approval by the General Education Committee, we now had a clearly formatted plan that faculty could consult. A solid foundation was now available from which to reinforce existing concepts and introduce new and more sophisticated ones.

Librarians at UD now had a clear framework on which to build subject specific library instruction requested by professors for more advanced classes. This is a growing area of attention that the library must address and it is becoming increasingly difficult to keep up with the demand. Each librarian has liaison and subject collection duties with several departments on campus. It is up to the librarian to encourage collaboration with the faculty with whom they interact by involving them in the instruction process wherever possible. This is something at which some librarians are better than others, but it is the goal toward which we strive. With few exceptions, all faculty attend instruction sessions requested for their classes. Librarians discuss the material being covered by the class and work with the professor to determine which materials and examples best suit content. Several librarians regularly create web pages to accompany class presentations, and all faculty are encouraged to include links to any of several guides, subject as well as skill related, created by the librarians. Most recently, the requirement that any library session must be tied to a specific assignment is encouraging interaction between faculty and librarians. Librarians serve on a number of key university committees such as the Faculty Development and e-Learning committees. The Writing Across the Curriculum program regularly includes a presentation by a librarian.

Since the information literacy competency was written to include the participation of faculty as an integral part of the program, there have been a number of workshops given to help faculty members understand the competency and their role in its success. With the assistance of the Learning Teaching Center, the implementer of the Reading and Writing Competency organized a series of competency workshops over the last two years. Each implementer had the opportunity to offer as many as three sessions a semester to explain what each competency involved and suggest ways to reinforce competence in the classroom. The departmental role in developing its graduation competencies and assessment methods was also covered.

Faculty workshops were seen as especially critical for information literacy. Given the less than enthusiastic initial response to the idea of information literacy, the main theme of the workshops for that competency was to let faculty know that the concept of information literacy was not as foreign as it might first appear and that help was readily available from the librarians. The first workshop explained the rationale for information literacy, the competency requirement at UD, and what each component of the competency meant. The next three workshops focused on those competencies that were thought to be most confusing or difficult to understand. Topics included the value of choosing a variety of resources to improve research, how to vary search strategy depending on the type of information sought, and how knowledge of the publication cycle and the availability of information generated directly affect success or frustration levels for student research. Two more workshops covered using research logs as a reflective process and assessment tool and creating electronically enhanced syllabi with links to specific library resources and websites of value to the class. The final workshop encouraged faculty to use the QuickPlace tool as a platform for a web enhanced syllabus. QuickPlace allows the user to create links to documents and web pages, as well as share work in progress and carry on discussions. The idea was to introduce faculty to an easy way to incorporate computer skills in a very practical and valuable fashion for themselves and their students.

Information literacy workshops tried to reinforce the topics presented for the reading and writing competency because the material was closely related. The theme for all workshops was that, if faculty are truly interested in helping students improve research skills leading to better papers and assignments, professors must help guide students to the resources they need and build into their syllabi opportunities and time for students to master the new skills. The library regularly offers workshops on recently acquired resources and refresher sessions on enhanced features of existing databases. Faculty are consistently encouraged to direct their students to those tools that lead to proficiency and understanding in the discipline. While attendance at workshops was never overwhelming, faculty who attended agreed that the information presented was useful on a practical level and helpful in explaining the concepts involved in information literacy.

As work on implementing information literacy continues, the entire delivery structure of the competency has recently been assessed. We examined the matrix for delivery of information literacy and decided to look at what content could be best delivered through a computerized approach. This move grew out of the request from the College of Arts and Sciences to make better use of the Virtual Portfolio that was developed in part to house the content for the First Year Experience course. Librarians and those involved with the First Year Experience were concerned for some time that the study skills portion of the course that included information about the library was not being adequately and consistently addressed. The decision was made to transfer selected content of an introductory nature to the Portfolio. With the assurance that all freshmen would be required to read the information and submit a response (a feature available in the Portfolio), basic library orientation material was selected for transfer to the Portfolio format. Some of this material can be viewed at (http://portfolio.udayton.edu/learning/libraryresources).

The English 101 class visit to the library was also re-examined with the intent of presenting content via a computerized tutorial. Librarians had determined that material was often being presented in a vacuum with no specific assignment in mind. Even though, theoretically, the parts of the information literacy competency for that class had been specifically chosen to respond to the need for instruction in helping with the resource based papers assigned in class, faculty were hard pressed to coordinate the usual library presentation with their class schedules. While the English department was somewhat reluctant to give up the familiar library visit, they did see the value of presenting a conceptual approach to searching any electronic resource versus a detailed explanation of how to use the online catalog. Today's students are technologically oriented, and a computerized tutorial available would ensure access to the information at any time, not just when the class visited the library. A well-planned and easily modified tutorial would free librarians to apply their expertise for subject specific classes during an otherwise very busy time of the semester. The librarians also discovered that the most important information literacy material scheduled for English 101 was actually conceptual in nature and that too much time was being devoted to demonstrating the online catalog and the recommended multidisciplinary database for locating periodical articles. Computerized instruction modules would offer a solution on many levels.

The decision was made to break with tradition and take away the face-to-face contact with the English 101 classes. The material normally presented in the class was transferred to a tutorial that will cover different sources of information, what electronic tools are appropriate for locating the information, and the difference between scholarly and popular sources. Demonstration of the online catalog and database will be handled in a series of short automated interactive modules. These are intended to be accessed through the Portfolio and will be available at any time and as often as necessary for review.

English 102 will also have online content covering how to refine a search topic, searching techniques, and explanations of different useful databases. The English 102 class visits to the library will continue, but will incorporate more time for hands-on instruction covering the research process, choosing the right tool for an information need, and the evaluation of information sources. These concepts offer an opportunity for librarians to concentrate more on discussion in the class and less on repetitive demonstrations. Engaging the students in problem solving with the hands-on portion of the class was seen as the most valuable and productive form of librarian/student interaction. Realigning the content for English 101 and 102 will also enable librarians to devote more time to the increasing requests for subject specific library instruction. We want to develop a strong instruction model based on teachable moments, times when students are most receptive because they have a clearly defined information need. To encourage and assist librarians in their teaching mission, a shared course portfolio for the library component of English composition was developed. Librarians can evaluate themselves on teaching techniques and include examples of their class presentations and strategies. The portfolio can be viewed at (http://academic.udayton.edu/LibraryPortfolio).

We feel that the information literacy program at UD is capable of building the solid foundation needed for academic success. It gives faculty a clear picture of what skill level students are bringing to advanced classes as they continue their degree programs. The UD model has the advantage of placing the delivery of information literacy in both the departments' and librarians' hands. Librarians acting as subject specialists and department liaisons can position themselves to serve in a resource capacity of what and how to introduce appropriate level information literacy competencies. Faculty are encouraged to reinforce the basic competencies and consider what additional skills are needed to pursue the research component of advanced classes. The Basic Competencies Program includes a requirement meant to address acquiring those advanced research skills. Each department is required to develop a set of graduation competencies for reading and writing, oral communication, and quantitative reasoning as well information literacy. The graduation information literacy competency is to be directed specifically at the research skills needed for success in upper level classes. To allow as much autonomy as possible, departments were given the choice of adopting the general competencies as graduation competencies or examining the requirements particular to their disciplines and coming up with competencies that reflect those special needs.

To encourage departments to adopt the latter approach, each department chair was visited individually. At the meeting, each chair was given an explanation of the information competency, the general competency matrix, an explanation of the options available for developing graduation competencies, and an offer of assistance from a librarian, meeting with the entire department if requested. In an effort to persuade the department to develop graduation competencies specific to its discipline, each chair was given several discipline specific subject guides to the literature and databases in the field as well as associations and libraries known for strong collections in their area. It was suggested that the guides be used as starting points for departmental discussions about what skills they would require of graduates in their discipline. Due to poor timing, near the end of the semester when faculty are particularly busy, lack of interest, other priorities, or lack of direction, only three progress reports were submitted. To spur the departments along, the implementation committee approved a template developed by one of the members that was sent to departments. The committee has not seen any department graduation competencies, but has been assured that they will be forthcoming.

PROBLEMS AND THE FUTURE OF
INFORMATION LITERACY AT UD

It is difficult to assess the success of the information literacy program at this point. The General Education Committee has approved the delivery of the competency as presented on the grid. Librarians have not found structuring instruction classes within the framework of the competencies too rigid or overly confining. The ongoing assessment of the program has proven the flexibility of the matrix approach. We have the endorsement of the administration and financial support to purchase software as well as pay for additional help to develop the planned tutorial. The University is more than committed to making information literacy an important part of the educational goals for its students.

The future is not without problems however. Widespread acceptance and belief in the value of a basic competency program that includes information literacy will probably never be a sure thing. Winning over the faculty whose agendas are sometimes more concerned with dispensing content than with finding out the best way to help students learn, will never be easy. Librarians will have to deliberately make information literacy a priority in the classes they teach and a point of discussion in the contacts they have with faculty, especially those new to the university. Librarians will also have to develop an "information literacy mindset" so that each contact with students, even at the reference desk, is viewed as a teachable moment. The laptop requirement for students entering the university makes it imperative that we offer those students every opportunity to understand and use the wealth of information at their fingertips. Students' tuition goes to paying for a growing and frequently bewildering array of databases made possible through UD's participation in the OhioLINK consortium. We will have to continue to encourage the responsible use of those increasingly expensive library resources by both students and faculty. Existing partnerships with the faculty must be maintained and strengthened so that additional collaborative efforts can take root.

A Competencies Resource Center (http://academic.udayton.edu/crc) has been developed to support faculty and students across the curriculum with practical implementation suggestions, examples, and background for all the competencies. Each of the four competencies will be represented with links to publications, workshop resources, and helpful best practices sites and examples. Keeping contributions current and useful will be a continuing challenge. Assessment poses its own set of problems. Assessing how well a specific instruction class went and whether the students retained the material presented that single time is not the same as assessing how the instruction impacts students' performance in class, much less their learning for a lifetime. Any true assessment effort must be tied to working with the faculty, and we must certainly look for additional opportunities for collaboration. Another area for collaboration lies with K-12 educators and librarians. Several high school classes visit the university library each semester, and it would be valuable to work with teachers and school librarians to help them understand what skills and concepts should be considered essential entry-level competencies on the college level.

A fairly recent opportunity for future collaboration is the partnership that the University of Dayton has begun with the Dayton Public Schools. UD and DPS will be starting a school, tentatively called the Early College Academy, with a goal of challenging at risk students to remain in school and earn college credit at the same time. The information literacy program has enjoyed some notoriety in this joint endeavor since the organizing committee included information literacy and technology as one of the initial advisory committees.

CONCLUSION

The University of Dayton's vision statement, "To be a national leader in Catholic higher education," is expressed in four key outcomes. Three of them,

- *Distinctive Graduates*, prepared for life and work, who combine competence in a discipline or a professional field, broad liberal learning, strength of character, and skills in building community into a commitment to lifelong learning, leadership, and service.
- *Connected Learning and Scholarship* that explore the connections among disciplines, extend beyond the campus to integrate theory with the realities of professional practice, and contribute to the strengthening of public and community life.
- *Outstanding Resource Management* that enables us to allocate resources in a way that is both mission-driven and market-focused, improve the educational quality of our facilities and campus, strengthen our financial position, raise substantial and sustainable gift support for our vision, and strengthen our reputation for educational leadership (University of Dayton Vision 2005 document).

resonate strongly with the importance of information literacy.

Distinctive graduates must have the skills to make a difference in the community. The phrase "Learn, Lead, Serve" is frequently used on campus to describe what the University of Dayton is about. Bruce (1997) listed the seven faces of information literacy, the final characteristic of which is a person who uses information wisely for the benefit of others. A strong emphasis on the information literacy competency will empower graduates to use what they have learned and experienced for changing their environment through leadership and service. *Connected learning and scholarship* are supposed to focus on solving problems to improve the human condition. Information literacy is the best way to ensure the proper perspective on problems and questions, apply knowledge to real-life situations, and communicate solutions to a variety of audiences. Information literate graduates can make a difference on the local and global level. The commitment to *outstanding resource management* provides a practical rationale for insisting on information literacy. Students and parents are right to expect value for their investment. Instruction for the efficient use and appropriate choice of resources is a necessary part of any information literacy program. The true value of a college education is more than a coveted diploma, professional credentials, or status that accompanies graduation from a prestigious university. Higher education should mean the passion, zest, and the skills to continue learning for a lifetime, and information literacy is a key component of that goal.

REFERENCES

Barclay, D. A. (1994). The role of freshman writing in academic bibliographic instruction. *The Journal of Academic Librarianship, 20,* 213–217.

Black, C., Crest, S., & Volland, M. (2001). Building a successful information literacy infrastructure on the foundation of librarian-faculty collaboration. *Research Strategies, 18,* 215–225.

Blandy, S. G., & Libutti, P. O. (1995). As the cursor blinks: Electronic scholarship and undergraduates in the library. *Library Trends, 44,* 279–305.

Boff, C., & Johnson, K. (2002). The library and first-year experience courses: A nationwide study. *Reference Services Review, 30,* 277–287.

Boyer, E. L. (1987). *College: The undergraduate experience in America.* New York: Harper & Row.

Bren, B., Hillemann, B., & Topp, V. (1998). Effectiveness of hands-on instruction of electronic resources. *Research Strategies, 16,* 41–51.

Brock, K. B., Brenenson, S., & Lenn, K. (2002). Problem-based learning: Evolving strategies and conversations for library instruction. *Reference Services Review, 4,* 355–358.

Bruce, C. (1997). *Seven faces of information literacy in higher education.* Retrieved May 15, 2003, from http://sky.fit.qut.edu.au/~bruce/inflit/faces/faces1.htm.

Carlson, D., & Miller, R. H. (1984). Librarians and teaching faculty: Partners in bibliographic instruction. *College & Research Libraries, 45,* 483–491.

Clay, S. T., Harlan, S., & Swanson, J. (2000). Mystery to mastery: The CSU information competence project. *Research Strategies, 17,* 157–166.

Colborn, N. W., & Cordell, R. M. (1998). Moving from subjective to objective assessments of your instruction program. *Reference Services Review, 26,* 125–137.

Cunningham, T. H., & Lanning, S. (2002). New frontier trail guides: Faculty-librarian collaboration on information literacy. *Reference Services Review, 4,* 343–348.

Dabbour, K. S. (1997). Applying active learning methods to the design of library instruction for a freshman seminar. *College & Research Libraries, 58,* 299–308.

Elmborg, J. K. (2003). Information literacy and writing across the curriculum: Sharing the vision. *Reference Services Review, 31,* 68–80.

Emmons, M., & Martin, W. (2002). Engaging conversation: Evaluating the contribution of library instruction to the quality of student research. *College & Research Libraries, 63,* 545–560.

Farber, E. (1999). College libraries and the teaching/learning process: A 25-year reflection. *The Journal of Academic Librarianship, 25,* 171–177.

Fosmire, M., & Macklin, A. (2002). Riding the active learning wave: Problem-based learning as a catalyst for creating faculty-librarian instructional partnerships. *Issues in Science and Technology Librarianship, 34,* Retrieved on May 15, 2003, from http://www.library.ucsb.edu/istl/.

Hardesty, L. (1995). Faculty culture and bibliographic instruction: An exploratory analysis. *Library Trends, 44,* 339–367.

Harley, B. (2001). Freshmen, information literacy, critical thinking and values. *Reference Services Review, 29,* 301–305.

Iannuzzi, P. (1998). Faculty development and information literacy: Establishing campus partnerships. *Reference Services Review, 26,* 97–102, 116.

Knox, W. E., Lindsay, P., & Kolb, M. N. (1993). *Does college make a difference?: Long-term changes in activities and attitudes.* Westport, CT: Greenwood Press.

Kuhlthau, C. C. (1987). An emerging theory of library instruction. *School Library Media Quarterly, 16*(1), 23–28.

Leckie, G. J. (1996). Desperately seeking citations: Uncovering faculty assumptions about the undergraduate research process. *The Journal of Academic Librarianship, 22,* 201–208.

MacDonald, B., & Dunkelberger, R. (2000). Full-text database dependency: An emerging trend among undergraduate library users? *Research Strategies, 16,* 301–307.

Macklin, A. S. (2001). Integrating information literacy using problem-based learning. *Reference Services Review, 29,* 306–313.

Nimon, M. (2001). The role of academic libraries in the development of the information literate student: The interface between librarian, academic and other stakeholders. *Australian Academic and Research Libraries, 32*(1), 43–52.

Nugent, C., & Myers, R. (2000). Learning by doing: The freshman-year curriculum and library instruction. *Research Strategies, 17,* 147–155.

Oberman, C. (1991). Avoiding the cereal syndrome, or critical thinking in the electronic environment. *Library Trends, 39,* 189–202.

Owusu-Ansah, E. K. (2001). The academic library in the enterprise of colleges and universities: Toward a new paradigm. *The Journal of Academic Librarianship, 27,* 282–294.

Rader, H. B. (1995). Information literacy and the undergraduate curriculum. *Library Trends, 44,* 270–278.

Rockman, I. F. (2002). The importance of assessment. *Reference Services Review, 30,* 181–182.

Shumaker, J. W. (2003). *The higher education environment and the role of the academic library.* Retrieved on May 15, 2003, from http://acrl.telusys.net/acrl/charlotte/program/shumakerpaper.pdf.

Snavely, L. (2000). The learning library. *Research Strategies, 17,* 79–84.

Sonntag, G., & Ohr, D. M. (1996). The development of a lower-division, general education, course-integrated information literacy program. *College & Research Libraries, 17,* 331–338.

State University of New York (1992). SUNY 2000, college expectations: The report of the SUNY Task Force on college entry-level knowledge and skills. Albany, NY: State University of New York.

Tiefel, V. M. (1995). Library user education: Examining its past, projecting its future. *Library Trends, 44,* 318–338.

Valentine, B. (1993). Undergraduate research behavior: Using focus groups to generate theory. *The Journal of Academic Librarianship, 19,* 300–304.

Valentine, B. (2001). The legitimate effort in research papers: Student commitment versus faculty expectation. *The Journal of Academic Librarianship, 27,* 107–115.

INFORMATION LITERACY INITIATIVES IN HIGHER EDUCATION: ORIGINS, OPTIONS AND OBSERVATIONS

Nancy P. Thomas

INTRODUCTION

It should come as little surprise that the technological advances in information storage and retrieval have led many in the information professions to renewed concerns for educating student users in college libraries. The introduction of electronic information retrieval methods and an explosion in the amount of information available online and across media have created a sort of instructional imperative, to which many in the academic community have responded. This move, which characterizes so many programs in public, school, and academic libraries, is consistent with contemporary models of librarianship that emphasize information access over information acquisition and storage. This agenda has important implications for 21st century library administrators, reference professionals, and LIS educators, even though the practice of "teaching the use of books and libraries" (Rothstein, 1955, p. 14) has 19th century roots. Indeed, from an early date academic librarians viewed "bibliographical information" provided by "the librarian of their college or university" (Adams, 1887, quoted in Rothstein) as key in enabling students "in all their after lives to do their individual work more readily and successfully (Barnard, 1838, quoted in Rothstein).

The articles by Donham and Tiller in this issue of *Advances in Library Administration and Organization* describe two contemporary efforts to provide comprehensive instruction to undergraduates within multi-faceted, systematically

Advances in Library Administration and Organization
Advances in Library Administration and Organization, Volume 21, 257–266
© 2004 Published by Elsevier Ltd.
ISSN: 0732-0671/doi:10.1016/S0732-0671(04)21016-1

planned, content-based, collaboratively taught instructional programs. Donham's project has been in place for several years, although, as she notes, it is still very much a work in progress. In addition to describing strategies and structures that have helped make the program a success, Donham provides a snapshot of what it means to integrate an information skills agenda into a variety of disciplines and departments, and to tailor such a program to meet the exigencies of a particular (e.g. a one-course-at-a-time academic calendar) institution and its unique requirements. In her article, Tiller steps us through her initial efforts at program planning and implementation at a private university that operates on a more traditional academic schedule. Taken together, the articles by Donham and Tiller provide valuable insights into the dynamics at work in the implementation of a comprehensive information literacy program, while drawing attention to the role that institutional context plays in launching, building, and sustaining interdisciplinary initiatives. At another level, however, the projects described have much to say about contemporary academic library programs as they relate to un-dergraduate education, the skills demanded of reference librarians involved in such programs, and about information literacy as it is understood and promoted in the library community.

The Lessons of History

The contributions that Donham and Tiller make to our appreciation of the problems and processes involved in creating information literacy programs at an undergraduate level can best be understood when considered within the larger framework of American library history and tradition. The fact that neither author references this history speaks eloquently to the widespread acceptance as best practice of specific ideas, strategies, and frameworks that actually developed over time in a variety of contexts and programs. However, enthusiasm for "instruction and aid to undergraduates" (Barnard, 1883, quoted in Rothstein, 1955, p. 14) surfaced relatively early among 19th century college librarians. "A librarian should be more than a keeper of books," wrote Otis Robinson, "he [sic] should be an educator" (quoted in Tuckett & Stoffle, 1984, p. 58). "All that is taught in college amounts to very little," Robinson continued, "unless we can send students out self-reliant in their investigations" (p. 58).

One of the first to actively encourage library staff to provide search assistance to student users was Justin Winsor (1831–1897), the "professor of books" at Harvard University. "If our colleges would pay more attention to the methods by which a subject is deftly attacked, and would teach the true use of encyclopedic and bibliographic helps," Winsor wrote, "they would do much to make the library more serviceable" (quoted in Rothstein, 1955, p. 24). For his part, William Frederick Poole (1821–1894), favored the creation of a university course in the "scientific methods of using books" and sought faculty status for professor-librarians to whom would fall the responsibility for providing such instruction. Raymond C. Davis (1836–1919) created such a course at the University of Michigan as early as 1881.

As forward looking as these early library educators were, it was Melvil Dewey (1851–1931) who, at the turn of the 20th century, finally regularized reference, established "organized personal assistance," as an integral instrument of the Columbia College's library's educational purpose. For Dewey, the "first and paramount duty of the Reference Librarian" was to set an example, counsel students, and train library users in the delights of the library and the "habit of hunting" information (Rothstein, 1955, p. 28). William Warner Bishop (1871–1955) was among the first to envision instruction in the use of books and libraries as a sequential program beginning in elementary school and continuing until a student graduated from college. These early themes were taken up by Lucy Maynard Salmon (1853–1927), a history professor at Vassar, who, at an ALA conference in 1913, argued persuasively for the incorporation of library skills instruction within the context of regular college courses. In order to put her ideas on library instruction into play, Salmon (1986) created a course for new students that included a library tour, and designed "bibliographical work" within a..."definitely planned,... systematically carried out" progression of courses, "involving college librarians and teaching faculty working together" (p. 93).

The assumptions, objectives, and structures advanced as frameworks for the projects being implemented by Donham and Tiller are also informed by programs launched and conducted at Stephens College, Peabody College, Wayne State University, and Earlham College. These programs, which flourished in the middle of the last century, were specifically designed to ensure that instruction in library skills was directly tied to the curricular context of regular college classrooms. The first of these, the program launched at Stephens College (Columbia, MO) in the early 1930s was the brainchild of B. Lamar Johnson (1904–1995). Johnson's project emphasized the development of good study skills as prerequisites for learning in addition to instruction in the use of the library resources. Through a sequence of carefully designed courses, Johnson sought to place library use at the vortex of the instructional process. The fact that Johnson occupied positions as both the college librarian and the dean in charge of instruction greatly facilitated the implementation of his ideas at Stephens, and he himself admitted that the adoption of his program would have been impossible had he not had the authority to impose it on both faculty and students (Hardesty et al., 1986).

Johnson's faith in the value of the library as the linchpin of a college education was shared by Louis Shores (1904–1981) at Peabody College for Teachers (Nashville, TN), who in the 1930s and early 1940s launched an ambitious program based on his idea that the library is the college and the college, the library. Shores (1986) vision presupposed an academic environment where all the teachers would be library-trained and charged with supervising and tutoring students in reading and research projects. Two significant contributions to the discourse of academic librarianship were Shore's ideas that learning should be student-centered and interdisciplinary and that creating independent learners was the appropriate goal of education.

A third major and influential program was created by Patricia Bryan Knapp (1914–1972) at Wayne State University (Detroit, MI) in the early 1960s. Incorporating themes from earlier initiatives, Knapp's (1977, 1986) projects provided library instruction as a cooperative effort between university librarians and the teaching faculty. Among insights developed through her research were an understanding that library use is a multidimensional activity involving "knowledge, skills, and attitudes" (Farber, 1995, p. 24), and that library use skills are best learned over time and when presented within the context of ongoing classroom assignments. In fact, the systematicity of the instructional program, her emphasis on "process" over "content," and her understanding of the key roles played by course instructors are now regarded as "givens" for the successful implementation of instructional programming.

No review of the development and history of bibliographic instruction would be complete without noting the exemplary program created at Earlham College (Richmond, IN) in the mid 1960s. Implemented by librarians Evan Ira Farber, Thomas B. Kirk and James R. Kennedy, Earlham's program was founded on the bedrock of active cooperation between departmental scholars and college librarians, and featured three central principles: integration, demonstration, and gradation (Kennedy, 1986, p. 233). Integration was achieved by embedding all library instruction within courses that most often required students to use library resources. Demonstration was chosen as the central instructional strategy and included an introduction to the search process as well as to specific types of library resources. Gradation was achieved through the implementation of a planned sequence of instructional sessions, which were conducted over the four years of a student's college career. Elements identified as key to the implementation of the program included: rapport and synergy between the librarians and the teaching faculty; the selection of appropriate courses for library skills integration and appropriate projects within the courses; small class size; and a "just in time" approach, which based decisions related to course scheduling directly on the needs of students.

A Tale of Two Libraries

It is evident that Donham and Tiller's programs owe much to insights gleaned from the work of these academic library pioneers. It is worth noting as well that in both instances, program implementation is addressed within a college and university with strong commitments to liberal arts education – also reminiscent of earlier comprehensive programs discussed above. In particular, a systematically planned and conducted, fully-integrated and " spiraling" information skills curriculum, faculty-librarian partnerships, and point of need instruction, and an emphasis on process skills over tool skills, are but a few of the elements that characterized earlier programs. This is not to say that the projects Donham and Tiller describe are merely derivative. On the contrary, Donham and Tiller make an important contribution to a discussion of comprehensive, integrated information literacy programs in undergraduate settings in that they provide a clearly delineated theory base anchored in constructivism, and models that delineate activities and roles to guide program planning and implementation. Important as well to both programs is their emphasis on intercollegiate relationships and trust, the alignment of information literacy standards with academic standards and competencies recognized across campus; and the use of web-based strategies as an integral part of program delivery. In addition, both Donham and Tiller make unique contributions in explaining program specifics relative to the size and complexities of their own particular situations.

In her article, Donham provides both conceptual and theoretical frameworks for an integrated information skills curriculum, and the strategies used for its implementation. Donham's model outlines the processes involved, delineates roles for librarians and departmental faculty in teaching and learning, and illustrates the many steps and complexities involved in information seeking and making sense of information through the creation and completion of students' information-based projects.

The intent of program planners in the project at the University of Dayton described by Tiller is to work from the "inside out," embedding information literacy goals within a discipline-articulated agenda of core competencies. However, at this point in time, library professionals appear to be championing the project, but from the outside. This observation is based on an apparent emphasis in the article on raising awareness and expectations through campus workshops, and references to cultural constraints and faculty foot-dragging. However, one of the values of Tiller's article lies in the description of the preliminaries to program implementation and the serious barriers and challenges – both external and internal, that the program faces in a university of this size and complexity. The problems Tiller has encountered speak directly to the issues that exist for librarians on campuses where the centrality of their instructional role has yet to be fully realized. One advantage of considering the Donham and Tiller articles together is that the strategies employed in the one may help readers understand how the problems encountered in the other can be resolved. The fact that strategies Tiller plans to implement have proven successful in Donham's program is reassuring.

The experiences recounted by Donham and Tiller are useful, too, as reminders there are no quick fixes when it comes to creating integrated literacy programs at the college level, and no single template can be devised that will be appropriate for all of them: academic departments and disciplines will dictate approaches, and their issues will vary from one university or college to the next as they do among departments within the same institution. They also point to the continuing dilemma experienced by many academic libraries whose programs are considered irrelevant to departmental courses. Although Donham's librarians have success-fully negotiated places for information literacy goals with competencies adopted in a number of departments, there are still many departments and faculty members who have yet to participate fully. Donham's scheduling of library instruction in sessions outside the normal classroom, which "eases the pressure for faculty who are concerned about using too much class time for information literacy topics" is suggestive that faculty understandings of the contribution of information literacy skills can make to content learning is still incomplete.

The truth is that full acceptance cannot be mandated by the administration or gained through professional hand waving. As Donham suggests, they will probably have to be built one relationship at a time. For her part, Tiller describes a higher-education culture resistant to change and one where tradition holds the individual classroom as sacrosanct. This assertion seems to be born out in the reported reluctance of professors at the University of Dayton to take advantage of the instructional potential the library represents. This begs the question, what accounts for the failure of some faculty to "buy into" the importance of library-assisted teaching and learning opportunities? While marginalization may be too strong a term to use in characterizing the library's situation on many college campuses, it is clear that there is still much "educating to be done before library professionals are considered instructional resources."

Reference, Research, and Information Processes

One strategy to gain legitimacy is surely to anchor an argument for the inclusion of information literacy within conceptual frameworks and discipline-based research activities. Indeed, one of the most valuable aspects of Donham's work is the description of how information seeking and information skills instruction can be seen to fit within a systematic program of scholarly research. Having said that, it is important to note that library use or reporting (here defined as an the retrieval and examination of primary and secondary source materials to make an argument, report findings, or defend a thesis statement) is not the same as undertaking original, basic, or applied "research" as it is understood in the academy. Stoan (1984) describes academic research as "a quest for knowledge" (p. 165), entailing the "systematic collection of original and "uninterpreted" data (p. 100). Although this seems like a straightforward idea, the fact is that many times librarians do not make the distinction between information seeking and "research" in its academic meaning in discussing information literacy and/or information skills. As Stoan argues, the two are not equivalent and in fact do not "bear any organic relationship to each other" (p. 105). It should be noted here that it is not being claimed that librarians do not understand the difference between information and gathering for an information project and academic research, but that their use of the term "research" when describing the former can be confusing and misleading.

Stoan (1984) has argued that the failure to make this distinction is more than a semantic gaff, because the misunderstandings between librarians and academic faculty that can occur when librarians fail to distinguish between the two leads many academic researchers to discount librarians as capable collaborators in guiding students. It is perhaps for this reason, that for example, Kuhlthau (1991) labels her model the ISP (Information Searching Process), and frames her work in terms of information seeking and learning from information rather than as "research." Donham also draws attention to the distinction articulately when she writes: "Strategies, skills, techniques, and even concepts in information literacy vary, sometimes subtly, sometimes dramatically, across disciplines. Students ought to have the opportunity to experience information seeking in a variety of disciplinary contexts as one way of considering the research disposition of scientists as compared to artists as compared to psychologists, etc." While not addressing the issue of research vs. information seeking directly, Donham's description of the integrative practices at Cornell College appears to resolve the problem in structuring lessons so that professors "especially qualified to provide education related to the later steps of the information process," do so, whereas librarians provide education related to the earlier stages. The Cornell approach also reflects Stoan's (1984) view that college students should not be taught a single set of generic strategies, but should rather develop their own personal style, one that reflects their own personal experience in information seeking and the particular academic discipline within which the information seeking and academic research is undertaken.

Library/Librarian Models

It is probably unnecessary to point out that an academic library up to the challenge of supporting such ambitious plans as those described by Donham and Tiller is the very antithesis of the old warehouse model. Indeed the library constructed in these articles is a dynamic workspace and campus resource staffed by pro-active, flexible, technologically adept, politically astute, service oriented individuals committed to promoting the goals of the parent institution through the library's program. In addition, the librarians upon whom the responsibility for making connections across campus appears to rest, must, along with acquiring, organizing, and maintaining resources, be capable teachers and staff developers, with the ability to deliver instruction and professional services within an array of scheduled and point of need venues. In a very real sense, the multifaceted, multitasking roles created for librarians within the projects Tiller and Donham describe raise a series of issues with implications not only in terms of hiring library personnel but for recruitment and pre-service training of the next generation of academic library professionals.

Information Literacy

As mentioned earlier, technological innovations, the proliferation of electronic databases, and widespread Internet use have caused the LIS community to re-think and re-frame library skills as information skills. In turn, recent discourse, reflected in the Donham and Tiller articles, employs information literacy as terminology to discuss information skills that appear isomorphic with an array of cognitive skills, including the ability to think critically, and to locate, evaluate and use information for problem solving and decision-making. Defining information literacy in this way presents what is essentially a set of cognitive skills in a distinctly utilitarian light, an emphasis that is reinforced when the library takes skills for lifelong learning and the workplace as its instructional goals. While the redefinition of library skills in this way can certainly be defended on both theoretical and pragmatic grounds, especially when it works to strengthen a library's claims to legitimacy and value, it also raises some issues and questions that it might be of use to consider. In particular, might there be losses as well as gains in predicating the library agenda exclusively in terms of information literacy as it is defined in this way?

The widespread acceptance of the term information literacy by the LIS community has made it a trope referenced by practitioners and the academy alike to orient and justify an agenda for practice and research. Both Donham and Tiller accept the term in a self-evident way, and they are at pains to show that aspects of the libraries' information literacy (e.g. critical thinking, life long learning, etc.) program line up well with the educational values and agendas of their parent institutions. This is a sound strategy in that it, in each case, it explicates the library's connections to the college/university and its commitment to the college's/university's instructional project. However, one might ask whether or not a strong information literacy agenda runs the risk of appearing to reduce the importance of disciplinary competence and other kinds of intellectual skills (e.g. those related to human creativity, notions of justice, aesthetics etc.) and to dictate for all educational endeavors one evaluative criteria (e.g. utility in the workplace)? Of course, framing connections to academic competencies as the authors do in their programs inevitably draws attention to certain aspects of a project at the expense of others. And, to be sure, both authors make passing reference to the benefits derived from a liberal arts education. However, the emphasis on skill development at least suggests a valuing of the utilitarian over intellectual goals. To what extent this view is embraced more generally on the authors' respective campuses might be an issue worth pursuing, particularly if the adoption of an information literacy orientation could be interpreted as a move to professionalize liberal arts or shape its agenda.

Finally, one aspect of information literacy that goes unexplored by Donham and Tiller is worth a mention here – the notion of what constitutes information. While the fact that Donham and Tiller do not consider this issue in their articles is not unusual given their goals in describing their instructional programs, their implicit acceptance of information as transparent and unproblematic – as something to be "searched for" or retrieved from information resources – obscures the fact that information is a social construction reflective of a particular world view. The implications for LIS in adopting information literacy as a trope by researchers and practitioners also goes unexamined. When this occurs, LIS misses an opportunity to explore new and complex issues and problems related more generally to both information and information literacy.

REFERENCES

Farber, E. I. (1995). Bibliographic instruction, briefly. In: The fifteen anniversary task force (Comp), *Information For a New Age: Redefining The Librarian* (pp. 23–34). Library Instruction Round Table of the American Library Association. Englewood, CO: Libraries Unlimited.

Hardesty, L. L., Schmitt, J. P., & Tucker, J. M. (Comps) (1986). *User instruction in academic libraries: A century of selected readings.* Metuchen, NJ: Scarecrow Press.

Kennedy, J. R., Jr. (1986). Integrated library instruction. In: Compiled by L. L. Hardesty, J. P. Schmitt & J. M. Thatcher. *User Instruction in Academic Libraries: A Century of Selected Readings* (pp. 231–242). Metuchen, NJ: Scarecrow Press, 1986.

Knapp, P. B. (1986). A suggested program of college instruction in the use of the library. In:
L. L. Hardesty, J. P. Schmitt & J. M. Tucker (Comps), *User Instruction in Academic Libraries:
A Century of Selected Readings* (pp. 151–166). Metuchen, NJ: Scarecrow Press.

Kuhlthau, C. C. (1991). Inside the search process: Information seeking from the user's perspective.
Journal of the American Society for Information Science, 42(5), 361–371.

Rothstein, S. (1955). *The development of reference services through academic traditions, public
library practice and special librarianship.* Chicago, IL: Association of College and Reference.

Salmon, L. M. (1986). Instruction in the use of a college library. In: L. L. Hardesty, J. P. Schmitt
& J. M. Tucker (Comps), *User Instruction in Academic Libraries: A Century of Selected
Readings* (pp. 86–101). Metuchen, NJ: Scarecrow Press.

Shores, L. (1986). The liberal arts college, a possibility in 1954? In: L. L. Hardesty, J. P. Schmitt
& J. M, Tucker (Comps), *User Instruction in Academic Libraries: A Century of Selected
Readings* (pp. 121–29). Metuchen, NJ: Scarecrow Press.

Stoan, S. K. (1984). Research and library skills: An analysis and interpretation. *College and Research
Libraries, 45*(2), 99–108.

Tuckett, H. W., & Stoffle, C. J. (1984). Learning theory and the self-reliant library user. *RQ, 24*(1),
58–66.

A HISTORY OF LIBRARY ASSESSMENT AT THE UNIVERSITY OF NORTHERN COLORADO: FIFTEEN YEARS OF DATA ANALYSIS AND PROGRAM CHANGES

Lisa Blankenship and Adonna Fleming

INTRODUCTION

In 1985 the Colorado State Legislature mandated, in Article 13 of HB 1187, that institutions of higher education become "accountable for demonstrable improvements in student knowledge, capacities and skills between entrance and graduation" (Colorado Revised Statutes, 1988). As a result, the University of Northern Colorado Libraries became involved in the assessment process. In 1988 the UNC Libraries formed the University Libraries Assessment Committee, comprised of library faculty, classified staff and an administrator in an ex officio position. The Assessment Committee conducted the first survey to assess user satisfaction in the fall of 1988. Since that time, the committee has conducted an assessment program on an annual basis. Today, the UNC Libraries are evaluated in three areas: collections, services, and instruction. Over time, the assessment tools and survey methodologies have evolved, and a variety of program changes have resulted. In this article, we will summarize the history of the assessment program at the UNC Libraries, track selected questions through the years, and describe the resulting changes in the UNC Libraries programs.

Advances in Library Administration and Organization
Advances in Library Administration and Organization, Volume 21, 267–282
© 2004 Published by Elsevier Ltd.
ISSN: 0732-0671/doi:10.1016/S0732-0671(04)21017-3

BACKGROUND

The University of Northern Colorado was founded as the State Normal School in 1889 to train qualified teachers for the state's public schools. Its first class had 96 students who received teaching certificates after completion of two years of instruction. It became the State Teachers College of Colorado in 1911, with expanding its curriculum to support a four-year Bachelor of Arts program. In 1935, the program was expanded again to include graduate programs, and the name was changed to Colorado State College of Education at Greeley. UNC achieved university status in 1970. The present mission of UNC is to offer a comprehensive liberal arts education at the baccalaureate level and master's and doctoral degrees primarily in the field of education. There are five colleges, Arts and Sciences, Education, Health and Human Sciences, the Monfort College of Business, and Performing and Visual Arts, with an approximate enrollment of 11,000 students.

UNC Libraries presently consists of two locations, the James A. Michener Library and the Music Library. In 1988, there was also a Laboratory School Library and Educational Materials Services. Michener, the main library, was named after writer James A. Michener, who attended UNC from 1936–1937 and taught as a Social Science educator from 1936 to 1941. His novel *Centennial* was conceived during his time at UNC. The building was opened in 1972 and its collections hold approximately 1.5 million items in monograph, periodical, government document, audio-visual and microform formats. Michener Library also houses the University Archives, the James A. Michener Special Collection, and the Mari Michener Art Gallery. Staffing includes 33 classified staff, 14 faculty, and three administrators.

The assessment program began in 1988 with the establishment of the University Libraries Assessment Committee. According to the first committee report (University Libraries Assessment Committee, 1989), the charge, as directed by Gary Pitkin, Dean of the UNC Libraries, was to "create, implement, and evaluate an assessment procedure at least annually. The results will be used by the University Libraries Administrative Staff to analyze and strengthen services provided to students, faculty and staff." Today, the committee is responsible for writing an annual plan outlining the upcoming year's activities and, at the end of the fiscal year, an annual report summarizing the survey results and including recommendations to program changes. In addition, the committee keeps a profile of its activities on the Libraries web site, including any program changes that have come about due to its recommendations. Outcomes and recommendations are accessed by Libraries Administration and become part of the Libraries' strategic planning process. The UNC Libraries undergo an official program review every five years from the UNC Administration. This review includes outcomes and recommendations made by the Assessment Committee over this time period, as well as the implementation of any recommendations to the program. Furthermore, data from the Assessment Committee reports is also collected for the university accreditation process conducted by the North Central Accreditation (NCA) organization.

THE FIRST FIVE YEARS OF ASSESSMENT

The first Assessment Committee decided to create a general library user survey and a separate faculty survey, both focusing on collections, services, and the environment in Michener Library and including basic demographic information such as UNC status (freshman through doctoral student, faculty, or staff), UNC college affiliation, sex, ethnicity, and age. Because the surveys had to be created in a brief amount of time, they did not include actual measurement of library skills, although the general library user survey did explore self-assessment of skill levels.

One of the committee goals was to gain an understanding of library users in terms of their awareness of library resources and services, their self-assessed success in using the library, and their general attitudes toward the library. The survey created for this purpose was handed out to 1500 people as they entered the library during the course of one day. The committee received 989 returned responses, a 66% return rate. The second goal of the committee was to gain an understanding of faculty perceptions of library resources and services relevant to library-related class assignments, library skills needed by students, and general attitudes toward the library. This survey was mailed to 551 teaching faculty at UNC, and 240 responses were received for a return rate of 44%.

The committee found that, in general, those who reported more frequent library use also reported a higher level of skills and a greater awareness of services. In its final report (1989), the committee notes, however, that "self-evaluation of 'success' speaks to the self-confidence of the library users and may not be an accurate assessment of actual library skills of the respondents."

After the first year, the committee was referred to as the Library Assessment Committee (LAC), reflecting the fact that the survey focused on questions about using Michener Library and was distributed there. (Over the years, the questions have been broadened in scope and now refer to collections and services in the UNC Libraries as a whole.) With more time for preparation, the second survey was revised to include questions to actually measure library skills and compare this objective data with self-assessed skill levels. Efforts were focused on surveying general library users, since it was felt that a good base level of information had been collected from the previous faculty survey and that little would be gained from conducting another faculty survey so soon. This time, rather than including any questions measuring general user satisfaction with the library resources and services, the assessment was aimed at providing "a foundation for measuring changes made by students in the area of library literacy and to determine whether significant differences exist between the skills and knowledge of freshmen and seniors" (Library Assessment Committee [LAC], 1990). They identified library literacy according to the components listed in the Colorado Academic Library Master Plan (1988):

(1) Knowledge of the function and use of information sources.
(2) Ability to select relevant information.
(3) Knowledge of the physical arrangement of materials.
(4) Knowledge of the options available for utilizing local, state, regional and international systems.

The survey began with a few demographic questions followed by questions about frequency of library use, bibliographic instruction experiences, and a self-assessed rating of the respondent's library skills. Several questions about success in the use of specific materials and services were asked. Ten questions designed to objectively measure library skills concluded the survey. In a 1991 article in *College & Research Libraries*, committee members noted that their literature search showed "that most library questionnaires geared to an academic population resemble UNCs 1988/1989 survey in principally addressing issues of user satisfaction relative to ambiance, quality of service, or access" (Greer et al., 1991), so this was new territory for the committee. The questions that they developed addressed the library literacy components from the Colorado Academic Library Master Plan listed above, ranging from questions about specific locations and services in the library to questions about selection of appropriate sources and structuring a database search. Surveys were distributed to arriving library users during the spring of 1990 (1000 distributed and 694 returned). Although "negative comments about the presence of test questions were written on some of the instruments or made when the surveys were returned" (Greer et al., 1991), the committee was generally pleased with the level of response and felt that the information collected from the survey was valuable. The self-assessment data showed definite trends toward higher scores for seniors as compared to freshmen. Although the tested knowledge levels for seniors were also higher than for freshmen, the increases were not as dramatic. The committee felt that the survey results demonstrated a need for more bibliographic instruction, and recommended that a new library faculty position be added for this purpose. The survey, with only minor changes, would be used for the next several years.

An interesting follow-up to the 1990 survey was an analysis conducted during spring of 1991 after the annual survey was administered. Results from that year's survey were compared to those of a group of nursing students who had received a series of four library instruction sessions during one of their required courses and were given the same survey. In their conclusions, published in a 1993 *Research Strategies* article, the authors noted that bibliographic instruction did seem to play an important role in improving certain types of library skills (Fox et al., 1993).

In preparation for a library program review that takes place every five years, the 1992/1993 LAC prepared a report comparing the spring 1993 survey results with those from 1990, the first year that library skills were measured. Again, surveys were handed out at the door of Michener Library, but the rate of return had steadily dropped each year, and in 1993 only 337 of the 1000 distributed surveys were returned with enough of the questions completed to be usable. Judging by comments given by some library users as they were handed the surveys, people who had filled out the survey in previous years recognized it and weren't enthusiastic about being "tested" again. The survey remained largely the same through the years, but the format of some of the skills questions had been simplified. The average scores for the knowledge questions were significantly higher this time (LAC, 1993). For the revised questions, it was difficult to tell which had the greater effect, instruction efforts or the revised format. However, higher results were also seen on most of the questions that had not been revised. In particular, questions about constructing database searches showed considerable improvement. There was also an overall increase in self-reported excellent library skills (Table 1).

A Bibliographic Instruction Librarian position had been created and the entire instruction program had been revised along with the creation of new guides and handouts, so it was not surprising to see that participation in bibliographic instruction provided by a librarian increased. It was gratifying to see a particularly large increase in the numbers of students reporting excellent skills whose primary

Table 1. Question: Using Computer Search Techniques on ERIC, Medline, Psyclit, Sociofile, or ABI/Inform, a Search Might Best be Constructed for the Topics as Shown Below.

	1989/1990 –% Correct	1992/1993 –% Correct
Topic: Child Abuse by Alcoholic Parents		
Freshmen	34	42
Sophomores	34	67
Juniors	42	61
Seniors	46	68

influence in library use was a librarian-led class or handouts. The major programmatic recommendation from the committee was to explore ways to introduce
more students to the library earlier. Revisions to the survey and exploring better
methodologies for administering the survey to improve the response rate were
also recommended.

During the first five years of Assessment Committee activities, a unique evaluation instrument was developed, and from the results recommendations were made.
The most important of these, the addition of a Bibliographic Instruction Librarian
position, resulted in a more active instruction program and more efforts to reach
students earlier, which in turn led to improved library skills in UNC students.

DEVELOPMENTS IN THE SURVEY
AND THE METHODOLOGY

During the 1995/1996 academic year, the LAC decided to rewrite the survey,
eliminating the objective library skills questions. Because the library now had
a well established bibliographic instruction program, it was felt that this type of
assessment could be better handled in classroom settings with students attending
instruction sessions. The new questionnaire focused on user experiences and
attitudes with regard to Michener Library, particularly in terms of whether or not
the collection supported curricular needs, student use of electronic resources, and
satisfaction with public services. The format of the survey was updated as well,
to include a machine readable response sheet to make the survey results easier
to tabulate.

The original method of distributing the survey, handing it to people entering the
library, had the disadvantage of only reaching library users. The LAC was also
interested in learning something about members of the campus community who
were not regular library users. In an effort to get information from a broader section
of the campus, the 1995/1996 LAC decided, in addition to handing the surveys out
at the library door, to distribute surveys at the University Center and the various
cultural centers on campus (such as the International Student Center). Ultimately,
the committee didn't feel that handing out the surveys in different locations was
particularly successful.

Teaming With a Marketing Class

The 1996/1997 LAC decided to make a complete change in the process. Committee
members had long felt that it would be desirable to give the survey in a setting that

would encourage respondents to answer more thoughtfully and thoroughly. The LAC enlisted a Marketing class on campus to conduct the library survey as part of a class project. The Marketing students created a survey, with input from the LAC members and from various groups of students through focus group interviews, and distributed it to classes with enrollments providing a representative sample of the undergraduate population at UNC. This method had the advantage of giving the library a chance to survey students within a classroom setting and giving the students a real-life project to manage.

One of the interesting aspects of having students take a large role in developing the survey was that questions were asked that the LAC had never before thought of asking. For example, the Marketing students included questions about how safe students felt in the library and walking from and to the parking lot. Interestingly, this turned out to be of great concern to many students who evidently didn't feel safe walking between the library and the parking lot after dark. The experience of working with the Marketing class was generally successful, although the LAC members felt that they would like to have had more input on the wording of the questions (LAC, 1997). This same procedure was used the following year, and with a year of experience, the survey was edited more carefully and the chair of the LAC was able to contribute a final proof-reading.

Surveying Faculty

Beginning with the 1998/1999 academic year, the LAC decided to once again survey the faculty. It had been ten years since the first survey, which included a version that was mailed to all faculty members on campus. Since that time, the survey had targeted the undergraduate population. The LAC decided to try alternating the populations surveyed each year, with the 1998/1999 survey given to faculty and graduate students, then the 1999/2000 survey given to undergraduates, and so on. That pattern was followed for four years.

The faculty surveys for 1999 and 2001 were mailed to faculty members, and the return rate both years was approximately 23%. Survey questions focused on the library collections, satisfaction with staff, and instruction services. In 1999, the LAC members were not surprised to see disappointing numbers of faculty respondents reporting that the collections supported their own professional research (of those with an opinion, there were 52% positive responses about the monograph collection and 55% about the journal collection). They were slightly more positive about whether the collection supported their students' needs. They were very positive about the assistance efforts of the library staff (over 96% positive responses). When asked about library instruction, 46% reported scheduling a library instruction session, with 94% of those reporting that the session was very useful or somewhat useful, 78% reporting that the session was also useful to their own research, and 68% reporting a difference in the quality of student work as the result of the library instruction session (LAC, 1999). The 2001 results were similar.

Continuing Evolution of the Student Survey

Although the LAC no longer partnered with the Marketing class for the under-graduate or the graduate surveys, they did continue to administer the surveys to classes with populations reflecting the makeup of the overall UNC population, as selected by the UNC Institutional Research office. Rather than continuing to collect demographic information as part of the survey, the committee decided to ask students to supply student ID numbers. Institutional Research was then able to provide accurate demographic information, including information that had not been previously collected on the library surveys, such as cumulative grade point average. After receiving the list of classes from Institutional Research, the LAC contacted the professors for the classes and set up times to give the surveys. Occasionally, a faculty member would not give permission to the LAC to give the survey in a particular class, usually due to inflexibility of class plans during the survey period. This sometimes resulted in the over-sampling of students in certain colleges and under-sampling in others.

The 1996 survey omitted the questions that objectively assessed library skills, but because the LAC was interested in measuring information literacy skills in a variety of ways, they were reinstated for the 2000 undergraduate survey. Five multiple choice questions about basic information seeking techniques were included, covering skills such as understanding the purpose of a periodical index and the library catalog, using Library of Congress subject headings, and finding items if they are not available in the UNC Libraries collections. In the past, the committee received negative comments about the existence of "test" questions on the survey, but that was no longer the case once the survey was administered by LAC members in classroom settings. In this setting, a verbal explanation could be given about the fact that these questions were included so that the Libraries' faculty members could gauge the effectiveness of their instruction efforts.

Updating the Assessment Plan

In 1999/2000, the LAC also updated and expanded the assessment plan. According to the assessment report on that year's undergraduate survey, the committee planned to collect data to be used to evaluate the UNC Libraries with these objectives in mind:

(1) Ensure that library resources support class assignments, professional research, and other types of UNC scholarship.
(2) Provide our users with superior assistance in finding and using information from internal collections as well as remote resources.
(3) Increase user awareness of library resources and services in a rapidly evolving information environment.
(4) Maximize the information literacy skills of students and faculty to enable them to become effective library users, information consumers, and lifelong learners (LAC, 2000).

This data has been collected through the continued use of the annual survey, along with pre- and post-tests given through the library instruction program. The LAC encouraged the future use of a wider variety of assessment activities. As a response to the expanded assessment plan, LAC invested in two new assessment tools in 2003, LibQUAL, an online web survey, and the Automated Collection Assessment and Analysis Service (ACAS) from OCLC.

Moving to an Online Survey for 2003

Instead of conducting the faculty survey for the spring of 2003, LAC chose to participate in the LibQUAL+ project. LibQUAL+ is a web-based library assessment survey sponsored by the Association of Research Libraries (ARL) in collaboration with the Texas A&M University Libraries. This survey instrument measures user satisfaction in terms of the collection, facilities and service. It is based on the SERVQUAL survey instrument which utilizes the "Gap Theory of Service Quality" and was developed by the marketing research team of A. Parasuraman, V. A. Zeithaml, and L. L. Berry. The focus of LibQUAL is to measure service quality. The instrument measures the library users' perceptions of service quality and identify gaps between desired, perceived and minimum expectations of service and assigns quantifiable variables to the outcomes.

LAC chose to replace the in-house survey with LibQUAL for a variety of reasons. First, LibQUAL has the advantage of allowing participants to compare their results with other participating institutions around the country. In 2003, 316 academic libraries, including several Colorado institutions, were participating in LibQUAL, and, since the University would be undergoing its ten year accreditation process from NCA in 2004, LAC felt it was imperative to have comparative data from peer institutions. Secondly, the committee thought that an online survey would reach more of the Libraries' users, specifically off campus students and faculty. Thirdly, LAC thought that an online survey, which could be taken from the convenience of a computer anywhere and at anytime, would be perceived easier to take, and thus more amiably received. Finally, LAC felt that once the parameters were set up to use LibQUAL on an annual basis, the committee would have to spend less time implementing the survey and analyzing the outcomes than they did with the in-house version. This was an important issue due to the staff reductions and budget cuts the Libraries were facing.

LAC opened LibQUAL+ to the UNC community for a three week period beginning March 31, 2003, with the expectation that the results would be available from ARL sometime in the summer of 2003. For the first year, they wanted to reach as much of the UNC community as possible, and made it available to all faculty, staff and students. (Library faculty and staff were welcome to take the survey, but their answers would be excluded from the analysis.) The UNC community was notified about the survey through a series of email announcements, and advertising both in the University's newspaper as well as posters within the Libraries. Incentive gifts, such as pizza coupons, were offered to qualified participants. The UNC community could access the survey from the Libraries webpage as well as the email notices. Through LibQUAL+, LAC was able to reach larger numbers of UNC community members than through the printed surveys.

OCLC ACAS Project

Although showing a slight improvement between the 1999 and 2001 faculty/graduate student surveys, the negative responses relating to the quality of the monograph collection were still high enough to cause concern. In 1999, 48.1% reported dissatisfaction with the collection, followed by 31.6% in 2002. Whereas the implementation of *Prospector*, a union catalog which includes libraries in Colorado and Wyoming from which UNC faculty and students may borrow books and have them delivered to UNC, has relieved some of this negativity, LAC decided it was time to assess the monograph collection and look for subject areas that were inadequate to support UNC curriculum needs.

LAC contracted with OCLC in the fall of 2002 to perform an automated analysis of UNC Libraries' collection based on the holdings in the online catalog. OCLC provided LAC with a title list arranged by WLN (Western Library Network) Conspectus subject levels: 24 divisions, 500 categories and 4,000 subject descriptors. The titles were categorized by subject and broken out by publication date. In addition, OCLC also provided a separate analysis of the classified serials as well as a comparison of UNC's titles to the *Choice Outstanding Academic Books* lists from 1991 through 2002.

LAC plans to use this data to recommend changes to the collection development formula which is currently undergoing review. In addition, subject bibliographers will be able to use the data to request special funds from the James A. Michener Endowment to fill in some of the weak areas in their respective subject areas.

TRENDS IN RESPONSES

Responses were easy to compare during the first several years of assessment activities because the survey wasn't significantly altered, but many changes have been made to the instrument in subsequent years. The early versions focused on library skills, with a change to general user satisfaction questions in the 1996 survey. Each year, the survey has been revised, sometimes slightly and sometimes in major ways, to reflect the interests of the current LAC members and the changes happening in the library with regard to collections and services.

Since 1996, questions about the services provided by the library faculty, staff, and student employees have always been included, and these questions have always yielded large percentages of positive results. Demographic information has been collected since the beginning, either through questions or through information provided by Institutional Research, and results for the other questions have been cross-tabulated with this information. The results have never shown any particular long term trends or differences with respect to ethnicity or gender. Occasionally, differences emerged in a particular survey, for example, the 1998 survey showed that female students and older students were more likely to ask for assistance.

Technological advances resulted in the addition of certain questions. For example, a question about whether or not the respondent has used the Internet for class-related research first appeared on the survey in 1996, with approximately 45% answering yes. That question has been asked in all subsequent undergraduate and graduate student surveys, and not surprisingly, the positive responses increased (Table 2).

Another change was seen when the Libraries migrated to a new integrated library system. In the 1996 survey, many respondents reported unhappiness with their experiences with our text-based online catalog and article indexes. Comments suggested that the systems were complex, unfriendly, and slow. In 1998, after the Libraries migrated to a new system, 70% of the respondents reported that both the catalog and the article indexes were easy to use.

During the first several years, the question "How often have you used the library in the past year" was asked. Choices were almost daily, once a week, once

Table 2. Percent Reporting Use of the Internet for Class-Related Research.

Year	%
1995/1996	44.8
1996/1997	60
1997/1998	86.4
1998/1999	90.5 (graduate students)
1999/2000	98.2 (undergraduates)
2000/2001	93.7 (graduate students)
2001/2002	98.3 (undergraduates)

a month, and occasionally. The responses showed that approximately 70%–80% of undergraduates were daily or weekly library users. The 1998 survey was updated to measure the number of times students used the library's collections for class-related research rather than measuring physical presence in the library. This made sense as many of the library resources and services had become available remotely. In spite of the large numbers of students using the Internet for research, the library's collections are still heavily used. In 1998, over 96% of the undergraduates reported at least some use of the library's collections for class-related research. This number dropped to 91.5% in 2000, and rose to 93.3% in 2002. Another interesting finding in the 2000 report came from comparing frequency of use of the library's collections for class-related research to cumulative grade point average. There appeared to be "a clear relationship between the use of library resources and cumulative GPA" (LAC, 2000). The exception came in the most frequent use category (16+ times), but further analysis showed that many respondents in this group had not actually been given regular admittance status to the University, but were part of a program that includes extensive tutoring (including many library visits) to prepare students for regular admittance. The original question included use of the library for purposes other than use of library collections. In the 2002 survey, the LAC decided to look at the variety of reasons that students use the library. Students were asked about their use of the libraries and library resources, and use of the libraries' computers. Results (LAC, 2002) showed that the main use of the libraries was for course related research (84.3%), followed by use as a place to study (63.3%), use of reserve readings (44.6%), use as a computer lab (39.3%), and as a place to socialize (7.2%). The computers were used most frequently to access library resources (93.8%), followed by use for course related web use (56.4%), email use (50.2%), Microsoft Office software (43%), and recreational web browsing (35.1%).

When questions objectively measuring library skills were asked, results have demonstrated that library instruction has a positive effect on library skills. This was noted in the 1993 *Research Strategies* article (Fox et al., 1993) and in the LAC report of 1993 that compared 1990 and 1993 survey results (LAC, 1993). In the report of the undergraduate survey of 2000, an interesting comparison was done among participation in library instruction, attitude toward the instruction, and the results of the objective questions. The highest number of correct responses (67.6%) was for the question "What resource should you consult to determine if UNC Libraries owns a particular book." The lowest number (14.1%) was for the question "When searching for books in Michener Library, how can you determine the official subject heading(s) for your topic." The results were cross-tabulated, and showed that having attended a library instruction session greatly increased the likelihood of answering certain questions correctly ("When searching for books in the Michener Library, how can you determine the official subject heading(s) for your topic," "What is the BEST procedure to follow if UNC Libraries does now own a magazine or journal article that you need," and "Which is an advantage of subject heading searches"). Of those who had not received library instruction, the average number of correct answers out of the five questions was 2.13. For those who had library instruction, the average score was 2.48. For those who had library instruction and reported that they found it helpful, the average score was 2.52, compared to 2.35 for those who had library instruction but didn't feel that it was useful (LAC, 2000). The next year, in the report of the 2001 graduate student survey (LAC, 2001), results were similar.

Questions about library instruction services have been asked most years since the 1990 survey. That year, 53% of the survey respondents (45% of the freshmen and 68% of the seniors) reported having participated in a bibliographic instruction session provided by a librarian. By 1993, with the addition of a more formal instruction program, the numbers increased to 63% (50% of the freshmen and 71% of the seniors) (Table 3).

Table 3.   Survey Results.

Year	Number of Instruction Sessions	% Having Had a Library Instruction Session	Notes
1989/1990	199	53	First year question was asked.
1992/1993	217	63	A 0.75 FTE Instruction Librarian was added.
1996/1997	182	42	Instruction Librarian used electronic tutorial for some classes.
1997/1998	242	61	FTE was added to the Instruction Department during the year.
1999/2000	205	49	Instruction Librarian focused on creating LIB 150 course.

Since then, the results have shown significant rises and falls. The survey results wouldn't necessarily be expected to mirror the actual numbers of library instruction sessions held during a particular year since the question asked about past instruction experiences and not only instruction experiences during the current year. However, the actual statistics do show similar variations, mostly explained by programmatic and staffing changes. The rate of change is not the same for the survey results as for the actual statistics though, and this suggests the importance of collecting statistical information and assessment data in a variety of ways.

CHANGES BASED ON SURVEY OUTCOMES

Several changes to the Libraries' program have been made based on the recommendations of the LAC committee. Following is a chronological order of the most significant.

1989 – LAC recommended an increased emphasis in library instruction and a bibliographic instruction librarian was hired in the fall of 1990.

1996 – LAC recommended increasing efficiency and stability of the online catalog or replacing it, and as a consequence, UNC Libraries contracted in the fall of 1997 with Innovative Interfaces, Inc. to provide the online catalog. In the same year, based on the LAC recommendation to provide public Internet access, four Internet workstations were added to the reference area.

1997 – LAC recommended that, since the library has taken a leading role in providing expertise for accessing Internet based information to UNC, we should promote our expertise and make Internet access more visible to students. Many did not know whether or not the Internet was available in the library but reported that they would probably use it if it was. As a consequence, the Libraries increased the number of computers in the library and more librarians began presenting information about web use in bibliographic instruction classes. In addition, the Libraries started providing online document delivery of journal articles through Uncover, and later Ingenta.

1998 –Three changes were made based on the 1998 survey. First, LAC wanted to assess interest in a credit-bearing information literacy course. The results showed that 38.5% of those surveyed responded positively, and, because the Libraries were only investigating the possibility of offering one or two sections of such a class, this was deemed enough of a positive response. In 2000, it was 44.5%. The class was offered beginning fall of 2000.

Secondly, gradual changes in the food and drink policy were implemented based on the 1998 survey. Students were asked to rank which of the following they would

like to see added. Responses included: Room where eating and drinking are allowed
– 26%; open computer lab – 46%; more individual and group study space – 25%.
As a result students are allowed to have food and drink on the first floor and a
coffee cart is planned for the summer of 2003.

Thirdly, in response to the same question, the Information Commons was established in the fall of 2000. Beginning with eight computers, this area was established
as a place where students could work on research assignments. Each computer
workstation has a fully functional computer offering Internet access, email and
Microsoft Office, as well as the Libraries online resources. The area was upgraded
to 16 computer workstations in the fall of 2001 and 32 in the summer of 2002. In
January 2003, Microsoft Office was added to 15 of the 30 existing Internet-only
computers in Reference.

1999 – To address collection deficiencies that had been noted over a number
of years, the UNC Libraries became a member of the *Prospector* union catalog.
This catalog combines the holdings of the 16 academic libraries in Colorado and
Wyoming as well as Denver, Jefferson County and Fort Collins public libraries.
Patrons may search this catalog and request books that their home library does not
own.

2000 – LAC recommended that the committee monitor data from national surveys and use it to supplement and inform our other assessment activities. As a
result, the Libraries joined the LibQUAL+ online national survey project in 2003.

2002 – Over the years there has been increasing demand to provide more study
space and upgrade furniture. In 1998, 25% of those surveyed selected "more individual and group study space" as a priority. In 2002, from a list of four options,
25% requested a 24 hour study area, and 11% wanted to replace existing furniture
with updated furniture. In response, the Libraries formed a Furniture Task Force to
look at purchasing new furniture, investigate compact shelving, and re-group the
current furniture to create more study space. Presently, the Libraries have received
$75,000 to reupholster and replace some of the existing furniture.

CONCLUSION

For the past 15 years the UNC Libraries have been involved in assessment.
Although the methodology and the instrument have gone through many changes,
the focus has not. Users have been asked in one form or another to evaluate the
Libraries in terms of service, collections, and instruction. In response to these
evaluations, the Libraries have instituted many changes over the years; the most
significant include focusing on instruction and information literacy through the
hiring of a bibliographic instruction librarian in 1990 followed by implementing

LIB 150, a credit-bearing course, in the fall of 2000. To respond to the ever-increasing demand for computer access and the importance electronic resources play in information gathering, the Libraries developed the Information Commons in 2000. This area allowed students to access information, evaluate it, and compose their research papers all within the library. Finally, in response to collection deficiencies, the Libraries became a member of the *Prospector* union catalog, thus allowing academic libraries in Colorado and Wyoming to share access to their collections, a must in these economic times.

REFERENCES

Colorado Academic Library Committee (1988). *Colorado academic library master plan* (3rd ed.). Denver: Colorado Commission on Higher Education.

Colorado Revised Statutes (1988). Section 23-13-101.

Greer, A., Weston, L., & Alm, M. (1991). Assessment of learning outcomes: A measure of progress in library literacy. *College & Research Libraries*, *52*, 549–557.

Library Assessment Committee (1990). Second annual library assessment committee report. Greeley: University of Northern Colorado, University Libraries.

Library Assessment Committee (1993). Library assessment committee report, 1992–1993. Greeley: University of Northern Colorado, University Libraries.

Library Assessment Committee (1997). Spring 1997 student survey report. Greeley: University of Northern Colorado, University Libraries.

Library Assessment Committee (1999). Report on the annual user survey. Greeley: University of Northern Colorado, University Libraries.

Library Assessment Committee (2000). Report on the undergraduate survey 2000. Greeley: University of Northern Colorado, University Libraries.

Library Assessment Committee (2001). *University libraries assessment plan*. Greeley: University of Northern Colorado, University Libraries.

Library Assessment Committee (2002). Report on the undergraduate survey 2002. Greeley: University of Northern Colorado, University Libraries.

University Libraries Assessment Committee (1989). Final 1988–1989 report. Greeley: University of Northern Colorado, University Libraries.

ISO 9000 IMPLEMENTATION IN THAI ACADEMIC LIBRARIES

Malivan Praditteera

INTRODUCTION

The academic library is an important component of any university and is responsible for providing academic and research support to all members of the university community. At present, higher education institutions in Thailand are trying to evaluate and improve their quality by implementing quality assurance models/mechanisms. Libraries, as critical supporting organizations in these institutions, also need to improve their quality. As a service organization, academic libraries are faced with the need to satisfy their clientele and to measure and evaluate their services. There is a need, therefore, for librarians to take positive steps to insure that their clients receive quality services.

Excellent library service is one requirement in the guidelines for quality assurance established by the Thai Ministry of University Affairs (Ministry of University Affairs, 1998). There are many models for quality management and quality assurance such as accreditation, benchmarking, total quality management (TQM), and ISO 9000 series standards. A challenge for academic libraries is to investigate and determine which model/mechanism is appropriate for improving and ensuring the quality of their library service programs.

There are several popular management techniques and trends available to help improve library quality. Such techniques are mostly business and industrial oriented (e.g. TQM and ISO 9000). Because they are built on the fundamentals of good business practice, most nonprofit organizations, especially libraries, believe that quality methodologies are of more relevance to

Advances in Library Administration and Organization
Advances in Library Administration and Organization, Volume 21, 283–297
© 2004 Published by Elsevier Ltd.
ISSN: 0732-0671/doi:10.1016/S0732-0671(04)21018-5

industry and commerce in general, and particularly to large organizations, and fear the cost and the time-consuming nature of implementing such models (Brockman, 1997).

But, methodologies and measures for using them are emerging. ISO 9000, for example, a quality assurance model from industry developed by the International Organization of Standardization, is a set of international quality assurance and quality management standards. The standards are necessarily generic, but they are an important step in the direction of establishing quality standards worldwide. Because the certification of an organization's performance in accordance with these standards (called "registration" in America) is acknowledged through third-party examination, the ISO 9000 program is useful, providing objective measurement standards (St. Clair, 1997).

In a paper concerned with the application of the ISO 9000 quality assurance standard to libraries, Tann (1993) suggests that fitness for purpose would include:

- knowing the customer's needs – stated and/or implied;
- designing a service to meet them on or off the premises;
- faultless delivery of service;
- suitable facilities – car park, cafe, crèche;
- good accommodation – seating lighting, heating, toilets;
- good "housekeeping";
- reliable equipment – computers, videos;
- efficient administration – welcome, queries answered efficiently and effectively;
- helpful, courteous staff;
- efficient backup service;
- monitoring and evaluation including customer expectations, complaints, recommendations for improvement; and
- feedback loops to build-in improvement procedures and or checking that improvements are put in place.

(Tann, 1993, cited in Brockman, 1997, p. 11.)

Accordingly, it can be seen that the key issue is for quality to become a meaningful concept linked to the aim of total customer satisfaction. It does not matter whether the context is an industrial company involved in metal fabrication, a government department preparing legislation, a finance department operating internally within a local authority, or a library lending books. All have to meet customer needs. This idea challenges academic libraries to apply and implement ISO 9000 for quality assurance in spite of its being an industrial model.

Significance of the Study

At present, academic libraries in Thailand are involved in establishing institutional quality assurance processes. On December 2–4, 1998, the Thai Public Academic Libraries Cooperation Committee organized its annual conference around the theme "Academic Libraries and Educational Quality Assurance" in order to enhance and disseminate quality assurance knowledge and techniques. Many different quality assurance approaches were discussed and suggested for academic libraries, especially the ISO 9000 series standards (Thai Academic Libraries Cooperation Committee, 1999). It indicated that the trend of adopting ISO 9000 Standards was appropriate for library organizations.

Problem Statement

This study examined the quality assurance models and practices currently utilized in Thai academic libraries with a special focus on the ISO 9000 implementation process that has been completed by Thai academic libraries. The current status of implementation, facilitators, obstacles, benefits, strengths and weakness of the ISO 9000 implementation and certification process was determined. Case studies were done in ISO 9000 certified academic libraries in order to examine how they conducted the ISO 9000 implementation and certification process. The results should be beneficial for other academic libraries, which have not yet developed and/or applied any quality assurance model.

Research Methodology

This study utilized surveys to determine which quality assurance models were being used in academic libraries. Case studies were then prepared and presented on those libraries that have implemented and certified ISO 9000 standards through questionnaire and personal interview. The survey was administered at the end of the year 2000, and the data was collected and analyzed in the year 2001.

The population for this study included academic libraries located at the 54 main campuses of higher education institutions under the supervision of the Thai Ministry of University Affairs. The senior librarians of all 54 Thai academic libraries were asked to complete a questionnaire concerning the current status of quality assurance approaches being utilized in their libraries. Responses were received from all 54 of the senior librarians who received the questionnaire.

A second questionnaire was then distributed to the senior librarians at four academic libraries who had been certified as meeting ISO 9000 standards. It asked for general information about the ISO 9000 implementation, facilitating factors, benefits of and obstacles to ISO 9000 implementation and certification in their libraries. Additionally, the follow-up interviews were done with this group after the questionnaires were returned. The main objective was to investigate the ISO 9000 implementation process.

Research Findings

Part I: Quality Assurance in Thai Academic Libraries: Current Status
The results indicated that several quality assurance approaches had been utilized in Thai academic libraries. Of 54 participant libraries, 20 libraries had implemented quality assurance systems/approaches. Of those, it was found that self-accreditation was the most used approach.

As shown in Table 1, a self-accreditation approach was used in ten libraries, a Ministry of University Affairs (MUA) model in six libraries, ISO 9000 in eight libraries, and a total quality management (TQM) model, a benchmarking approach, and a self-developed model in one library each.

Additionally, six of those 20 libraries had implemented more than one quality assurance system. Four of those six were implementing self-accreditation and the ministry of University Affairs system together. One library was implementing the self-accreditation with a benchmarking model whereas another, which had already received ISO 9002 certification, was implementing self-accreditation and TQM approach. It should be noted that 20 libraries had been utilizing the quality assurance models/approaches for a period of from 3 months to more than 21 months. This indicated that quality assurance and improvement had been under consideration in Thai academic libraries for a relatively short period of time.

Table 1. Quality Assurance Models in Thai Academic Libraries: Current Status.

QA Models	Number of Libraries ($N = 20$)
Self-accreditation	10
ISO 9000	8
Ministry of University Affairs' model	6
TQM	1
Benchmarking	1
Self-developed model	1

Note: There were 6 libraries implementing more than one quality assurance system in their libraries.

Table 2.   The Quality Assurance Models in Thai Academic Libraries: Future Implementation.

QA Models	Number of Libraries ($N = 50$)
Self-accreditation	8
ISO 9000	24
Ministry of University Affairs' model	13
TQM	6
Benchmarking	2
Self-developed model	2

Note: There were 9 libraries considered implementing more than one quality assurance system.

Part II: Quality Assurance in Thai Academic Libraries: Future Trends
Based on the findings, most (50 of 54) Thai academic libraries were planning to develop and implement quality assurance systems/approaches in the future. The most popular choice was ISO 9000. As shown in Table 2, 24 libraries were considering using the ISO 9000 standards model, compared to 13 using the Ministry of University Affairs model, eight libraries using self-accreditation, six using Total Quality Management, two using benchmarking, and two using self-developed models.

Also the findings indicated that nine of the 50 libraries considered implementing more than one quality assurance systems together, ISO 9002 with the TQM model, ISO 9002 with the Ministry of University Affairs model, TQM with benchmarking, and self-accreditation with benchmarking. This indicated that libraries could implement more than one quality assurance model together in pursuing the best quality.

Part III: ISO 9000 Implementation in Thai Academic Libraries
The findings indicated that eight Thai academic libraries were utilizing ISO 9000. The four that had implemented and received ISO 9002 certification were the libraries of Saint Louis College, Saint John's University, Dhurakijpundit University and Ramkhamhaeng University. All but Ramkhamhaeng University were private institutions.

ISO 9002 (1994 version) was indicated as the suitable standard for academic libraries. Four ISO 9000 certified libraries had implemented the ISO 9002 standards series. In addition, two types of implementation and certification processes were used in Thai academic libraries: the institutional level and the independent level. Three private academic libraries (Saint Louis College, Saint John's University, and Dhurakijpundit University) had implemented ISO 9002 at the institutional level. Ramkhamhaeng University Library, a public institution, also had implemented

ISO 9002 at the institutional level initially, but it subsequently went independently for certification.

The findings also showed that there were four other libraries in the initial stages of ISO 9000 implementation. They were the libraries of Prince of Songkla University, Kasem Bundit University, King Mongkut Institute of Technology in North Bangkok, and South East Asia University. Prince of Songkla's and South East Asia's library programs were being implemented independently, but Kasem Bundit's and King Mongkut's were being implemented as part of an institutional initiative. They all were planning to complete the certification process by 2001.

The aims to be standardized and to improve library service quality were indicated to be the most important reasons for choosing ISO 9000 as a quality assurance model in Thai academic libraries. The following factors were also indicated as priorities: the Ministry of University Affairs' requirement; university support and commitment in implementing ISO 9000; and the need to improve the library organization and work systems.

An ISO 9000 consultant was apparently necessary for Thai academic libraries in ISO 9000 implementation. All four ISO 9002 certified libraries hired external consultants for assistance with ISO 9002 implementation. Each library used two consultants and met an average of five times with each of those consultants. The consultants were most useful in documentation work and ISO 9002 training. Only a limited number of ISO 9000 consulting agencies were identified in the findings; to include HR Business Partners and the Training Lead Consultancy (TLC) pilot project under the supervision of the Thai Industrial Standards Institute. This suggests that there are a relatively small number of ISO 9000 consultants available to libraries or for other education-related organizations in Thailand.

Regarding the overall organization of university implementation of ISO 9002, similar committees were established at each university: a Steering Committee, a Quality Management Representative Committee (QMRC), Documentation Subcommittee, and an Internal Quality Audit Committee. The library top administrators were named as members of all four committees. In addition, Ramkhamhaeng University Library had a Library QMR Committee, which was set up later to evaluate the feasibility of implementing the certification process independently. The quality management representative (QMR) of the library was usually the top administrator or library director. Only at Ramkhamhaeng University Library was the QMR a mid-level administrator.

Library personnel in those four libraries had high levels of knowledge of ISO 9000 and quality assurance. Senior librarians perceived that librarians had a better understanding of ISO 9000 and quality assurance than did other library staff.

ISO 9002 Implementation Model in Library

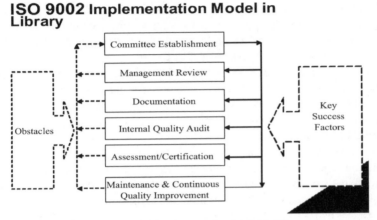

Fig. 1. ISO 9002 Implementation Model in Library.

This suggests that academic libraries should put more effort into library personnel training, not only for librarians, but also for non-professional staff. The training should be adapted and given according to employees' levels of responsibility, education and professional experience.

ISO 9000 training was conducted for all personnel in these libraries, and orientation programs were conducted for new library personnel at least twice a year. The libraries also conducted review activities and retraining of ISO 9002 library practices for all library personnel. This suggests that continuous training and quality activities are important in ISO 9002 implementation and in continuous quality improvement.

Five major procedures were similarly employed in the ISO 9002 implementation process in Thai academic libraries. As seen in Fig. 1, they were:

- Management review procedure.
- Documenting procedure.
- Internal quality audit.
- Assessment/certification process.
- Maintenance and continuous quality improvement.

The findings indicated that unlike other organizations, Thai academic libraries did not experience much difficulty in ISO 9002 implementation and certification. The ISO 9002 certified libraries felt that the overall difficulty in ISO 9002 implementation was only at a moderate level. However, among the five major procedures,

ISO 9002 certification maintenance and continuous improvement was perceived to be extremely difficult by senior librarians. The certification process itself and conducting effective ISO 9002 training for all library administrators and staff were also perceived as being at a high level of difficulty.

The average time for the ISO 9002 implementation and certification process in the four libraries was 178 calendar days. The longest time was spent on documentation writing and preparation. This relatively short average time suggests that the ISO 9002 implementation and certification process was not difficult for the libraries.

The ISO 9000 certification body was selected and employed by an institutional quality management representative committee (QMRC). Bureau Veritas Quality International Co. (BVQI Thailand) was named to be the ISO 9002 certification body by three institutions. The other used two certification bodies: EIT-CBO and Energy & Environment Accredited Quality Assessment Co. (EAQA-UK). This suggests that a limited number of ISO 9000 certification bodies have experience in education-related fields.

Thai academic libraries were likely to undergo re-engineering during the ISO 9000 implementation process. Three libraries had restructured their organizations before, during, and after ISO 9002 implementation. Some library departments and divisions were merged, downsized or eliminated, according to the redundancy of their activities. Senior librarians stated that the procedure used in documenting library operations helped the libraries analyze clearly the workflow of products and services and learn how effective their communications channels were. Despite the restructuring, no library laid off employees during reorganization.

The finding that ISO 9002 certified libraries had, through reengineering, reorganized without the necessity of terminating staff was attributed to a number of factors. For example, based on the results of the restructuring, senior librarians reassigned staff to other areas of the library or made temporary assignments until staff vacancies occurred through normal attrition. In some cases, such as in the public university libraries, the staffs have long-term contracts with the government, and it is difficult to rotate people out of the library.

Nevertheless, librarians and library staff felt satisfied with ISO 9002 implementation. Senior librarians reported a better working environment and improved customer service, suggesting that ISO 9002 was involved in creating these improvements. It was clearly stated that, to implement the ISO 9002 system in Thai academic libraries, top administrators of the institutions had to be involved on several levels, providing not only funding support, but also commitment to adopting the quality assurance system, and the findings of this study support that conclusion.

Table 3.   Key Success Factors and Obstacles in ISO 9000 Implementation Process in Thai Academic Libraries.

Key Success Factors	Obstacles
Funding support	High costs
High level of administrative commitment	Amount of time required for document and
Administrator's attitude	implementation
Cooperation of subcontractors	A lack of ISO 9000 training in library
Efficient committees	
Success of staff training	

Key Success Factors and Obstacles

Table 3 shows that the key success factors of ISO 9000 implementation came from senior management. Funding support, a high level of commitment, and the attitude of administrators were perceived as critical factors affecting the success of ISO 9002 implementation. The cooperation of subcontractors, the effectiveness and efficiency of the ISO 9002 committee, and the success of staff training were also important factors.

As shown in Table 3, high costs in the implementation and certification process, documentation work, and the amount of time demanded to support certification were perceived as major obstacles in Thai academic libraries' implementation of ISO 9002. A lack of ISO 9002 education and training for library staff was also identified as an obstacle.

This suggests that academic libraries need to establish a detailed plan for ISO 9000 implementation. The four m's – Money, Men, Materials and Machines – are crucial factors that libraries have to consider in planning their ISO 9000 implementation.

Benefits of ISO 9000 Certification

A number of benefits resulted from ISO 9002 implementation. The accountability of their parent institutions was indicated as the most important benefit. Promoting a good image and improving the awareness of quality services of the libraries were also perceived as being of a high level of importance. In addition, greater quality awareness by library employees was an important benefit in promoting better morale and greater worker efficiency. This suggests that the implementation of ISO 9000 provides important benefits for both the libraries themselves and their

Table 4. Strengths and Weaknesses of ISO 9000 Model as Perceived by Thai Academic Librarians.

Strengths	Weaknesses
Good business practices	Costs of training, consultant, auditing
Elimination of duplication document of activities	and certification process
Creating a formal training system	Time consuming documentation work
Employees involvement and participation	Difficult to interpreting ISO 9000
Evaluation tool	requirement to library work

parent institutions. Nevertheless, promoting a good image, improving services, and increasing quality awareness of library employees are important benefits for libraries.

Strengths and Weaknesses of ISO 9000

Senior librarians identified the following issues as the strengths of ISO 9002: the encouragement of good business practices; the evaluation tools; elimination of the duplication of activities; the creation of a formal training system; and employee involvement and participation (Table 4).

However, as shown in Table 4, several librarians perceived the weaknesses of ISO 9002 implementation as the costs of training, consultants, auditing and the certification process; its focus on documentation, which was time-consuming; and the difficulty encountered in interpreting and adopting the requirements of certification to library work.

Additional Findings

(1) A study of library service satisfaction was not conducted in any library following ISO 9002 certification. Nevertheless, in three ISO 9002 certified institutions, the Quality Management Representative Committee conducted institution-wide user surveys in order to receive feedback on the ISO 9002 certification every six months. The surveys included an evaluation of library services. Recent results showed a high level of library user satisfaction.

(2) All four libraries agreed with the conclusion that ISO 9000, and especially 9002, was well-suited for use in library environments. Viewing the library as a service organization, they agreed that ISO 9002 was the most appropriate quality assurance model to adopt for the assurance of quality service.

(3) Some useful suggestions in adopting ISO 9002 were given by the senior librarians. The most important things in ISO 9002 (or any ISO 9000) implementation were to have library employees involved from the beginning of the process; to obtain senior administrators' support and involvement; to provide ISO 9000 training; to use experienced ISO 9000 consultants; and to select an experienced certification body.

DISCUSSION AND CONCLUSION

Quality Assurance in Thai academic Libraries: Present and Future Trends

Twenty Thai academic libraries had implemented quality assurance systems. Several models were utilized, including self-accreditation, ISO 9000, the Ministry of University Affairs' model, TQM, benchmarking and self-developed models. Self-accreditation was mentioned most frequently, being used in 10 of the libraries.

From the literature reviewed, it was found that self-accreditation had been informally utilized since 1986 when the Ministry of University Affairs announced Thailand's Standards for Academic Libraries (Ministry of University Affairs, 1986). Minimum standards for university libraries were established to guide libraries of higher education institutions in maintaining, collecting, and disseminating educational resources effectively. In addition, the standards required that the number of qualified personnel available, the budget, and the collections of materials to support research and teaching be sufficient. Services should be organized and offered related to the needs of the patrons in the university and the community (Ministry of University Affairs, 1986). Every higher education institution needs to pass the library standards assessment of the Ministry of University Affairs before a license may be granted. Also, the re-assessment is continuously done every two years for each program offered. The number of books and journal holdings per faculty and per student is a major indicator. Since these standards are basic requirements for all higher education institutions, librarians may not recognize them as a quality assurance model at the beginning. However, since the quality issue has been raised recently, self-accreditation has become significant in terms of guiding libraries to achieve minimum standards. Nevertheless, the standards were initially more quantitative than qualitative. Thailand's Standards for Academic Libraries Committee was set up under the supervision of the Ministry of University Affairs in order to revise and update the standards. At the beginning of 2001, the new revision was released. The 2001 revised standards are more qualitative and focused on information technology management (Ministry of University Affairs, 2001).

There has been a trend whereby academic libraries quite often implement more than one quality assurance system in their libraries. Based on the findings, among 20 libraries, six were implementing more than one quality assurance system. Four of them were implementing self-accreditation and the Ministry of University Affairs system together. One library was implementing self-accreditation with a benchmarking mode, whereas another, which already had received ISO 9002 certification, was also implementing self-accreditation and TQM together. This might indicate that some of the quality assurance systems they used may not be suitable for libraries, or that the libraries may need to use different systems at different times or for different aspects of quality improvement. In addition, when more than one quality assurance system is implemented in one library, it may be for the reason that both systems have different scales for quality development. For example, self-accreditation might help the library in improving quality in one specific aspect whereas TQM might be more useful for total quality improvement.

The findings indicated that some Thai academic libraries have been involved in quality assurance processes for more than 21 months. Seven public institution libraries stated that they had started their quality assurance activities more than 21 months prior to the survey. The literature review showed that the Ministry of University Affairs announced and promoted quality assurance guidelines in 1997. Since then, quality assurance has become more significant in higher education institutions in Thailand. Academic libraries in Thailand became involved in establishing quality assurance processes when the Thai Public Academic Libraries Cooperation Committee organized its annual conference on "Academic Libraries and Educational Quality Assurance" from December 2–4, 1998, in order to enhance and disseminate quality assurance knowledge and techniques (Thai Academic Libraries Cooperation Committee, 1999).

Nevertheless, it is interesting that there was a large time gap between the durations of the quality assurance activity involvement in Thai academic libraries (from three months to more than 21 months). The quality assurance policies and guidelines were announced and have been promoted in higher education institutions since 1997 by the Ministry of University Affairs, but only a small number of universities were interested in implementing the quality assurance approaches they recommended. Because of a lack of clarity in the Ministry of University Affairs' quality assurance guidelines, Thai higher education institutions began to pursue quality assurance models from industry and business, and this occurred in the academic libraries as well.

There are still several quality assurance models that Thai academic libraries are interested in implementing, such as ISO 9000, TQM, and benchmarking.

Regardless of the model used, this indicates that academic libraries in Thailand are eager to pursue quality in their libraries.

ISO 9000 Implementation in Thai Academic Libraries

ISO 9000 is one of the quality assurance models that has been used in Thai academic libraries. Among eight libraries that were implementing this quality assurance system, four had already received ISO 9000 certification whereas four others were moving towards implementation but had not yet completed the certification process.

Twenty-one additional libraries were planning to implement ISO 9000 and another 24 libraries were considering implementation. This indicates a general trend in library quality management. Nevertheless, while the findings revealed a growing number of ISO 9000 implementations, there were also some factors that might be obstacles to their success. These include a lack of consultants available, the time-consuming nature of implementation, the cost associated with the process, and difficulty encountered in interpreting ISO 9000s generic standards. Training for ISO 9000 was indicated as a priority for libraries. These factors should be considered by other libraries who are considering future selection and implementation of quality standards.

ISO 9000, originally an industry-based model, is now widely used in education organizations, not only in higher education but also in all kinds of education and non-profit organizations in Thailand. ISO 9000 has also been implemented in libraries in many other European and Asian countries, especially in academic libraries. The most notable example of this is the University of Central Lancaster Library in the U.K.s implementation of these standards in 1992 (Lundquist, 1997). This suggests that ISO 9000 may be appropriate for education organizations, and, specifically, for service organizations like libraries. Mostly, the adoption of ISO 9000 in academic libraries was found to be one segment of overall institutional implementation. ISO 9000 was also found to be an appropriate context for development of total quality management in the library.

However, in Thailand, none of ISO 9000 certified libraries has conducted a customer satisfaction survey or an evaluation of how library users feel about their ISO 9000 quality accreditation. Thus, it has not yet been determined how much the libraries have improved the quality of their services in terms of satisfying the library users' needs. Furthermore, the question of whether ISO 9000 is the best fit for academic libraries in pursuing and assuring quality has yet to be satisfactorily answered.

Even though ISO 9000 will be utilized and considered for future implementation in Thai academic libraries, one thing the senior librarians learned was that it was difficult to interpret ISO 9000 requirements. Since it is a generic standard, it is time-consuming to learn and develop to fit an organization. This clearly suggests that ISO 9000 consultants and training activities are very important in the ISO 9000 implementation process.

Further Study Recommendations

(1) A study should be conducted to determine the type of organizational changes that occur as a result of implementing an ISO 9002 quality process and how they affect library services. This should include an identification of indicators of quality service as well as associated user satisfaction measures.
(2) Senior administrators play an important role in ISO 9000 implementation and success in each institution. Therefore, a study can be developed to reveal what the administrative roles and characteristics are in supporting ISO 9000 implementation or the adoption of any quality assurance approach. Variables could include leadership, attitudes, and university administrative policies.
(3) Cost-benefit and cost-effectiveness studies regarding the implementation of ISO 9000 or any quality assurance are needed. All libraries stated that their institutions have spent a lot of money and effort on the ISO 9000 implementation process. They all felt it worthwhile for institutional accountability and image. However, this perception could be subjective and biased. A study should be conducted to investigate how much money the institutions invested and how many benefits the institutions believed that they received in return.
(4) The utilization of ISO 9000 consultants and accreditation organizations in Thailand has become an interesting issue. The findings of this study show that a small number of certification bodies and consulting agencies are used in Thai academic institutions. This suggests that, although the trend in ISO 9000 is growing, there is a shortage of consultants and certification bodies that have experience in education accreditation.

ACKNOWLEDGMENTS

The author would like to acknowledge Dr. John L. Yeager, Dr. Sean Hughes, Dr. Rush G. Miller, and Dr. Glenn M. Nelson (University of Pittsburgh, Pennsylvania, USA) for their generous help and support with doing this research. The gratitude also goes to all academic libraries in Thailand, especially the four ISO 9002 certified libraries of St. Louis College, Saint John's University, Dhurakijpundit University, and Ramkhamhaeng University. Last but not least, special thanks go to Dr. Delmus Williams and his co-editor for editing this publication.

REFERENCES

Brockman, J. (Ed.) (1997). *Quality management and benchmarking in information sector: Results of recent research.* London: Bowker.
Lundquist, R. (1997, June). Quality systems and ISO 9000 in higher education. *Assessment & Evaluation in Higher Education, 22*(2), 158–172.
St. Clair, G. (1997). *Total quality management in information services.* London: Bowker.
Thai Academic Libraries Cooperation Committee (1999). Academic libraries and educational quality assurance: Annual conference. December 2–4, 1998. Bangkok: Thai Academic Library Cooperation Committee.
Thailand. Ministry of University Affairs (1998). *Quality assurance in Thai higher education.* Bangkok: Chulalongkorn University Press.
Thailand. Ministry of University Affairs. Academic Library Standards Committee (1986). *Standards for academic libraries.* Bangkok: Office of Ministry of University Affairs.

INTERVIEWS

1. Library Director of Dhurakijpundit University. December 13, 2000.
2. Library Head of Saint John's University. November 24, 2000.
3. Senior Librarian of Saint Louis College. December 2, 2000.
4. Senior Librarian and Library's QMR of Ramkhamhaeng University. November 28, 2000.

ABOUT THE AUTHORS

Lisa Blankenship is Head of Reference and web site coordinator at the James A. Michener Library, University of Northern Colorado. Her former positions include Health Sciences Librarian and instruction Librarian at UNC, and Science Librarian at Colorado State University. She served as chair of the UNC Libraries Assessment Committee during 1992/1993, and began another three-year term on the Committee in 2001.

Richard F. Bowman, Jr. is Professor of Educational Foundations at Winona State University in Minnesota. His research interests include community as an organizing principle, leadership without power, generative coaching, dialogue process, and change based upon living-systems principles.

Janet Carson received her doctorate in sociology from Carleton University, Ottawa, Ontario and her Masters of Library Science from the University of Western Ontario, Ontario. Her research interests are the professional labour process and the social aspects of information technologies. She divides her time between research and teaching in these areas, and reference librarianship at the Carleton University Library.

Patricia J. Cutright is the Director of Libraries at Eastern Oregon University in La Grande, Oregon. She is the 2003 recipient of the LITA/Gaylord Award for Achievement in Library and Information Technology and the 2002 recipient of the Oregon Librarian of the Year award from the Oregon Library Association.

Jean Donham is College Librarian at Cornell College in Iowa. Prior to her appointment in 2000, she was associate professor of Library and Information Science at The University of Iowa. She is co-author of *Inquiry Based Learning: Lessons from library Power* and author of *Enhancing Teaching and Learning: A Leadership Guide for School Library Media Specialists*.

Adonna Fleming is a Reference Librarian at the James A. Michener Library, University of Northern Colorado. She currently serves as chair of the Library

Assessment Committee and is the library faculty representative to the University Assessment Coordinating Council. Previously, she was the Electronic Resources Librarian at the Owen Science and Engineering Library, Washington State University.

Edward D. Garten has been Dean of Libraries and Professor at the University of Dayton since 1985. His research interests include leadership and transformation in higher learning communities, accreditation and quality assurance processes, and organizational behavior.

Elaine Heras is Associate Director of the Aubrey R. Watzek Library at Lewis & Clark College in Portland, Oregon where she has been employed since 1985. She also has worked at Portland State University and the Boston Public Library.

Richard W. Hines is the Dean of Information Resources and University Librarian at the University of Portland in Portland, Oregon. Prior to his current appointment, he held positions at Colorado State University, Duke University, and the Massachusetts Institute of Technology.

Cynthia A. Klinck has been the Director of the Washington-Centerville Public Library in Ohio for 29 years, a library that has been ranked #1 for several years in Hennen's American Public Library Rating. She is an accomplished trainer, presenter and consultant with an MSLS from the University of Kentucky and a passion for organizational design, managing change, learning new theories, developing employees, and pleasing patrons.

James J. Kopp is the Director of the Aubrey R. Watzek Library at Lewis & Clark College in Portland, Oregon. His previous appointments include positions at the University of Portland, Washington State University, Columbia University, and the National Library of Medicine.

Ellen Martins is co-director of Organisational Diagnostics, a management consultancy that focuses on organizational assessments. She holds Masters degree (cum laude) from the University of South Africa (Unisa) and has completed an Advanced Program in Organisational Development (cum laude) at Unisa. Since 1993 she has participated in at least 200 organizational surveys for several companies in various organizational behavior areas. She was a librarian at the Rand Afrikaans University Library and the Institute of American Studies in Johannesburg for 6 years, (1988–1992).

Nico Martins is the co-director of Organizational Diagnostics, a closed corporation that focuses on organizational assessment. He also published several national and international articles on organizational culture, organizational diagnoses and diversity and presented papers at several national and international conferences on the mentioned subjects. Nico holds a Ph.D. in Industrial Psychology and is a registered industrial psychologist and personnel practitioner. He is also a Professor in Organizational Psychology at the University of South Africa.

Lt. Col. Per-Arne Persson graduated from Linköping University in 2000 in informatics (media and communication). He has worked within information systems since the mid-1980s and has studied command work and human understanding of technology in action. He is currently assigned to the Swedish Armed Forces Joint Command, while also lecturing at the Swedish National Defense College on command/control theory and information systems.

Malivan Praditteera is the Director of the Library and a faculty member in the Department of Information Management, Faculty of Information Technology at Rangsit University in Lak Hok, Pathumthani, Thailand. She received her Ed.D. at the University of Pittsburgh in 2001.

Scott Alan Smith is Regional Sales Manager, Pacific Northwest/Northern Tier, Blackwell's. He has been a key player in several library activities in the Northwest, including the Timberline Acquisitions Institute.

Fransie Terblanche is Head of the Department of Information Science at the University of South Africa. She taught library and information management for 22 years. Her special interests are human resources management and development, information and knowledge management, creativity and innovation in organizations. She consults, lectures, trains, and publishes nationally and internationally LIS practice and has supervised many Masters and Doctoral students in the field of the library and information service.

Dan Terrio is the Chief Technology Officer at Lewis & Clark College in Portland, Oregon. He previously held positions as CTO at Lewis-Clark State College in Idaho, Director of Information Technology for the Richard T. Farmer School of Business at Miami University in Ohio, and Manager of Academic Computing at Augsburg College in Minnesota.

Nancy Pickering Thomas Ph.D., graduated from the School of Communication, Information and Library Studies of Rutgers, The State University of New Jersey in 1996 and is an associate professor at the School of Library and Information Management at Emporia (KS) State University. She is the author of Information

Literacy and Information Skills Instruction: Applying Research to Practice in the School Library Media Center, published by Libraries Unlimited in 2004.

Kathleen Tiller has been an information literacy consultant at the University of Dayton's Roesch Library for the last 3 years. Prior to 16 years as a reference librarian actively involved with library instruction, she taught high school English for 10 years.

AUTHOR INDEX

SUBJECT INDEX

Set up a Continuation Order Today!

Did you know you can set up a continuation order on all JAI series and have each new volume sent directly to you upon publication. For details on how to set up a continuation order contact your nearest regional sales office listed below.

To view related Library & Information Sciences series, please visit

www.ElsevierSocialSciences.com/lis

30% Discount for Authors on all Books!

A 30% discount is available to Elsevier book and journal contributors ON ALL BOOKS plus standalone CD-ROMS except multi-volume reference works.

To claim your discount, full payment is required with your order, which must be sent directly to the publisher at the nearest regional sales office listed below.

Elsevier Regional Sales Offices

For customers in the Americas:

Customer Service Department
11830 Westline Industrial Drive
St. Louis, MO 63146
USA
For US customers:
Tel: +1 800 545 2522
Fax: +1 800 535 9935
For customers outside the US:
Tel: +1 800 460 3110
Fax: +1 314 453 7095
Email: usbkinfo@elsevier.com

For customers in the Far East:

Elsevier
Customer Support Department
3 Killiney Road, #08-01/09
Winsland House I,
Singapore 239519
Tel: +(65) 63490200
Fax: + (65) 67331817/67331276
Email: asiainfo@elsevier.com.sg

For customers in Europe, Middle East and Africa:

Elsevier
Customer Services Department
Linacre House, Jordan Hill
Oxford OX2 8DP
United Kingdom
Tel: +44 (0) 1865 474140
Fax: +44 (0) 1865 474141
Email: amstbkinfo@elsevier.com

For customers in Australasia:

Elsevier
Customer Service Department
30-52 Smidmore Street
Marrickville, New South Wales 2204
Australia
Tel: +61 (02) 9517 8999
Fax: +61 (02) 9517 2249
Email: service@elsevier.com.au